Latino Identity in Contemporary America

This edited collection brings together original research papers that explore an important aspect of race and ethnic studies, namely the processes that are shaping the making of Latina and Latino identities in contemporary America. This is a question that has received much attention in the USA over the past decade, and these papers make an original contribution to these debates. Much of this attention towards Latino/a communities in the USA can be seen as the outcome of public debates about the growth of these communities over the past three decades, and the consequences of this growth for social and political constructions of Latino identity. The papers in this collection highlight some of the key facets of contemporary research in this field. As original pieces of research they are at the forefront of current debates about Latino/a identities in contemporary America, and they provide research based insights into the changing experiences of these communities.

This book was originally published as a special issue of *Ethnic and Racial Studies*.

Martin Bulmer is Emeritus Professor of Sociology at the University of Surrey, UK. He retired in 2008, prior to which he was also Director of the ESRC Question Bank. He has edited the journal *Ethnic and Racial Studies* since 1993.

John Solomos is Professor of Sociology at City University London, UK. He has carried out extensive research on race, politics and social change and on theories of race and ethnicity. He is co-editor of *Ethnic and Racial Studies*.

Ethnic and Racial Studies

Series editors: Martin Bulmer, *University of Surrey, UK*, and John Solomos, *City University London, UK*

The journal *Ethnic and Racial Studies* was founded in 1978 by John Stone to provide an international forum for high quality research on race, ethnicity, nationalism and ethnic conflict. At the time the study of race and ethnicity was still a relatively marginal sub-field of sociology, anthropology and political science. In the intervening period the journal has provided a space for the discussion of core theoretical issues, key developments and trends, and for the dissemination of the latest empirical research.

It is now the leading journal in its field and has helped to shape the development of scholarly research agendas. *Ethnic and Racial Studies* attracts submissions from scholars in a diverse range of countries, fields of scholarship and crosses disciplinary boundaries. It has moved from being a quarterly to being published monthly and it is now available in both printed and electronic form.

The Ethnic and Racial Studies book series contains a wide range of the journal's special issues. These special issues are an important contribution to the work of the journal, where leading social science academics bring together articles on specific themes and issues that are linked to the broad intellectual concerns of *Ethnic and Racial Studies*. The series editors work closely with the guest editors of the special issues to ensure that they meet the highest quality standards possible. Through publishing these special issues as a series of books, we hope to allow a wider audience of both scholars and students from across the social sciences to engage with the work of *Ethnic and Racial Studies*.

Other titles in the series include:

The Transnational Political Participation of Immigrants
Edited by Jean-Michel Lafleur and Marco Martiniello

Anthropology of Migration and Multiculturalism
Edited by Steven Vertovec

Migrant Politics and Mobilisation: Exclusion, Engagements, Incorporation
Edited by Davide Però and John Solomos

New Racial Missions of Policing: International Perspectives on Evolving Law-Enforcement Politics
Edited by Paul Amar

Young People, Ethnicity and Social Capital
Edited by Tracey Reynolds

Cosmopolitan Sociability
Edited by Tsypylma Darieva, Nina Glick Schiller and Sandra Gruner-Domic

Retheorizing Race and Whiteness in the 21st Century
Edited by Charles A. Gallagher and France Winddance Twine

Theorising Integration and Assimilation
Edited by Jens Schneider and Maurice Crul

Ethnic and Racial Minorities in Asia: Inclusion or Exclusion?
Edited by Michelle Ann Miller

Diasporas, Cultures and Identities
Edited by Martin Bulmer and John Solomos

Gender, Race and Religion: Intersections and Challenges
Edited by Martin Bulmer and John Solomos

Latino Identity in Contemporary America
Edited by Martin Bulmer and John Solomos

Migration: Policies, Practices, Activism
Edited by Martin Bulmer and John Solomos

Nationalism and National Identities
Edited by Martin Bulmer and John Solomos

Methods and Contexts in the Study of Muslim Minorities: Visible and Invisible Muslims
Edited by Nadia Jeldtoft and Jørgen S. Nielsen

Latino Identity in Contemporary America

Edited by
Martin Bulmer and John Solomos

First published 2012
by Routledge
2 Park Square, Milton Park, Abingdon, Oxfordshire OX14 4RN

Simultaneously published in the USA and Canada
by Routledge
711 Third Avenue, New York, NY 10017, USA

First issued in paperback 2016

Routledge is an imprint of the Taylor & Francis Group, an informa business

© 2012 Taylor & Francis

This book is a reproduction of *Ethnic and Racial Studies*, volume 32, issue 6. The Publisher requests to those authors who may be citing this book to state, also, the bibliographical details of the special issue on which the book was based.

All rights reserved. No part of this book may be reprinted or reproduced or utilised in any form or by any electronic, mechanical, or other means, now known or hereafter invented, including photocopying and recording, or in any information storage or retrieval system, without permission in writing from the publishers.

Trademark notice: Product or corporate names may be trademarks or registered trademarks, and are used only for identification and explanation without intent to infringe.

British Library Cataloguing in Publication Data
A catalogue record for this book is available from the British Library

ISBN 13: 978-1-138-67654-1 (pbk)
ISBN 13: 978-0-415-68634-1 (hbk)

Typeset in Times New Roman
by Taylor & Francis Books

Disclaimer
The publisher would like to make readers aware that the chapters in this book are referred to as articles as they had been in the special issue. The publisher accepts responsibility for any inconsistencies that may have arisen in the course of preparing this volume for print.

Contents

Notes on contributors viii

Introduction
Martin Bulmer and John Solomos 1

1. 'Latino before the world': the transnational extension of panethnicity
   Wendy D. Roth 4

2. Latinidad and masculinidad in Hollywood scripts
   Ana S. Q. Liberato, Guillermo Rebollo-Gil, John D. Foster and Amanda Moras 25

3. Contexts of bilingualism among US-born Latinos
   April Linton and Tomás R. Jiménez 43

4. 'I am somebody': barrio Pentecostalism and gendered acculturation among Chicano ex-gang members
   Edward Flores 72

5. 'It is their nature to do menial labour': the racialization of 'Latino/a Workers' by agricultural employers
   Marta Maria Maldonado 93

6. New immigrant destinations and the American colour line
   Helen B. Marrow 113

7. An assessment of the Latin Americanization thesis
   Christina A. Sue 134

8. Are the Americas 'Sick with Racism' or is it a problem at the poles? A reply to Christina A. Sue
   Eduardo Bonilla-Silva 147

Index 159

Notes on contributors

Eduardo Bonilla-Silva is Professor in the Department of Sociology at Duke University, USA.

Edward Flores is a PhD candidate in the Department of Sociology at the University of Southern California, USA.

John D. Foster is Assistant Professor in the Department of Social and Behavioral Sciences at the University of Arkansas at Pine Bluff, USA.

Tomás R. Jiménez is Assistant Professor of Sociology at Stanford University, USA, and an Irvine Fellow at the New America Foundation.

Ana S.Q. Liberato is Assistant Professor in the Department of Sociology at the University of Kentucky, USA.

April Linton is Assistant Professor in the Department of Sociology at the University of California, San Diego, USA.

Marta Maria Maldonado is Assistant Professor in the Department of Sociology and the U.S. Latino/a Studies Program at Iowa State University, USA.

Helen B. Marrow is Robert Wood Johnson Postdoctoral Scholar in Health Policy at the Universities of California at Berkeley and at San Francisco, 2008–10, USA.

Amanda Moras is Assistant Professor in Residence in the Department of Sociology at the University of Connecticut, USA.

Guillermo Rebollo-Gil is Assistant Professor in the Department of Sociology at the University of Connecticut, USA.

Wendy D. Roth is Assistant Professor in the Department of Sociology at the University of British Columbia, Canada.

Christina A. Sue is Assistant Professor in the Department of Sociology at the University of Colorado, Boulder, USA.

Introduction

Martin Bulmer and John Solomos

The question of the evolving nature of Latino identity in contemporary America has been the subject of much scholarly research and debate over the past two decades. The changing composition of Latino communities in the U. S., combined with processes of social and cultural change, has led to intense scholarly and policy debate about the position of these communities within the changing ethnic and racial identities that help to shape American society. In addition we have seen a growing body of research and scholarly debate about the shifting boundaries of Latino identity within the contemporary U.S., in the period both before and during the Obama presidency (De Genova and Ramos-Zayas, 2003; Gracia and De Greiff, 2000; Marrow, 2009).

The various chapters we have put together in this edited collection were all originally published in a themed issue of the journal *Ethnic and Racial Studies*. Though by no means exhaustive of the wide range of research in this field they do provide an insight into the shifting terrain of research and scholarship on Latino identity.

Outline of chapters

A recurring theme in all the chapters in this edited collection relates to the processes that are shaping the making of Latina and Latino identities in the contemporary United States. This is a question that has received much attention in the U.S. over the past decade and more. Much of this attention towards Latino/a communities in the U.S. can be seen as the outcome of public debates about the growth of these communities over the past three decades and the consequences of this growth for social and political change (McClain et al., 2007; Portes, 2007; Gracia and De Greiff, 2000). While the chapters in this volume are not exhaustive in the depth of their coverage we have put them together in order to highlight at least some of the key facets of contemporary research in this field.

The first chapter in this volume by Wendy D. Roth focuses on the formation of panethnic identities within a transnational framework. Roth's account draws on extensive ethnographic research and qualitative interviews in Puerto Rico and the Dominican Republic in order to analyse the complex mechanisms in which panethnicity is shaped by globalized Spanish media and interpersonal transnational contact. In the context of this analysis Roth is able to illustrate the importance of the relationship between sending and receiving societies in framing mechanisms of identity transmission, and she argues that studies of transnational social fields need to focus both on the sending and receiving contexts.

Roth's account of the transnational extension of panethnicity is followed by the chapter by Ana S.Q. Liberato *et al* on the representation of Latino masculinity in a range of crime films. Central to this representation are questions about the intersections between marginality, class and culture. Liberato and her colleagues suggest that Latinos are often represented in these films through class, ethnic and racial presumptions about power, masculinity and success. These images draw heavily on ideas about the cultural backwardness of Latino/a communities. The chapter does suggest, however, that different narratives about Latino/a identities are emerging in the current social and political environment that question such images.

An important theme in discussions of Latino/a communities is the issue of bilingualism. April Linton and Tomás R. Jiménez focus on this dimension by exploring the determinants of bilingualism among Latino/a adults who were born in the U.S. or who were past of '1.5' generation who went to the U.S. aged 10 or younger. Linton and Jiménez draw on detailed research from census data and ethnographic data to explore the factors that influence bilingualism. They identify the replenishment of an immigrant population as a strong predictor of bilingualism, but they also suggest that it is important to explore the role of factors such as institutional contact with Spanish, labour-market rewards and cosmopolitanism.

The chapter by Edward Flores explores the thesis that second-generation immigrants today are at risk of downward acculturation and socio-economic mobility, and that dense co-ethnic communities provide the greatest resistance. Flores uses his research at a Pentecostal church among Chicano ex-gang members to question this line to analysis and to set out an alternative argument. He highlights the role of American-origin religious institutions as a potential shelter against downward mobility. Flores's approach suggests that it is over-simplistic to dichotomize the values of immigrant groups against those of native-born blacks and Latinos. He uses a race-gender analytical framework to explore the trajectories of the ex-gang members.

This is followed by Marta Maria Maldonado's chapter, which focuses on the racialisation of Latino/a workers by agricultural employers. Given the history of immigration in the U.S. in recent decades this is an important social and political question. Maldonado's research highlights the ways in which the racialisation of Latino/a workers draws on a whole range of cultural and racial imagery about these communities in order to provide employers with usable stereotypes that shape the interactions between employers and workers.

The final substantive chapter is by Helen B. Marrow, and it examines the ways in which Hispanic newcomers are being incorporated into the American Colour Line. It provides a useful reminder of the persistence of the colour line in shaping the racial-ethnic identifications of new Hispanic migrants in the rural South. Marrow's account focuses particularly on the distancing strategies that are adopted by newcomers to reinforce their separation from blacks in the American racial hierarchy, and she provides an exploratory account of the likely impact of these strategies for the future of race relations.

We have also included in this volume a debate on the 'Latin Americanisation thesis' that was outlined by Eduardo Bonilla-Silva in *Ethnic and Racial Studies* in a classic article in 2004 (Bonilla-Silva, 2004). The debate starts with a critical analysis by Christina A. Sue of the core arguments outlined by Bonilla-Silva. This is followed by a response from Bonilla-Silva that takes up Sue's comments directly as well as reflecting on more recent debates about race in the U.S., including the debates surrounding the election of Barack Obama as the first black President.

The chapters in this volume do not exhaust the questions that need to be discussed in relation to this field. We hope, however, that they help to prompt further research and debate about the racial and ethnic politics of the U.S as well as other societies.

References

BONILLA-SILVA, E. 2004 'From Bi-Racial to Tri-Racial: Towards a New System of Racial Stratification in the USA', *Ethnic and Racial Studies,* vol. 27, no. 6, pp. 931–50.
DE GENOVA, N. & RAMOS-ZAYAS, A. Y. 2003 *Latino Crossings: Mexicans, Puerto Ricans, and the Politics of Race and Citizenship,* New York: Routledge.
GRACIA, J. J. E. & DE GREIFF, P. 2000 *Hispanics/Latinos in the United States: Ethnicity, Race, and Rights,* New York: Routledge.
MARROW, H. B. 2009 'New Immigrant Destinations and the American Colour Line', *Ethnic and Racial Studies,* vol. 32, no. 6, pp. 1037–57.
MCCLAIN, P. D., LYLE, M. L., CARTER, N. M., SOTO, V. M. D., LACKEY, G. F., COTTON, K. D., NUNNALLY, S. C., SCOTTO, T. J., GRYNAVISKI, J. D. & KENDRICK, J. A. 2007 'Black American and Latino Immigrants in a Southern City', *Du Bois Review,* vol. 4, no. 1, pp. 97–117.
PORTES, A. 2007 'The New Latin Nation', *Du Bois Review,* vol. 4, no. 2, pp. 271–301.

'Latino before the world': the transnational extension of panethnicity

Wendy D. Roth

Abstract

Studies of panethnic boundary formation focus on multi-ethnic environments like immigrant receiving nations. Central to these accounts are the structured interactions between the ethnic majority and the minorities they perceive as a homogenous group. I argue that theoretical models of panethnicity overlook how panethnic identities may be extended transnationally to migrant sending societies lacking local ethnic interactions. Using multi-sited ethnography and qualitative interviews in Puerto Rico and the Dominican Republic, I illustrate the transmission of panethnicity through globalized Spanish media and interpersonal transnational contact. The political relationship between sending and receiving societies shapes these mechanisms of identity transmission, illustrating the need to make these relationships central to the emerging concept of transnational social fields.

> Even though the one who saw himself as Latino was the immigrant, and not us because we haven't emigrated, and we should feel before the world, 'We're white, we're black,' or whatever. It's curious but ... today we say, 'Yes, we're Latino.' ... What you can be sure of is that every Puerto Rican is going to tell you that he's Latino ... and that he sees himself as Latino before the world. (Roberto, San Juan, Puerto Rico)

An expression of panethnic sentiment from a Puerto Rican living in the mainland US would surprise few scholars of migration or racialization. Puerto Rican migrants, like many Latin Americans who have settled in the mainland US, often embrace a panethnic identity such as Latino or Hispanic (Diaz McConnell and Delgado-Romero 2004). Yet in the above quote, Roberto, a 21-year-old in San Juan, is discussing a different phenomenon: why do many Puerto Ricans who have never migrated also adopt Latino identities?

Studies of panethnic boundary formation focus on multi-ethnic environments and immigrant-receiving societies like the United States. Central to these accounts are the structured group interactions between a dominant ethnic majority and the ethnic minorities whom they perceive as homogenous, as well as relations between those ethnic subgroups. Several studies detail how ethnic groups developed panethnic identities in response to government policies and external threats from the majority. For example, Padilla (1985) describes how Mexican-Americans and Puerto Ricans in 1970s Chicago developed Latino consciousness in protesting their joint exclusion from employment. Espiritu (1992) reveals how Asian panethnicity in the US is institutionalized through government efforts to lump Asian Americans together in electoral politics, social service funding, and census classification, and through panethnic responses to anti-Asian violence from whites. Okamoto (2006) identifies the structural conditions that produce panethnic identities and collective action. In these studies, structured interactions between majority and minorities foster panethnic boundaries by heightening in- and out-group distinctions.

How, then, can we explain widespread expressions of panethnicity by the majority group in a society that lacks such ethnic diversity? The 2005 Puerto Rico Community Survey estimates that 98.5 per cent of Puerto Rico's population is Latino or Hispanic and 95 per cent is Puerto Rican. How are panethnic boundaries maintained in a context where interactions outside the panethnic group are not a feature of daily life?

I argue that theoretical models of panethnicity fail to capture how panethnic identities, once created, may extend into new social contexts lacking the local interactions that gave rise to them. Past research concentrated on the construction of panethnic boundaries. Although scholars note that panethnic identity may persist and grow beyond the circumstances that fostered it (Padilla 1985; Espiritu 1992), these accounts do not address how panethnicity may extend spatially into new regions. Specifically, the literature does not consider how transnational migration reshapes the fields of reference that influence ethnic boundary construction. Transnational practices allow migrants to link together the communities they enter and those they leave behind (Glick Schiller, Basch and Blanc-Szanton 1992). When sending and receiving societies have strong, enduring links and high levels of transnational activity, a transnational social field develops, providing nationals with a dual frame of reference that makes each location relevant for daily life in the other (Guarnizo 1997; Itzigsohn *et al.* 1999; Levitt 2001). Within such fields, it is not merely local level interactions that shape ethnic boundaries, but the numerous links that make ethnic groups in distant societies appropriate reference groups. Those links allow non-migrants to form symbolic identifications with other Latino groups and create panethnic consciousness.

This article demonstrates, through multi-sited ethnography and qualitative interviews with non-migrants (people who have not lived outside their home country) in San Juan, Puerto Rico and Santo Domingo, the Dominican Republic, how panethnic identity extends to migrant-sending societies within a transnational social field. At the micro-level, panethnic identities are transmitted through individual contact between migrants and non-migrants. At the macro-level, they are communicated through transnational media whose attempts to foster panethnic identification promote the consumption and expansion of their cultural products. I illustrate how panethnic identities take on new meaning among non-migrants, assuming a symbolic content divested of the social consequences they bear in the US. The paper thus builds a bridge between studies of panethnicity and the literature on transnationalism.

Puerto Rico and the Dominican Republic provide distinct sending-society contexts because of their different political relationships with the US. Puerto Rico's political affiliation produces transnational linkages that are supported by political and institutional infrastructure, facilitating the extension of panethnicity. This is not the case with the Dominican Republic, even though its connections to the US are sufficient to create a transnational social field. I focus on these groups precisely to illustrate how political relationships shape the mechanisms that allow identities to extend from one context to another.

In doing so, I critically investigate the concept of transnational social fields. At present, societies are simply dubbed transnational social fields, with little attempt to differentiate them or their impact on people's lives. Yet such fields are influenced by the relationships of the societies that comprise them and therefore produce qualitatively different types of transnational exchanges. This study argues that political relationships need to be brought into the concept of transnational social fields to move them beyond theoretical observation and towards becoming an informative analytical tool.

The origins of panethnicity

Panethnic groups extend ethnic boundaries to incorporate several groups that previously considered themselves distinct ethnicities. Such groups can reshape political interests and affiliations, and are theoretically important for illustrating how and why ethnic boundaries may shift.

Panethnicity develops through distinct processes of *ascription*, *accommodation* and *identification*. Panethnic labels typically originate in *ascription* by outsiders who fail to recognize the diverse origins within the group and see them as homogenous (Cornell 1988; Espiritu 1992). *Accommodation* often follows, as individuals within the group initially assume the panethnic label to conform to outsiders' expectations. This does not imply acceptance of those labels, but the need to interact with a society that organizes itself around such classifications. However, panethnic groupings also serve as a basis for political mobilization. As ethnic groups organize around their common structural conditions, they create or enhance the cultural solidarity that leads to panethnic *identification*. Several studies detail distinct national origin or tribal groups organizing around an imposed panethnic identity to secure common resources, while simultaneously creating greater symbolic identification with that panethnic group (Padilla 1985; Cornell 1988; Espiritu 1992; Nagel 1995).

Latino or Hispanic identities[1] exemplify this pattern of panethnic group formation. The panethnic label 'Hispanic' originated in the early 1970s as an official designation by state agencies to identify people of Latin American and Spanish descent in the US (Oboler 1995). Thus, it began with *ascription* by government offices, which treated all Spanish-origin ethnicities as homogenous. Members of various Hispanic groups were forced to *accommodate* this terminology to fit into the US classification system. Padilla's (1985) study illustrates the process of *identification* with Latino panethnicity. This process occurred for Mexican-Americans and Puerto Ricans in 1970s Chicago as they mobilized to protest local corporations' refusal to hire minorities under Affirmative Action regulations. The group mobilization aroused sentiments of 'common origin', particularly in the symbol of their shared Spanish language.

It is through the mobilization process that communities develop the group consciousness to transform from a 'panethnicity in itself' into a 'panethnicity for itself'. However, individuals need not be involved in the collective action process to identify panethnically. Past research on panethnicity has focused mainly on the organizational dimension of panethnic groups – how they are organized as collective actors (Padilla 1985; Cornell 1988; Espiritu 1992; Nagel 1995; Okamoto 2006). Yet Espiritu (1992) describes a second, conceptual dimension to 'groupness' in individual behaviour and attitudes – how group members view themselves. By overlooking this dimension, scholarship fails to address how panethnicity is spread or reinvented by individuals who did not participate in collective action.

In the literature, panethnicity is created and located entirely within the host society, as a result of a minority group's struggle for resources controlled by the majority. Padilla states that 'Latino ethnic identity and consciousness ... is largely a phenomenon of American urban life' (1985, p. 144). Because Latino panethnicity develops in the meeting of the Latino and non-Latino communities, it is believed not to exist in sending-country environments where nearly everyone is Latino.[2] According to Tinker Salas, Latino and Hispanic designations are 'not generally used by Latin Americans as terms of identification in their native lands. Rarely do Mexicans, Venezuelans, Puerto Ricans or Peruvians, within their own countries refer to themselves as Hispanic or Latino' (1991, p. 67). Thus, Puerto Rican non-migrants do not adopt panethnic identities simply because of their US affiliation. Americans are an important reference category in the construction of *Puerto Rican* identity, but this does not necessitate *panethnic* identification. It is the interaction of Latino groups in a context where they are similarly classified and marginalized that produces panethnic consciousness.

Transnationalism and ethnic boundaries

How, then, are identities formed in the receiving society spread elsewhere? Transnational migration facilitates this transmission. Once in their host society, many international migrants continue to orient themselves towards their home society by maintaining regular contact and a range of economic, political or socio-cultural involvements. Glick Schiller, Basch and Blanc-Szanton describe this pattern as *transnationalism*, 'the processes by which immigrants forge and sustain multi-stranded social relations that link together their societies of origin and settlement' (1992, p. 7).

Ideas, practices and identities learned in the host society can be communicated back to the society of origin as *social remittances.* Levitt (2001) found that Dominican immigrants in Boston adopted more liberal ideas about women's roles from their involvement in the workplace and public sphere. They communicated these ideas to women back home, who began to embrace new gender identities.

The transmission of ideas and identities may also affect individuals with few or no transnational ties, as transnational social fields create a dual frame of reference that permeates the fabric of life itself (Guarnizo 1997; Itzigsohn *et al.* 1999). For example, residents of Miraflores, a small Dominican town, are conscious of the activities occurring in Jamaica Plain, a community in Boston where numerous Mirafloreños have settled, even if they have never visited and have no personal ties there (Levitt 2001). The web of micro-level interconnections sustained by many members of these locations are the threads that weave a macro-level social field, creating societies whose ideas, values and practices are shaped by the influences of both locations.

Barth (1969) reveals how interactions between groups reinforce ethnic boundaries. I maintain that transnational migration can influence ethnic identity within transnational social fields without regular local interaction, by making new societies and groups relevant comparison categories in the formation of ethnic boundaries.

Is it appropriate to think of Puerto Ricans as transnational migrants? Puerto Rico is not an independent country, even though most Puerto Ricans consider it a distinct nation and distinguish themselves culturally from *los americanos* (Flores 1993; Morris 1995; Duany 2002). Puerto Ricans have long held an ambiguous position in migration studies, resembling international immigrants in some respects and internal migrants in others (Pérez y González 2000). Massey *et al.* assert that 'movement between [Puerto Rico] and the US mainland replicates many of the features of transnational movement. ... As with migration from other independent nations in the Caribbean region, movement out of the Commonwealth of Puerto Rico entails crossing significant cultural, linguistic, and geographic boundaries' (1994, p. 702). I maintain that it would not be appropriate to consider Puerto Ricans as transnational migrants in a study of migration choices or patterns, given the lack of legal restrictions that distinguishes them from other Caribbeans and Latin Americans. However, when considering the cultural and social connections that migrants retain to their societies of origin, it is appropriate to think of Puerto Ricans as transnational migrants. Several scholars have chosen to conceptualize Puerto Ricans within a transnational framework for precisely this reason (Meléndez 1993; Alicea 1997; Duany 2002). Puerto Ricans' greater facility of movement then becomes a factor to be considered in the processes of maintaining cultural connections and exchanges.

Comparing Puerto Rico and the Dominican Republic

Transnational social fields have developed from the complex connections linking migrants with their home societies in both Puerto Rico and the Dominican Republic (Alicea 1997; Guarnizo 1997; Itzigsohn *et al.* 1999; Levitt 2001). Both societies experience frequent transnational contact and return migration. In 1980, return migrants comprised 19 per cent of the male population in Puerto Rico (Meléndez 1993). A 1991 survey in the Dominican Republic estimated that 28.6 per cent of the migrant population had returned to the country (Guarnizo 1997).

The colonial histories, populations and cultures of these nations are quite similar. Both societies were populated by indigenous Taínos at the time of Spanish conquest. The importation of African slaves and widespread miscegenation in both colonies created populations of mixed Taíno, European and African roots. Under Spanish rule, the nations shared a common language, religion and customs that blended the cultures of these three origin groups.

However, the nations have very distinct political histories. Puerto Rico became a US protectorate in 1898 during the Spanish-American war and in 1952 was established as a Free Associated State. Puerto Ricans' US citizenship allows them to move freely between the island and mainland, and a great wave of migration to the mainland extended from the mid-1940s through the 1960s. By 1973, 40 per cent of Puerto Rico's population resided in the mainland US (Pérez y González 2000).

Puerto Rico's status and national identity have long been contested. Politically, the island is divided fairly evenly between those who opt for US statehood and those who prefer the status quo; independence is advocated by a small minority, yet plays a considerable role in public discourse. Given these divisions, many question what Puerto Rican national identity means (Flores 1993; Morris 1995).

By contrast, the Dominican Republic became a sovereign nation in 1844, having proclaimed its independence not from Spain but from neighbouring Haiti, which had invaded in 1822. The nation's emergence from Haitian invasion allowed dictator Rafael Trujillo (leader from 1930 to 1961) to enforce a nationalist ideology of anti-Haitian stereotypes. This defined the Dominican people in contrast to their neighbours, creating a strong national identity as Spanish-speaking, Catholic and non-black (Moya Pons 1998).

The US also has a history of involvement in Dominican politics and economics. In 1872, part of Dominican territory was leased to a private US corporation. The US took over Dominican customs offices in 1905 and established control over the country's finances and the right to interfere in Dominican politics. US military forces occupied the nation in 1916–24 and 1965–6. The Dominican Republic remains highly dependent on US markets, public aid and private investment (Moya Pons 1998). Nonetheless, the nation lacks the political and institutional infrastructure of formal affiliation found in Puerto Rico.

The Trujillo regime restricted emigration to control its people. With Trujillo's assassination in 1961, massive emigration to the US began. Immigration increased through the 1990s, with significant jumps in the late 1980s and early 1990s (Levitt 2001). Yet, despite increasing Dominican migration, the overall mass exodus remains small compared to Puerto Rico; less than 8 per cent of the Dominican-born population lived in the US in 2000.[3]

Thus, Puerto Rican mass migration was beginning to decline as Dominican migration picked up in the 1960s and 1970s. While the nations share cultural and historical similarities, the Puerto Rican transnational social field is characterized by greater duration, scope and institutional infrastructure as a result of its political affiliation with the receiving society.

Data

This study relies on qualitative interviews with thirty Puerto Rican non-migrants in San Juan and thirty Dominican non-migrants in Santo Domingo, as well as participant observation during nine months of fieldwork. Each group was stratified by age, sex, occupational status and skin colour. Respondents had not lived outside their home country for more than six months;[4] identified both parents as Puerto Rican or Dominican, respectively; were age 21 or older; lived or worked in their nation's capital; and did not know any other respondents.

I collected samples using several methods. I distributed flyers in public locations, including malls and buses. I knocked on doors and recruited people I met during my daily interactions. Some respondents were referred by personal contacts, often by my research assistants or staff in the research institutes I visited. To find respondents with high occupational status, I asked professional organizations to contact their membership on my behalf.

I showed all respondents a photographic instrument of individuals representing the range of racial phenotypes typical in the Hispanic Caribbean[5] and asked respondents to identify the race of each person in open-ended terms. I was interested in racial identities, but found that many non-migrants used panethnic labels as racial identifications. Many Latin Americans identify strongly with ethnic or national identities, and use such terms to describe their race (Oboler 1995; Alcoff 2000; Rodríguez 2000; Gracia 2007). I also asked respondents to identify their own race in open-ended terms, and to complete the race and Hispanic origin questions from the 2000 US Census. Later, I probed how respondents hear panethnic terms and what they mean to them.

Interviews were conducted in Spanish; both a native research assistant and I were present. We varied who led the interview but did not find any interviewer effects, probably because my presence was sufficient to determine the respondent's audience. It is likely that both Puerto Rican and Dominican respondents would be more willing to describe themselves as Latinos when speaking to an American than to a fellow national. Thus, rather than taking claims of a Latino identity at face value, I probed the meaning respondents attribute to these identities. All identities are contextual, evoked more in some situations than others. A Latino identity is one of several nested identities that respondents maintain. To consider contextual effects further, I also discussed with my research assistants how they felt the respondents' answers might have differed if I, as an American, had not been present. These discussions form part of my data.

Latino identities in the sending societies

Embracing panethnic terms is much more common among Puerto Rican than Dominican non-migrants (Table 1). Considerably more Puerto Rican respondents used the panethnic terms 'Latino' or 'Hispanic' to identify the race of the individuals in the photographic instrument or to refer to non-migrants at any point during the interview. Most Dominican respondents claimed that panethnic terms were used to refer only to migrants in the US.

Most Puerto Rican respondents embrace a Latino identity, yet identify primarily as Puerto Rican and claim that these identities are consistent. One-fifth of Puerto Ricans used a panethnic label, alone or with another racial label (e.g. white Hispanic), as their primary racial identification, compared with 3 per cent of Dominicans. However, many more also identify as Latino. I distinguish between those who claimed they identify as Latino and those who expressed a strong panethnic identification, i.e. those who volunteered the identity without being asked or revealed a strong attachment to the group. Overall, 77 per cent of Puerto Ricans said they were Latino compared to 43 per cent of Dominicans. However, most Dominicans identified as Latino in response to a direct question, without expressing any attachment to the identity. This is consistent with accommodating other people's view of you as Latino. With the stricter criterion, the same 77 per cent of Puerto Rican non-migrants have a strong

Table 1. *Use of panethnic labels by Puerto Rican and Dominican non-migrants*

	Puerto Ricans %	Dominicans %
Uses panethnic labels on photo instrument	70	23
Uses panethnic labels to refer to non-migrants at any time during interview	77	37
Uses panethnic terms to refer only to migrants in US or says terms are not used much in home country	17	53
Uses panethnic label in primary racial identity	20	3
Identification with panethnic group	77	43
Strong identification with panethnic group	77	10
N	30	30

panethnic identification, but only 10 per cent of Dominicans do. Identifying as Latino is not associated with age, sex, occupational status or skin colour. Nor is it determined by Puerto Ricans' political affiliations concerning the island's status.

Latino panethnic terminology is commonplace in San Juan. A local establishment near my residence called itself 'Latino Dry Cleaners'. Yet qualitative interviews reveal how Puerto Rican non-migrants understand a Latino identity. Most believe there is a cultural connection among the people of Latin America and those who have moved elsewhere. It includes language, food, traditions and music. Leandro, a 45-year-old factory supervisor, feels a strong cultural bond with other Latin Americans:

[When I was younger] I thought, well, the Hispanics were Puerto Ricans, the ones on this island. The ones that are in the US ... I didn't see them as Latino or Hispanic. For me, as a child, race ... wasn't Hispanic or Latino race, it was Puerto Rican race. So I expanded my education and I was able to understand that we're all Hispanic and Latino. ... For example, I can know that Panamanians think a lot like us, that Mexicans see us as their equals ... in the sense of being Hispanic, of race, of being Latin American. I can tell you that I can go to Texas, for example, and I sit at a table to eat with some Mexicans, with some Cubans, with some Panamanians and we can eat the same thing. We don't have differences in ... tastes because we're raised more or less in the same way. (Leandro, Puerto Rican, factory supervisor)

Leandro developed this identification with non-Puerto Rican Latinos at the age of 16 or 17, before he had ever travelled outside Puerto Rico or knew any Mexicans, Panamanians or Cubans. He broadened the boundaries of his ethnic group identification without personal interactions to sustain it.

Relatively few Dominican respondents embrace a panethnic identity. The following quote from Rodolfo is typical of Dominicans' responses:

When you go to a different country you're already Latino ... because here in my country I'm Dominican. ... We're Dominicans. *Okay. So here, people don't say, 'We're Latinos'?*
No. I've never heard it here. Only when you go to another country, [do they say] 'the Latinos'. ... But I've never heard a Dominican say 'I'm Latino' in the Dominican [Republic]. Only 'I'm Dominican'. (Rodolfo, Dominican, social work assistant)

Many Dominicans strongly embrace their national identity, and while they recognize what it means to be Latino, this label has little resonance for them. Manuel, who earns money from odd jobs fixing electronics, describes how most Dominicans view the Latino identity: 'It has a meaning, but ... you don't carry that so deep inside, as a person with that pride. You don't carry it like that, not as you would say your nationality.'

Very few respondents who identify as Latino participate in collective action based on panethnic boundaries, a primary means by which panethnic boundaries develop. What role, then, do panethnic identities play in non-migrants' lives? For Puerto Rican non-migrants, embracing a Latino identity is a largely costless endeavour, expressed symbolically, with few structural repercussions. It has little impact on their daily lives, and, because it is an accepted form of identification that applies to the majority, it is not used to discriminate. It is often expressed through symbolic consumption of music, food or cultural products from other Latino nationalities. Eva, a young Puerto Rican reporter, lists favourite recording artists from Mexico, Spain and Venezuela as well as Puerto Rico. Others simply recognize that the products they consume resemble those of other Latino groups sufficiently to be considered part of the same genre: the rice and beans or fried meats they eat are not simply typical Puerto Rican food, but Latino food, because they are shared by many Latin American cuisines.

Just as the Irish feel Irish on St. Patrick's Day or Jews feel more Jewish when they read about Israel, cultural or political events can also heighten Latino identities. While Puerto Rican non-migrants rarely mobilize around a Latino identity to demand greater rights and resources, events occurring elsewhere can foster a symbolic political identity. Carmela explains that her Latina identity was reinforced by the Latino political mobilization around Proposition 187 in California:

> When there was the law ... I think it was 187, which was the law that wanted to ... leave some children of some Latinos ... without education ... in California. Well, when all those issues come up, I think that the issue is taken up again of, 'Look we're also Latinos ... the Latinos recognize each other in any place.' (Carmela, Puerto Rican, customer service representative)

Proposition 187 would not have affected Puerto Ricans, US citizens by birth. Carmela was not involved in mobilizing activities around it, but her identification feeds off the panethnic solidarity that others' mobilization created. A Latino identity can have real consequences in the mainland US, serving as the basis for discrimination or the distribution of resources. However, as panethnicity is exported to non-migrants, it takes on a new form with few structural repercussions.

How are panethnic identities that developed in the US extended to Puerto Rican non-migrants? Interviews and ethnographic observations reveal two important mechanisms: growing transnational media and contact between individuals in the home and host societies.

The globalization of Latino media

Scholars argue that the mass media have effectively shaped national and transnational identities (e.g. Meyrowitz 1985). Concepts of identity are communicated through media such as television, radio and the press. Media outlets may act as 'panethnic entrepreneurs' (Espiritu 1992): organizations with a vested interest in fostering panethnic identity. Here I focus on television media and illustrate how multinational Spanish-language television networks act as panethnic entrepreneurs to spread panethnicity across borders.

Dávila (2001) argues that Spanish-language television and marketing shape concepts of Latino identity in the US by creating a homogenized panethnic culture. These media promote a single concept of *Latinidad*, emphasizing cultural commonalities between Latino nationalities. Material is presented in generic Spanish with national references expunged, and newscasters lose their accents to hide national origins. Networks such as Telemundo and Univisión – literally, 'One Vision' – deliberately promote this model of panethnicity to broaden their markets by eliminating the need for culturally specific material.

The same programmes that promote a homogenized concept of Latino identity in the mainland US are also broadcast in Puerto Rico (and other Latin American countries). In Puerto Rico, Telemundo and Univisión are the dominant television networks, reaching the vast majority of the population. Puerto Rico's broadcast media infrastructure is relatively developed as a result of its close ties with the US. For many years, the island has had nearly universal television penetration (in 2000, 98 per cent of households had a television). In January 2006, nine of the top ten rated programmes in Puerto Rico were on Telemundo and Univisión (Foros Perú Website 2007).

The Dominican Republic's telecommunications industry was largely controlled by Trujillo until his death, with new national channels emerging in the 1970s (Menéndez Alarcón 1992). However, television ownership was considerably lower than in Puerto Rico until recently. Between 1991 and 1997, the percentage of Dominican households with a television rose from 53 to 83 (TableBase 2000). However, Telemundo and Univisión are available only on cable in the Dominican Republic, which is accessed by a small minority. Only some of their programmes are transmitted on local channels.

In non-migrants' discussions of how they learn what it means to be Latino, Puerto Ricans frequently refer to the media, particularly popular television shows targeted at multinational audiences, such as *Despierta America*, *Primer Impacto*, *Laura*, *Sabado Gigante* and *El Show de Cristina* – all of which appear on Univisión and Telemundo. The variety shows depict various Latino groups, promoting what producers describe as shared cultural elements. News programmes feature segments on different Latin American nations and Latinos in the US. Earlier, Leandro described his sense of connection to Latinos throughout the world. Explaining how he began to feel this connection before travelling outside Puerto Rico, he placed a heavy emphasis on the media:

Okay, I can tell you: through media of communication, through reading, through the press. ... I like to watch international news in Spanish that review the happenings in the Latin American countries and through that you learn about everything.
And all of these sources – the press, television, the news – are about Latin American countries? They're not about the US?
I see a lot about the US through cable and I make comparisons. ... Right now they talk a lot about the Hispanic race ... immigrants, the problem of legal documentation in the US. ... And you start identifying with that mass of Hispanics that are Spanish-speaking that look like you physically. ... For example, I never go to sleep without watching *Primer Impacto*. Why? ... Because they review everything that happens with Latin Americans in the US. (Leandro, Puerto Rican, factory supervisor)

Many Puerto Ricans learn about other Latino groups from these shows and come to see themselves as Latino. Roberto was one of my research assistants and also a non-migrant who would have been eligible for the study. He describes how these television programmes familiarize him with other Latino groups:

We're creating, all of the Latinos are creating, like the same culture even if we don't live in the same country.
And why does this happen? Many people here don't travel outside the country. How does that happen?
I consider that [it's] television ... it's like a continuous voyage of people. You turn on the television and Don Francisco can take you in *Sábado Gigante* ... to Chile, Guatemala. Therefore, I know that in Mexico there are pyramids, and I've never been to Mexico. ...
And I know many cultures and many foods that are eaten in

different countries and I've never visited them, but I've visited through the television. And the television is the connection of Latin America, that 'look, you're Latino just like me'.

Despierta America is on ... Univisión from Puerto Rico, and it's a program that's made in Miami. ... There are two Mexicans, one Puerto Rican, one Honduran. ... It's a program that presents the life of Latinos in New York. And every time there's a reporter and she's in a place ... she says, 'Here we are with the Latina community from Long Island', or 'the Latina community from Florida'. ... And they present people who are like us, who speak Spanish, who are in the US, they're the Latina community. Therefore [Puerto Ricans] say, 'Well, if they're the Latino community, then I'm Latino.'

The growing global focus on Latino communities unifies these groups. However, Roberto notes, it also reinforces boundaries between them and everyone else. 'All the messages that are coming, all our programs, present us as the Latino race. Every time there are Billboard Awards, there's the *Latino* Billboard Awards. There's the category of *Latino* rap music, category of *Latino* pop music. ... And "that's yours. Mine is pop music, yours is *Latino* pop music"' (emphasis his). By heightening their awareness of ethnic boundaries, foreign producers make Puerto Ricans, even in their own country, Latinos before the world.

Multinational programming was mentioned less often by Dominicans. Those who did mention similar programmes typically did so in the context of explaining how they hear the term Latino. None felt it had a strong impact on their ethnic identities. Some Dominicans felt that the media communicate the ascription of panethnic labels in the US. Marcela, a part-time office assistant, learned about panethnic labels from American television programmes where the police are chasing a thief and identify him as 'Latino male suspect'. From this, she concluded that Dominicans are seen as Latinos by Americans. The media bring panethnic labels into Dominicans' consciousness but these labels have little resonance for them. And, with less multinational programming, Dominicans are unlikely to embrace positive panethnic identities.

Transnational contact

Identities are also communicated at the individual level, through transnational contact between those in the sending and receiving societies. However, for the communication of identity, I argue that in-person contact and first-hand experience have a more powerful impact than word-of-mouth transmission or contact by telephone or writing. Respondents with the most frequent face-to-face contact with their US ties typically express the strongest panethnic identification, and describe the importance of these interactions for their identities. Because of their citizenship status, Puerto Rican non-migrants have and have had more first-hand experience in the US than Dominicans.

Most respondents have friends or relatives in the US and generally keep in frequent touch. In fact, Dominican and Puerto Rican respondents have comparable rates of contact with their US ties (see Table 2 below). In both groups, two-thirds of respondents communicate with their ties more than once a year; about two-fifths are in contact every month or more. However, the groups differ in visits to the US. With no entry restrictions, every Puerto Rican respondent except one has visited the mainland. Several non-migrants visit a few times a year, for a total of fifty to a hundred visits. Through their observations during these visits and their communication with friends, they learn first-hand how Puerto Ricans are classified in the US and how migrants identify. Only one-third of the Dominican respondents

Table 2. *Frequency of non-migrants' contact with the United States and percentages identifying with panethnic group by level of contact*

	Puerto Ricans		Dominicans	
	Frequency of contact	Percentage identifying with panethnic group[a]	Frequency of contact	Percentage identifying with panethnic group[a]
Total percentage identifying with panethnic group		77 [23/30]		43 [13/30]
Contact with US ties				
Every few months or more	67	92 [12/13]	67	65 [11/17]
Once per year or less	33	89 [8/9]	33	22 [2/9]
Visits to US				
Never visited US	3	0 [0/1]	67	47 [9/19]
Visited 1–2 times	30	88 [7/8]	13	25 [1/4]
Visisted 3+ times	67	100 [16/16]	17	60 [3/5]

Notes
[a] [% = number identifying as Latino/total with level of contact]
Cases with missing data are excluded.

have ever visited the mainland US; for those who have, the number of visits was much lower, typically three trips or fewer.

Yet Dominicans still access widespread word-of-mouth information about migrants in the US. Friends and neighbours in the Dominican Republic frequently tell stories about their own migrant ties. Dominicans even chat with strangers about Dominicans abroad. I frequently overheard conversations on street corners and buses that involved the migrant diaspora. In Santo Domingo, a cheap form of transportation is the *carros públicos*, cars that drive up and down the major avenues allowing as many people as possible to crowd in for a few pesos apiece. During this imposed intimacy, passengers chat with the strangers wedged next to them. Even in this forum, I heard stories about Dominicans' lives in the US and how they are treated, permitting a flow of information about the migrant experience that may be several degrees removed from a transnational connection. Such communications illustrate the transnational social field that entwines the Dominican Republic and the US. Nonetheless, non-migrants are less likely to adopt new identities from these casual exchanges than through personal interaction with known sources.

Through their interactions with their networks abroad, many Puerto Ricans learn why their migrant ties identify panethnically. Isandro has a vast network of between fifty and a hundred relatives in the US. He strongly identifies as Latino, partly because of what he has learned from them:

Do you think that people in the US perceive race differently than here in Puerto Rico?
Yes, at least my family has commented that they've noticed the difference. ... Over there the issue about race is ... like the extremes, [you're] either too white or too black or *trigueñito* [a little brown] and Latino. And that's where the Latinos fall. Which is actually another [reason] why I think that maybe we're a race, because we aren't either with the whites or with the blacks, but in the middle. (Isandro, Puerto Rican, tax auditor)

Through his many visits to the US, Isandro observed the similarities of different Latino groups first hand because his migrant networks broadened his contact with other Latin Americans. His father and his brother both married after moving to the US – to a Mexican and a Colombian woman, respectively. Through his visits to them and their visits to him, he has gotten to know his stepmother, sister-in-law and their extended families, reinforcing his Latino identity.

Visits to the US also provide first-hand experience of the discrimination Latinos face there. The only time Rubén, a Puerto Rican college student, experienced discrimination was on his one visit to the mainland. On a trip to Chicago, his school band entered a music store to buy instruments. A white American salesperson refused to sell to them, he claims, because they were Puerto Ricans. Even without sustained group interactions from living in the US, visits help non-migrants learn of the marginalized treatment Latinos experience.

Dominican non-migrants also hear from their ties abroad how Dominicans are treated in the US and they frequently hear the term 'Latino'. Yet their conversations are not communicating identification with these labels. Few of their discussions dwell on the meaning of Latino identity; this is not the type of subject raised in the precious moments of an international call. Nor does the word-of-mouth information about the diaspora that Dominicans pass along focus on the meaning of panethnic identity. Such mediated experiences do not have the same impact as closer, first-hand connections and observations.

Although the numbers are small and therefore only suggestive, Table 2 shows how level of contact with the US is associated with respondents' likelihood of identifying panethnically. For Dominican respondents who communicate with their US ties every few months or more, 65 per cent identify as Latino, compared with 22 per cent of Dominicans who communicate once a year or less. The frequency of communication has less impact on Puerto Rican respondents, partly because even those with little contact still visit the US. For both Dominicans and Puerto Ricans, those who visit the US three times or more are most likely to identify as Latino – 100 per cent of such Puerto Ricans and 60 per cent of such Dominicans do. Perhaps significantly, of the three Dominicans who expressed a strong Latino identity, one is married to a Dominican migrant who splits his time between New York and Santo Domingo and another was married to a Puerto Rican who has since returned to Puerto Rico yet visits regularly. Both of their spouses, they claim, identify as Latino. These first-hand interactions with panethnic identifiers have a stronger influence on identity than the word-of-mouth information Dominicans receive in public interactions. The close, personal quality of interaction is central to the micro-level transmission of ethnic or racial identities.

Conclusion

Latino panethnic identity is associated with immigrants and their children, the product of migration to a new society. This analysis shows that, once formed in the diaspora, panethnicity may also be extended transnationally. This occurs both through deliberate efforts of panethnic entrepreneurs in the media and through first-hand interactions between non-migrants and migrant communities. When identities are adopted, they differ from the original form in how they are expressed and the consequences they bear.

It is not surprising that Puerto Ricans, with their hundred-year affiliation with the US, should define themselves in contrast to the American 'other'. Yet those boundaries do not simply define their 'Puerto Ricanness' but take a panethnic form. In the transnational social field that incorporates them, awareness of US society and Latino panethnicity is an everyday reality. Non-migrants are touched simultaneously by the social orders at both ends of this dense social field, which changes the reference categories that shape their identities.

Yet such simultaneity does not have the same impact on all societies incorporated within transnational social fields. For Dominican non-migrants, the Dominican diaspora in the US is also a daily field of reference. But the history of political relations between the sending and receiving nations matters: it provides the infrastructure for the transmission of panethnicity. Puerto Rico's formal affiliation supported the development of the television industry and assists the movement of transnational Spanish networks into Puerto Rican markets. It allows Puerto Rican non-migrants to visit the US without administrative barriers, and provides economic development that facilitates overseas travel. Puerto Rico's political status also provides other forms of institutional support for a panethnic category – including using the category on census forms, federal college loan applications and other government documentation. The longer duration of mass migration from Puerto Rico than from the Dominican Republic also strengthens its transnational linkages. In these ways, Puerto Rico's relationship with the US supports the type of transnational connections that facilitate the extension of panethnicity.

Is Puerto Rico simply a unique case? Certainly its status as a Free Associated State differentiates it from other Latin American nations. But the mechanisms that spread panethnicity overseas are not dependent on a 'Commonwealth' status. Countries that are not politically affiliated may still develop similar institutional forms, trade and visa agreements. The likelihood of increased face-to-face interaction between Dominican non-migrants and migrants is high, given the current strengthening of US-Dominican relations, the extension of dual citizenship to Dominican migrants and the adoption of the Central American Free Trade Agreement. Lacking the political infrastructure of Puerto Rico, Dominicans are not likely to reach the same level of panethnic identification found there. But, as Dominican migration continues, US society will become an increasingly important field of reference for ethnic identity at home. Even in this research, a few Dominicans with very close, sustained ties to migrants came to see themselves as Latinos.

Studies of panethnicity maintain that panethnic boundaries develop from structured ethnic interactions in a multi-ethnic society. This article shows that other types of panethnic boundary formation are possible. People who have never lived abroad may also adopt panethnic identities that are created elsewhere and extended transnationally. The concept of transnational social fields reveals how individuals simultaneously reference distinct social orders in discrete locations. However, this analysis shows that different transnational social fields have qualitatively different impacts on the extension of panethnicity. To make the concept of transnational social fields analytically useful, comparative research needs to account for the political relationships that shape them.

Acknowledgements

This research was supported in part by grants from the National Science Foundation (SES-0221042 and IGERT grant #98070661). I would like to thank Irene Bloemraad, Prudence Carter, Felix Elwert, David Fitzgerald, Peggy Levitt, Helen Marrow, Katherine Newman, Mary Waters, and the anonymous reviewers for helpful comments.

Notes

1. I use the terms Latino and Hispanic interchangeably here. There are historical and symbolic differences between them (Oboler 1995), and their use is influenced by context. However, my respondents largely used these terms synonymously.
2. There are roots of *Latinidad* in Latin America (Padilla 1990), as residents of Latin America recognize cultural and historical commonalities among the peoples of the region. Such sentiments have developed independently, although they are reinforced when Latin Americans migrate to the US. However, the concept of an ethnic category comprising multiple Latin American nationalities, and the use of US-created labels such as 'Hispanic' to identify it, is born of the social processes Latin American migrants experience in the US (Oboler 1995).
3. Author's calculation based on Migration Policy Institute (2004) and Central Intelligence Agency (2000).
4. While six months was set as a criterion to distinguish those making short visits from those residing abroad, in fact almost none of the respondents had lived outside their home countries at all.
5. These photos range from light to dark and display a range of racial mixtures. I selected the photos in consultation with a Puerto Rican and a Dominican migrant in New York.

References

ALCOFF, LINDA MARTIN 2000 'Is Latina/o identity a racial identity?', in Jorge J. E. Gracia and Pablo de Grieff (eds), *Hispanics/Latinos in the United States: Ethnicity, Race and Rights*, New York: Routledge, pp. 23–44

ALICEA, MARIXSA 1997 ' "A chambered nautilus": the contradictory nature of Puerto Rican women's role in the social construction of a transnational community', *Gender & Society*, vol. 11, no. 5, pp. 597–626

BARTH, FREDERIK 1969 'Introduction', in Frederik Barth (ed.), *Ethnic Groups and Boundaries: The Social Organization of Culture Difference*, Boston, MA: Little, Brown, pp. 9–38

CENTRAL INTELLIGENCE AGENCY 2000 'The World Factbook', http://www.umsl.edu/services/govdocs/wofact2000/index.html
CORNELL, STEPHEN 1988 *The Return of the Native: American Indian Political Resurgence*, New York: Oxford University Press
DÁVILA, ARLENE M. 2001 *Latinos, Inc.: The Marketing and Making of a People*, Berkeley, CA: University of California Press
DIAZ MCCONNELL, EILEEN and DELGADO-ROMERO, EDWARD A. 2004 'Latino panethnicity: reality or methodological construction?', *Sociological Focus*, vol. 37, no. 4, pp. 297–312
DUANY, JORGE 2002 *The Puerto Rican Nation on the Move: Identities on the Island and in the United States*, Chapel Hill, NC: University of North Carolina Press
ESPIRITU, YEN LE 1992 *Asian American Panethnicity: Bridging Institutions and Identities*, Philadelphia, PA: Temple University Press
FLORES, JUAN 1993 *Divided Borders: Essays on Puerto Rican Identity*, Houston, TX: Arte Público Press
FOROS PERÚ WEBSITE 2007 'La Tormenta lider en Puerto Rico TOP 50', http://www.telenovelasperu.com/forostv/showthread.php?t=21352
GLICK SCHILLER, NINA, BASCH, LINDA and BLANC-SZANTON, CRISTINA 1992 'Transnationalism: a new analytical framework for understanding migration', *Annals of the New York Academy of Sciences*, vol. 645, pp. 1–24
GRACIA, JORGE J. E. 2007 *Race or Ethnicity? On Black and Latino Identity*, Ithaca, NY: Cornell University Press
GUARNIZO, LUIS EDUARDO 1997 'The emergence of a transnational social formation and the mirage of return migration among Dominican transmigrants', *Identities*, vol. 4, no. 2, pp. 281–322
ITZIGSOHN, JOSÉ, et al. 1999 'Mapping Dominican transnationalism: narrow and broad transnational practices', *Ethnic and Racial Studies*, vol. 22, no. 2, pp. 316–39
LEVITT, PEGGY 2001 *The Transnational Villagers*, Berkeley, CA: University of California Press
MASSEY, DOUGLAS S. et al. 1994 'An evaluation of international migration theory: the North American case', *Population and Development Review*, vol. 20, no. 4, pp. 699–751
MELÉNDEZ, EDWIN 1993 'Los que se van, los que regresan: Puerto Rican migration to and from the United Status, 1982–1988', Political Economy Working Paper Series No. 1, New York: Centro de Estudios Puertorriqueños
MENÉNDEZ ALARCÓN, ANTONIO V. 1992 *Power and Television in Latin America: The Dominican Case*, Westport, CT: Praeger
MEYROWITZ, JOSHUA 1985 *No Sense of Place*, New York: Oxford University Press
MIGRATION POLICY INSTITUTE 2004 *The Dominican Population in the United States: Growth and Population*, Washington, DC: Migration Policy Institute
MORRIS, NANCY 1995 *Puerto Rico: Culture, Politics, and Identity*, Westport, CT: Praeger
MOYA PONS, FRANK 1998 *The Dominican Republic: A National History*, Princeton, NJ: Markus Wiener Publishers
NAGEL, JOANNE 1995 'American Indian ethnic renewal: politics and the resurgence of ethnicity', *American Sociological Review*, vol. 60, no. 6, pp. 947–65
OBOLER, SUZANNE 1995 *Ethnic Labels, Latino Lives: Identity and the Politics of (Re)Presentation in the United States*, Minneapolis, MN: University of Minnesota Press
OKAMOTO, DINA G. 2006 'Institutional panethnicity: boundary formation in Asian-American organizing', *Social Forces*, vol. 85, no. 1, pp. 1–25
PADILLA, FÉLIX 1985 *Latino Ethnic Consciousness: The Case of Mexican Americans and Puerto Ricans in Chicago*, South Bend, IN: University of Notre Dame Press
—— 1990 'Latin America: the historical base of Latino unity', *Latino Studies Journal*, vol. 1, no. 1, pp. 7–27
PÉREZ Y GONZÁLEZ, MARÍA E. 2000 *Puerto Ricans in the United States*, Westport, CT: Greenwood Press

RODRÍGUEZ, CLARA E. 2000 *Changing Race: Latinos, the Census, and the History of Ethnicity in the United States*, New York: New York University Press
TABLEBASE 2000 'Global cable television', p. 181
TINKER SALAS, MIGUEL 1991 'El Inmigrante Latino: Latin American immigration and panethnicity', *Latino Studies Journal*, vol. 2, no. 3, pp. 58–71

Latinidad and masculinidad in Hollywood scripts

Ana S. O. Liberato, Guillermo Rebollo-Gil, John D. Foster and Amanda Moras

Abstract

We examined representations of Latinidad and masculinidad in a set of crime and independent films. Findings show that crime films emphasized marginality and suggested Latinos' inadequate cultural stock. They focused on violence and created notions of Latino inferiority based on class-specific presumptions of power, masculinity and success. The narratives suggest that Latinos lack the assertiveness and brilliance of the tough white gangster of the 1930s and 1940s. The deviant Latino is rather emotional and succumbs to his own vulnerabilities. He possesses an unfit masculinity which is linked to the presumed backwardness of his own ethnic community. The independent films reproduced some elements of these stereotypes, but one, *Girlfight*, situated Latinos in the context of racism, assimilation and multiculturalism. They offered a different narrative and a new Latino subject, one that somewhat destabilizes the coherence of racist and patriarchal messages found in the crime movies examined in this paper.

Introduction

The film industry is a culture- and knowledge-making institution. As such, cultural representations communicated in cinematic narratives convey meanings about a society's problems, anxieties and contradictions and reflect that society's view of itself and what is considered valued or undesirable (Denzin 1989). The work of cinema is thus highly sensitive to ideological scrutiny by professional critics who have the responsibility to 'politicize mass culture', paying attention to the ideological aspects around the production of film and interrogating the biases of filmmakers (McGee 1999).

With this in mind, this paper examines the set of generalizations and stereotypes about Latinidad and Latino masculinity portrayed in a selected number of Hollywood films. We examine the ideological frames and cultural assumptions that structure the narratives about Latino men and analyse the extent to which the narratives reproduce white racism. We also explore the extent to which these stereotypical representations help to promote a racialized view of Latinos in the United States, perpetuating the idea that Latinos/as do not want to and/or are not fit to be part of the fabric of American society.

Whiteness and Hollywood scripts

Hollywood filmmakers invoke ethnic difference as a means of constructing the Latino male's identity (Murji and Solomos 2005). They conceive and represent the Latino male as the Other in terms of their culture and 'moral, mental, and physical inheritance' (Roediger 2006). They render the Latino male as inferior to the white male in a codified narrative that subtly upholds WASPism.

A careful examination of the Othering of Latino men in Hollywood films demands an interrogation of whiteness. By definition, whiteness is involved with issues of power differences among whites and non-whites in the colonial and postcolonial context (Alcoff 1995; Kincheloe 1999; Barnett 2000). Whiteness is synonymous not with 'white people' but rather with a well-established epistemology in which the politics, culture, history, personality and phenotype of white Europeans are framed as if they would represent the natural and ideal way to be in the world (Kincheloe 1999; Barnett 2000). Whiteness acts as the common sense of people and represents sophistication, 'orderliness, rationality, and self-control' (Kincheloe 1999, p. 3). The ubiquity and pervasiveness of whiteness is possible due to its malleability and presumed 'social invisibility' (Frankenberg 1993; Keating 1995; Mahogany 1995; Dernersesian 1997). Racial divisions in the United States have been constructed on this dichotomous model – whites vs. non-whites – 'with the white self seeing racial others as monolithic' (Vera and Gordon 2001, p. 265).

An important consequence is the stigmatization of people of colour at all levels – from the institutional and governmental levels to microworlds such as that of cinematic storytelling. Another consequence is the reinforcement of emotional segregation, or European Americans' inability to see people of colour 'as emotional equals or as capable of sharing the same human emotions and experiences' (Beeman 2007, p. 687). The sense of worth, as well as the cultural and political citizenship, of people of colour is systematically diminished both in society and on screen.

Othering and stereotyping are precisely the lenses through which Anglo-American filmmakers have depicted Latinos in film (e.g. the caballero, the 'lazy greaser', the Mexican bandido, the harlot, the male buffoon, the female clown, the Latin lover and the dark lady) (Noriega 1992; Ramírez-Berg 2002; Rodriguez 2002). In particular, Chicano men started to be associated with urban violence in the late 1970s and early 1980s (Limón 1992; Noriega 1992; Ramírez-Berg 1998, 2002; Fregoso 1993a, 1993b; List 1996). This trend continued in the 1990s and early 2000s with Latino characters other than Mexicans. *White Men Can't Jump* (1992), *Collateral Damage* (2001), *Cocaine Cowboys* (2006) and *Illegal Tender* (2007) offer only a snapshot of the myriad Hollywood vehicles of vicious Latina/o stereotyping (Fuentes 1992; Ramírez-Berg 2002).

These cultural representations are such because they emphasize race and ethnicity following narrative recipes mediated by an ideology based on whiteness. They come to be a symptomatic manifestation of the existing 'structural relations of marginalization' and inequality that exist in our society, an indicator of 'the mental state of the dominant' (Murji and Solomos 2005). We look at stereotypes as a means to uncover this mental state. Our analysis is based on seven Hollywood films. The films included are: *Scarface* (1983), *American Me* (1992), *Carlito's Way* (1993) and *Blood In, Blood Out* (1993). We also include three recent independent films that offer audiences an alternative vision of Latina/o life, but in the end reinforce Hollywood race scripts based on whiteness. The three independent films are: *Girlfight* (2000), *Piñero* (2001) and *Empire* (2002). These films are under-studied and have generational representativeness. We included *Girlfight* because this film provides interesting insights into how filmmakers use race and gender in the construction of characters' personality. We talk about Cheech Marin's *Born in East L.A.* (1987) in several parts of this article as this movie features themes that are relevant to our discussion.

Methodological approach

We utilize the phenomenological-interpretative approach. We identify categories of meanings and discourses, 'ways of looking at and seeing things' emphasized in the narratives of Hollywood filmmakers. Carefully analysing the texts involved and repeatedly watching the movies, we began discovering themes and sub-themes, finally deciding which themes were more salient and establishing theoretical links between these themes and the literature. The recurrent themes found in the text were generalizations and stereotypes about deviant behaviour, marginality, diminished citizenship and machismo. These themes appeared pervasively in the narratives of the older films and persisted in the more recent films that, according to their producers, intended to portray Latinos/as in a more progressive, non-stereotypical way.

Latino masculinity in *Scarface* and *Carlito's Way*

Brian DePalma directed one of the most popular movies involving Latino themes in the 1980s, *Scarface* (1983), a remake of a 1932 mobster movie played mostly by Italian American actors. Unlike the original movie, the DePalma version incorporated Latino characters and themes (Rodriguez 1997). Al Pacino played Tony Montana, a Cuban refugee, who is the main character in the film. Brian DePalma and Al Pacino reunited again in *Carlito's Way* (1993); this time Pacino played Carlito Brigante, a Puerto Rican ex-convict who is in search of a second chance in life after his release from prison.

Tony is flamboyant, alluring, sexy and nasty. Carlito is sad, susceptible and broken. In time, it was Tony Montana, the most violent, deviant and flawed of the two characters, who became a cultural icon. It is the image of Tony Montana that appears on the bedroom walls of many young Latino men who admire him and see him even today as the epitome of Latino manhood and social rebelliousness; clear evidence of internalized sexism and racism among Latino men (see Sandoval Sánchez (2003) for a discussion of Latino audiences and criminal Salvador Agron in the theatrical production of Paul Simon's *The Capeman*).

Carlito 'Charlie' Brigante is a Puerto Rican from Spanish Harlem and Tony Montana is a recently arrived Cuban refugee living in Miami. Early in the films Tony and Carlito show awareness of the American ideals of progress and success. Tony and Carlito possess qualities that are highly regarded in the mainstream: intelligence, attractiveness, defiance, bravery and ambition. In the narratives, Tony and Carlito are not stripped of some of the qualities that marked Hollywood masculinity in the Reagan era: success, achievement, toughness and strength (Jeffords 1994). In particular, Carlito shows a strong sense of personal responsibility as he tries to take control and better his life after being in prison for several years on drug-trafficking charges.

These qualities make Tony and Carlito intriguing and thrilling characters, but at the same time their life stories are presented in problematic ways. For instance, Tony and Carlito play Latino men who live in a world of crime, sex, violence and drugs and who are obsessed with money and power. The narratives suggest that Tony and Carlito possess very dysfunctional personalities and shaky moral values. They grew up without fathers (like most Latino men in crime movies) and had turbulent relations with their families. Tony and Carlito *chose* criminality and terror as opposed to embracing the ideal notion of 'good old Americanness', which prescribes consistency between reaching success and respecting the rule of law (Jeffords 1994, p. 15). Even so, these characters expose a double standard in Hollywood and white hegemonic culture: that Anglo men who exhibit these characteristics are respected, even revered, while Latino men possessing the same qualities are detested; that is, a white (heterosexual) man acting macho is viewed positively (i.e. his ability to attract and seduce women and be in control) while a Latino (heterosexual) man exhibiting sexist traits is seen negatively (i.e. his propensity to dominate and terrorize women (see Mirandé 1997)). The criminal and corrupt behaviour of Tony and Carlito defines them as essentially not 'good old Americans'. They are only more dangerous since they are conceivably non-native and non-white.

Thus, characters like Tony and Carlito are effectively Othered in this process, symbolically defined in relation to the appropriateness, wholesomeness and righteousness of the dominant white male. Tony and Carlito are two maladjusted Latino males who cannot adjust to the otherwise sophisticated and rightful American way of life, and instead turn to crime and violence to earn money and respect. The narratives suggest that their inability to adjust resides in their maintaining a cultural identity that contradicts American values. One particular scene in *Scarface* illustrates this. In the scene, Tony Montana says to his best friend, right before joining a drug-trafficking organization, 'I didn't come to the United States to break my fucking back', indicating that he wanted money, power and success but he wanted them quickly and without having to play by the rules. The overall attitude system of Tony and Carlito, positioned as they are in the films as ethnic Others lacking an American identity, is subtly explained in relation to their cultural stock. Therefore, in both films, their characters are telling a story about a presumably identifiable and definable form of cultural identity and masculinity, a story about the nature of Latino men and Latino culture.

Tony killed and sold drugs to gain power *per se*; in a way he enjoyed being a criminal. This fact makes his character infamous. Carlito resented his past and showed some concerns for his future and some preoccupation over the effects of his behaviour on his family and community, but his defective character and his past are presented as such a burden that in the end he is unable to reshape his life. Alienated by criminality and trapped by passionate attitudes, both Carlito and Tony fail to create a healthy future for themselves and their kin. These two Latino characters, conceived within the ideological frameworks of whiteness, are represented as fragmented individuals, dangerous and tough, sexy and cruel, whose subjectivity can only be material for violent crime movies such as *Scarface* and *Carlito's Way*. With this background, Carlito and Tony become the prototype of the ethnic criminal, joining on screen the earlier Italian gangster in the urban criminal scene, the dangerous Chicano and the black gangster from the projects (Noriega 1992).

The masculinity of Tony Montana is highlighted through images of fearlessness and bravado. He is not afraid of the harshness of the American criminal justice system and has no regard for scruples. It is precisely his excessive bravado and aggressiveness that leads to the destruction of his self and his criminal enterprise. In the end, Tony builds a powerful and profitable criminal enterprise, but is defeated by his own desires and pathological personality. Passion over reason and pleasure over duty defines Tony's attitude systems in the Hollywood narrative.

Tony and Carlito experience life as if they are on the verge of an existential breakdown. Being emotional and highly subjective is not antithetical to masculinity in these two men. Carlito and Tony are never in control, even at the peak of their power. Their unpredictable, explosive and even childish behaviours are presented as the cause of such an emotional state and part of the cause behind their deviant lives. At times, Carlito and Tony show compassion and vulnerability in the films. There is a scene in *Scarface* in which Tony restrains himself from killing when he realizes his target is accompanied by his wife and child. On the other hand, Carlito struggles with his past, letting the audience know how much his emotional life has been affected by his criminal past. But the characters are too flawed and therefore their sensibility is actually dangerous. The subtle message is that Carlito and Tony possess a defective, even queer, masculinity (Negron-Muntaner 2000) and become victims of it. Furthermore, their actions throughout the film rationalize their brutal killings in the end (Rodríguez 1997, p. 181), while they justify Anglos acting violently against them (Ramírez-Berg 2002, p. 27).

Further, the controlling leadership style of Tony and Carlito reinforces stereotypes that Hollywood films have traditionally attributed to Latino men. They embody the 'machismo' that castrates, manipulates and controls other people's individuality and identity and that conceives interactions with other people through the lenses of clearly delineated hierarchies, where somebody always has a recognized power over others. These frames of representation of the Latino male resonate with the views of many western intellectuals that attribute certain backwardness to people of Latino descent. Arguments about backwardness have been frequently based on negative assumptions about the 'Catholic religion' and culture *vis-à-vis* 'Protestantism' (Harrison 1985).

Ideas about the inferiority of lifestyles, attitudes and culture of Latino men are conveyed through the criminalization of their place of residence and/or area of operation. Spanish Harlem and Miami are the settings of these films. They are negatively represented and depicted as being as dangerous as Tony and Carlito themselves. Miami and Spanish Harlem are sites of crises, lost territories disconnected from the quiet 'realities' of the rest of society. Only 'lesser whites' can risk coming close to these environments. A subtle connection is made in the narrative between failed masculinity and failed communities and between ethnicity and backwardness.

Defective in character and guided by non-US values, these men are depicted by these films as corrupt, irrational, contradictory, unsophisticated and therefore 'underdeveloped'. With their defective character, *they* built the barriers between them and American society. They resist the process of cultural assimilation, have a 'natural' tendency to failure and live in broken environments within broken families. Viewing dignity as a function of toughness and material exhibitionism, Tony and Carlito are portrayed as both glamorous and retrogressive. They are 'hotblooded and have an easy virtue' (Castro 1998). This male personality is essentially a threat to the constitution of stable and solid communities and to the society as a whole. With a fatalistic and authoritarian vision of life, they profess an overall attitude that contradicts those of US society. They are lacking not only the emotional resources and professional skills but also the discipline and talent needed to become, in a legitimate way, 'successful' Americans.

The masculinity of these two characters in many ways resembles hegemonic views of masculinity circulating in the society. The violence and aggression, the toughness, the readiness for emotional disconnection, the thrust for power and control are all there in rather excessive amounts. Their masculinity is not constructed in relation to women or to other men (Cohan and Hark 1993), but in connection to deviant behaviour. This deviance acts as a marker of masculinity and a stage for celebrating spectacular and racialized violence. But, while hypermasculine in their behaviour, Tony and Carlito are paradoxically feminized by their somewhat 'emotionalized' existence. In this way, DePalma produced the binary 'vs.', providing no plot about how these two male characters negotiate their male identities and roles *vis-à-vis* their experiences with urban life, sexuality, friendship, community, violence and drugs (Cohan and Hark 1993). In the end, DePalma created a coherent narrative of Latino life based on a monolithic and gendered concept of Latinidad.

The omnipresence of marginality in narratives of Latinidad and masculinity: *Blood In, Blood Out* and *American Me*

Marginality is an important theme in narratives of Latinidad and Latino masculinity. Just as in *Scarface* and *Carlito's Way*, an identifiable pattern of imagery helps construct notions of the marginal Latino man in *Blood In, Blood Out* and *American Me*. In both of these films, the camera takes us to dirty and isolated neighbourhoods or jails and exposes the audience to the problems of poverty, drug use, gang life and dysfunctional families. The neighbourhoods are ugly; there are clothes hanging on the walls, a lot of noise and a lot of Spanish signs on building walls. People walk down the neighbourhood streets and hang out, suggesting chronic idleness. Inside this world, the young inner-city population struggles to survive in the midst of drug violence, drug addiction and economic insecurity. Shootings, burglaries and gang confrontations form part of their everyday life.

In *Blood In, Blood Out* and *American Me*, Latino men are depicted as marginal men and marginal citizens. Marginality is presented as the common denominator of their life experiences in the United States. The marginality of Latino men is constructed on notions of gang membership, lower occupational status and income, and difference based on language and nationality. The narratives of marginality focus exclusively on accentuating a strong and exclusive relationship between ethnicity and deviant behaviour.

The constitution of the marginal Latino in these two films includes images of the unassimilated immigrant who cannot speak English fluently or hold a decent job. These images contrast noticeably with the dominant imagery of America as a wealthy middle-class nation. Neither physically nor behaviourally do these neighbourhoods represent American prosperity. Hence, these films represent Latino communities as peripheral, distanced culturally, technologically and economically from the mainstream and yet geographically close to the centre of it.

In these two films Hollywood filmmakers attach conditions of poverty, marginality and deviance to the Latino male experience. The constant focus on the street life of inner-city youths and delinquents make this attachment salient and exclusive and leaves out important aspects of Latino immigration and adaptation to US society. This is important since very few cinematic narratives actually tell stories about their lived experiences and status in US society and the particular historical, political, and economic circumstances in which they arrived (Flores 1993).

In essence, the narratives of these movies promote the sense that the poor and economically marginalized represent a threat to urban life and to society at large. They live broken lives in broken environments, and as a consequence have no future. Within this depiction, Latinos should not be 'rescued' or 'vindicated', since neither their families nor their communities are deemed able to cope with their problems or improve their situation. They live marginal lives and possess a marginal citizenship.

Chin Marin illustrated the consequences of marginalized experience and citizenship in his film *Born in East L.A.* Main character Rudy Robles' deportation to Mexico in this film reflects how marginal citizenship can be constructed through meanings of appearance and language capabilities in specific settings in the United States. Marin also shows how ethnic background, skin colour, class appearance and residency can fragment the status of people as citizens in American society. This film exposes how Chicano 'subjectivity resides in the space between and among cultural systems/orders' (Fregoso 1993b, p. 68). In the case of Rudy Robles in *Born in East L.A.*, his American citizenship was denied on the basis of his non-whiteness. Rudy is a third-generation Mexican-American who, despite speaking perfect English, could not prove his citizenship during an Immigration and Naturalization Services [INS] raid. Rudy was not carrying personal documents with him at the time of the raid and was captured and 'deported' to Mexico. Located in a poor immigrant setting, looking poor and being a person of colour, Rudy could not neutralize the strength of the images that associate those characteristics with illegal immigrant status in California. In the end, he had to put up with the mistreatment of INS officers. The persistent insinuation of questionable legal residency status sometimes took Rudy out of the category 'American all together' (Fregoso 1993b).

But marginal citizenship can be enacted on screen using other devices. For instance, portraying Latinas/os as culturally backward and unwilling to participate in the development of the country yields notions of second-class citizenship. Being consistently located in the margins of society in Hollywood narratives reinforces negative perceptions of the integrity of their communities and lowers their status as American citizens. When we see gangs killing each other in *Blood In, Blood Out* and *American Me* (and see the lives that Tony Montana and Carlito Brigante live), we witness the damage inflicted on urban life in America by mostly Latino delinquents. The actions and activities they are involved in legitimize ideas of exclusion and discrimination. These criminals are by no means represented as the protagonists of complex social problems and dramatic lives but rather themselves constitute the problems. They threaten the health of American life and institutions with their difference, deviance and marginality. Within the frameworks of whiteness, such individuals of colour should have fewer responsibilities to society and also many fewer rights. In essence, the marginal Latino does not and should not belong in America.

The marginal Latino is pitched against the notion of traditional US citizenship. In modern times, the concept of becoming or being an American has been linked to ideas of belonging to a society ruled by law, ethically inspired by the principles of freedom, democracy and material success (Gusteren 1998). Encapsulating Latinos within frameworks of marginality and criminality thus curtails the formation of positive perceptions regarding their participation in American society. This portrayal of Latinas/os as socially, culturally and personally unfit to form part of American society produces knowledge that recreates and perpetuates notions of their lower citizenship reinforcing the primacy of white citizenship and the lower citizenship of most recently arrived Latino immigrants (Rosaldo and Flores 1997).

It is the supremacy of these narratives that made success difficult for Edward James Olmos in his attempt to create an illuminating protest barrio film in *American Me* (Denzin 2002). Although the film is powerful, realistic and threatening in its indictment of Chicano male culture and capitalist values (Denzin 2002), Olmos employs the ultimate racialization narrative in it. The construction of his critique of machismo, racism and capitalism depends on attaching racial meanings to the social issues he presents in the story. This makes race, ethnicity and culture the key factors in defining and understanding criminality, marginality and violence. In the end, the film reifies the concept of race and ethnicity and invokes the biological, social and cultural unity of 'an arbitrarily Racialized group, that of Americans of Latino descent' (Murji and Solomos 2005).

Independent films as on-screen remedy

Latino actors from as far back as the 1930s have resisted negative scripts of Latinidad (Ramírez-Berg 2002). Today, when the trend in Hollywood is towards Latinization (Dávila 2001), Latinos are increasingly portrayed as visible outsiders. In this context, Latino actors and producers have put efforts into challenging uncomplicated narratives of Latinidad. Three recent independent films that offer audiences an alternate vision of Latino/a life and peoples are *Girlfight* (2000), *Piñero* (2001) and *Empire* (2002). Interestingly enough, all three films are set in New York City and give a glimpse into the life of predominantly Puerto Rican communities. Both *Girlfight* and *Empire* are fictional stories about boxing and the drug trade, respectively, while *Piñero* is the biopic of the famous Nuyorican poet, playwright and actor Miguel Piñero. Two of the productions, *Girlfight* and *Piñero*, received critical acclaim and certain accolades, with *Girlfight* being the more decorated of the two. *Empire*, though heavily criticized in several media outlets, is an important film to examine, considering the fact that it is the first feature production of the Latina/o-centred movie studio, Arenas. We analyse these films to ascertain exactly what are the different and genuinely progressive elements in their portrayal of Latinos/as on screen and what, if any, ideological concessions these films had to make in order to achieve box-office success.

Empire: *the sensitive man's* Scarface

Empire is the story of Victor Rosa, a respected Puerto Rican drug dealer in the Bronx who gets into business with a white American Wall Street con-artist who meticulously lures him into investing in several cutting-edge dot.com companies and then takes off with the money. The rest of the story unfolds in a predictable fashion as Victor, in his desire to move up out of the Bronx and leave the drug business behind, ends up cutting his interpersonal ties, upsetting his drug supplier and hitting rock bottom only then to seek out and kill the con-artist, getting his money back. In this sense, *Empire* does not break any new ground: drugs, shoot-outs, murders, cops and revenge invade the screen. *Empire*'s story however is twofold. Developing at the same pace as the traditional underworld storyline, there is the story of the clash between the white and non-white world in New York City. *Empire*'s contextual values lie in its conception and depiction of a clear class/colour demarcation between the world Victor Rosa inhabits and the world the con-artist offers him an entry to. The traditional and even clichéd gangster tale the movie tells is meant to serve simply as an attractive mechanism by which to present the more crucial issue of white/non-white relations. The problem is that the mechanism employed in the film ends up overtaking the principal message of the movie. Consequently, somewhere between the various scuffles and shoot-outs between opposing drug dealers and the cold and vicious murders of several of the film's primary characters, including the leading man, the issue of race is lost.

What remains is a sparse glimmer of hope that shines through every so often during the film. There is the loving relationship that Victor has with his girlfriend and his touching desires to be a father. There is the construction of Victor's posse as at once a frightening and deadly association of criminals and a loving and complex group of friends that go through an entire series of diverse emotions as their group is shaken by outside forces and almost torn apart. There is most importantly, for the purposes of the film, the equation of white legitimate business operations with the non-white drug world. Victor and the con-artist, Jack, are brought together by the kind of money they make and by the way they make it. They are both hustlers. However, since the audience views the action through Victor's eyes, and because the film does try, and in fact succeeds to a point, in depicting a more humanized version of the Puerto Rican drug dealer, Victor is the character one roots for. He is the character the people like. More importantly, his character, because he is given a girlfriend, a future child, a group of friends and a community, is the complex, three-dimensional person that the white American character is not and that makes all the difference.

This, in our estimation, is *Empire*'s most meaningful accomplishment. It manages to give a more complete view of a traditionally one-dimensional character. It does so, however, in the same fashion that Hollywood productions construct their white American heroes: it utilizes an image of the racial other as a mere foil (Vera and Gordon 2003). This is problematic for, in order to break out of the traditional Latino/a villain role, the film dehumanizes the white American character. Liberation here depends on an inversion or recreation of typical white vs. brown representations. The progressive character of the representation is thus compromised.

Piñero: *straight up, no chaser*

The film *Piñero* is compromised in a similar way. Based on the life and work of a founder of the 1970s Nuyorican poetry movement, this film is set up as a series of flashbacks that provide audiences with a dizzying look into the life of the deceased writer. The problem, however, is not with the cinematic style of the film, for one is able to get a good sense of what the man went through. The problem lies in the depiction of the man himself and the community he represented.

Miguel Piñero, the writer, is taken completely out of context in this film. While it is true that the movie goes to great length and succeeds in giving Piñero's work, especially his poetry, centre-stage on screen, the work is not placed adequately within the specific social circumstances under which it emerged. The migration of working-class Puerto Ricans to the US that took place following the Second World War and their settlement in some of New York City's poorest areas is only briefly acknowledged in the film by way of a facile nostalgia for better times on the island. This is problematic because Piñero's work, along with that of his fellow Nuyorican writers, was the direct product of that migration process and it arose out of an utter necessity to protest against the dire conditions in which they were forced to live in New York (Flores 1993). Further, their work served as the premier vehicle for the expression of socially conscious and politically motivated ideas among the Puerto Rican community (Flores 1993). Consequently, to strip the work from this context is to misconstrue both the nature and purpose of the work, as well as the life of the man who wrote it. Miguel Piñero is thus portrayed in this film as more of a junkie outlaw than a socially conscious poet. He comes off as a wayward and non-political petty thief with a unique and seemingly inexplicable gift for writing gut-wrenching plays and aggressive yet lyrical poetry.

Furthermore, the film's treatment of Piñero's sexuality leaves a lot to be desired. In the few instances in which Piñero's bisexuality comes to light in the film it is depicted as somehow deviant, immoral, or as a tragic consequence of the sexual abuse he suffered at the hands of his father when he was a child. His supposed truancy is further developed in the many scenes in the film where Piñero appears either drunk, high or getting drunk or high. Now, while it is true that Piñero's drug addiction and alcoholism did lead to an early death, and while it is also true that as his condition worsened he got more and more desperate and thus, more and more decadent, the film seems more concerned with this theme than with the relationship between the poet and his father, lover or best friend. The fact is that all these relationships, even though they do appear in the movie and even though they are at the base of some of the film's most touching moments, are overshadowed by the graphic and brutal drug scenes in which Piñero slowly but surely deadens himself with each hit.

A cloak of criminality thus seems to come over this character for even his most tender looks and heartfelt actions are somehow taken over by the moral and/or social defect he is presumed to have. Such is the span of this criminal persona that it eclipses the Puerto Rican community the writer represented. The film refuses to portray the people that made up Piñero's Puerto Rican New York. Consequently, it seems that the writer lived in some type of larger communal vacuum. It seems that he wrote for himself, that he believed in nothing and was read by no one.

Girlfight: *punching out racial/racist conventions*

Of the three independent films, *Girlfight* (2000) is the most successful in portraying multidimensional Latino/a characters. In the movie, Michelle Rodriguez plays the role of Diana Guzmán, a tough and stubborn yet sensitive Puerto Rican teenager from the Red Hook section of Brooklyn, New York. Diana lives with her obnoxious and domineering father and her little brother. The overall mood in their home is one of tension and anxiety. The two siblings get along and take care of each other, but their relationship with their father Sandro appears strained. He and Diana constantly clash. Diana's conflict with her dad stems from her mother's suicide which in Diana's mind was provoked by years of physical and emotional abuse from Sandro. The mother's presence in the movie is thus strikingly evident. Throughout the film, the audience witnesses the girl's trials and tribulations as she attempts to find a niche for herself. The movie, then, has much less to do with boxing than with this teen's urgent need to carve out, establish and assert an identity of her own.

Girlfight thus avoids all the trappings that could have made the film a female *Rocky*-type tale by having the boxing serve not as the centrepiece of the movie but rather as the metaphor for the much more interesting and important internal and interpersonal conflicts of the film's leading character. There is no glory, no fame and no money for Diana to make in this film. There is no visible change in her situation. On paper, she is no better or worse at the end of the movie than she was at the beginning. What *Girlfight* manages to do is to present the coming of age of a disenfranchised and doubly marginal character (she is in the margins of both mainstream white American society and the male-dominated Latina/o boxing community) in a difficult and dangerous social environment without having to resort to typical Hollywood depictions of 'people of colour' struggling to get by. Consequently, the violence prevalent in Diana's community, though acknowledged and somehow ever present, does not visibly appear in the film. By the same token, the abuse to which Diana's mother was submitted does not appear in visual recollections in the film even though it drives Diana's every move towards her father. What is played out for the camera is her attack on him. Physical violence is used here in a more positive manner: not as a reflection of the moral depravity of this community, but as the crowning symbol of self-assertion of one of this community's most subjugated members.

Furthermore, the ethnic character of the story is not developed within a context of criminality or overall illegality. On the contrary, the movie introduces the audience to a rich though economically humble and troubled community. There are loving relationships all through this movie. The movie is in fact built on the complex relationships of the different Latino/a characters. There is thus an overwhelming air of humanity that rises up in seemingly every scene and which gives the Latino/a characters in the film a tenderness rarely if ever seen in Hollywood productions. This tenderness, however, does not come at the expense of social consciousness or critique. On the contrary, the film harbours a very strong message against patriarchal thinking and male violence within the Latino/a community.

The character of Diana Guzman represents what Mary Beltrán refers to as the 'new Latina action hero'. The example of *Girlfight* is one of many, yet stands out as the most progressive. Beltrán writes:

Girlfight challenges gender typing with respect to the physical and mental training and qualities we associate with heroism ... in this regard, *Girlfight* comments on the qualities associated with masculinity in US culture, and the tradition of resistance to women demonstrating such so-called "masculine" traits. (Beltràn 2004, p. 194)

Whereas the representation of Diana challenges hegemonic notions of masculinity and heroism, Beltrán also points out that much of the construction of the Latina action hero relies on the emphasis on Latina bodies: because they are 'sexy' their aggression is more palatable, as is the case for instance in the myriad action roles Jennifer Lopez has played (*Anaconda, Enough, Angel Eyes, Out of Sight*). In contrast, *Girlfight* provides a welcome relief from these over-sexualized portrayals, the 'new macha heroine for a new era' (Beltrán 2004, p. 193).

Diana's character is a remarkably crafted and beautifully staged affront against traditional notions of manhood and femininity. Her character's ferocity represents the social and moral weight of the critique. The film then succeeds because it does justice to and humanizes Latinas/os on screen without having to shy away from the more troubling aspects of Latina/o culture and without compromising its commitment to female empowerment and overall social change.

Conclusions

Hollywood filmmakers construct ideological messages that safeguard whiteness through the systematic racialization of Latino men in film. Race and ethnicity are invoked to create a limited understanding of marginality and criminality, producing inferiorization of Latinidad and Latino masculinity. Accounts of gendered violence, cultural otherness and deficient cultural stock and class-specific presumptions of success, progress and normality help uphold white identity in the film narratives.

Although crime and marginality have been recurring themes, there are marked differences between these tales of crime and the frameworks used to tell crime stories involving white characters. It is obvious that the toughness of Latino criminals like Tony Montana and Carlito Brigante lacks the assertive manhood of the tough white gangster of the 1930s and 1940s (Neibaur 1989). The criminal Latino is defective in character and personality as it is his culture (Fregoso 1993a). In the case of Latinos, toughness and virility are revealed as counterproductive and extremely dangerous. Unlike the skilful and rational white villain, the marginal Latino is distracted by the confusion and contradiction of his emotions and succumbs to his own vulnerabilities.

Overall, the set of films analysed, except for *Girlfight*, fail to present and situate Latinidad and masculinidad in the context of racism, multiculturalism and assimilation. Even Edward James Olmos, who consciously tried to break the Hollywood mould, failed in this effort and reproduced Hollywood's narratives of Latino masculinity in his film *American Me*. These racialized images teach people about what it means to be a Latino male in the US (and what it means to be white), provide a reference for conceptualizing their citizenship and social worth, and help to jeopardize society's chances of increasing social closeness among groups (Feagin and Vera 1995; Honneth 1996).

Early twenty-first century films such as *Piñero*, *Empire* and *Girlfight* evidence the effort of challenging certain stereotypes of Latinas/os in Hollywood films as the number of Latinos/as increase in Hollywood and US society at large. They illustrate an attempt to define Latina/o ethnicity, community and identity from the standpoint of Latinas/os themselves as opposed to utilizing Hollywood's most traditional racial definitions (Molina Guzmán 2006). Latino/a actors have understood that the image of the dangerous Latino male is used to convey messages about the alleged dysfunctional character of families of colour. With an essential patriarchal premise, these messages link the goodness of a community to the goodness and fitness of their men. Movies like *Piñero* and *Empire* offer a different narrative and a new Latino subject, one that destabilizes the coherence of racist and patriarchal messages such as this.

As we write this conclusion, the number of Latina/o actors, producers, directors and singers continues to increase and become more visible in American movies and television. At the same time, the debate over the future shape of the American bi-racial order continues as the numbers of people of colour among the US population continue to increase. Bonilla Silva (2004) envisions a tri-racial system of stratification composed by whites (on top), honorary whites and collective blacks (at the very bottom). According to Bonilla Silva, the benefits of whiteness will be (unequally) shared by new white immigrants and lighter skin multi-racials while blacks, black immigrants and dark-skinned Asians will share the bottom of the hierarchy. George Yancey (2003) foresees a dichotomous system of stratification composed by whites and all minorities, on the one hand, and African Americans alone, on the other hand. Yancey's argument suggests changes in the definition of whiteness in a way that allows the integration of all non-black minorities.

As race and racial ideology are functional systems in our society (Haney Lopez 2006), we should expect these changes to reflect the dynamics brought about by the increased numbers of inter-marriage and multi-racial individuals and increased numbers of people of colour. We should expect films to reflect these tensions and new social, political and cultural realities (Noriega 1992). The challenge for professional critics is to expose the ideological underpinnings by which the stereotype of the dangerous, marginal, criminal Latino is maintained in the present and near future in the light of substantial transformations in the lives of Latinos and challenges to white supremacy by multiculturalism, new identity politics, progressive social policies and anti-racist social movements (Twine and Gallagher 2008).

References

ALCOFF, LINDA 1995 'Mestizo identity', in Naomi Zack (ed.), *America Mixed Race: The Culture of Microdiversity*, Lanham, MD: Rowman & Littlefield, pp. 257–78
BARNETT, TIMOTHY 2000 'Reading whiteness in English studies', *College English*, vol. 63, no. 1, pp. 9–37
BEEMAN, ANGIE K. 2007 'Emotional segregation: a content analysis of institutional racism in US films 1980–2001', *Ethnic and Racial Studies*, vol. 30, no. 5, pp. 687–712
BELTRÁN, MARY 2004 'Más macha: the new Latina action hero', in Yvonne Tasker (ed.), *Action and Adventure Cinema*, New York: Routledge
BONILLA SILVA, EDUARDO 2004 *Racism Without Racists: Color-blind Racism and the Persistance of Racial Inequality in the United States*, Lanham, MD: Rowan and Littlefield
CASTRO, D O. 1998 '"Hot blood and easy virtue": mass media and the making of racist Latino/a stereotypes', in Coramae Richey Mann and Marjorie S. Satz (eds), , *Images of Color, Images of Crime: Readings*, Los Angeles, CA: Roxbury
COHAN, STEVEN and HARK, INA RAE 1993 *Screening the Male: Exploring Masculinity in Hollywood Cinema*, London: Routledge
DÁVILA, ARLENE 2001 *Latinos Inc.: The Marketing and Making of a People*, Berkeley, CA: University of California Press
DENZIN, NORMAN K. 1989 'Reading tender mercies: two interpretations', *The Sociological Quarterly*, vol. 30, no. 1, pp. 37–57
—— 2002 *Reading Race: Hollywood and the Cinema of Racial Violence*, London: Sage
DERNERSESIAN, CHABRAM 1997 'On the social construction of whiteness within selected Chicana/o discourses', in Ruth Frankenberg (ed.), *Displacing Whiteness*, Durham, NC: Duke University Press, pp. 107–64
FEAGIN, JOE and VERA, HERNÁN 1995 *White Racism: The Basics*, New York: Routledge
FLORES, JUAN 1993 *Divided Borders: Essays on Puerto Rican Identity*, Houston, TX: Arte Publico Press
FRANKENBERG, RUTH 1993 *The Social Construction of Whiteness: White Women, Race Matters*, Minneapolis, MN: University of Minnesota Press
FREGOSO, ROSA LINDA 1993a 'The representation of cultural identity in Zoot Suit', *Theory and Society*, vol. 22, no. 5, pp. 659–74
—— 1993b *The Bronze Screen: Chicana and Chicano Film Culture*, Minneapolis, MN: University of Minnesota Press.
FUENTES, VICTOR 1992 'Chicano cinema: a dialectic between voices and images of the autonomous discourse versus those of the dominant', in Chon A. Noriega (ed.), *Chicanos and Film: Representation and Resistance*, Minneapolis, MN: University of Minnesota Press, pp. 207–17
GUSTEREN, HERMAN R. VAN 1998 *A Theory of Citizenship: Organizing Plurality in Contemporary Democracies*, Boulder, CO: Westview Press
HANEY, LÓPEZ and IAN, F. 2006 *White by Law: The Legal Construction of Race*, New York: New York University Press
HARRISON, LAWRENCE 1985 *Underdevelopment is a State of Mind: The Latin American Case*, Cambridge, MA: Harvard University Press
HONNETH, AXEL 1996 *The Struggle for Recognition: The Moral Grammar of Social Conflicts*, Cambridge, MA: MIT Press
JEFFORDS, SUSAN 1994 *Hard Bodies: Hollywood Masculinity in the Reagan Era*, New Brunswick, NJ: Rutgers University Press
KEATING, A. 1995 'Interrogating whiteness: (de) constructing race', *College English*, vol. 57, no. 8, pp. 901–18
KINCHELOE, JOE 1999 'The struggle to define and reinvent whiteness: a pedagogical analysis', *College Literature*, vol. 26, no. 3, pp. 162–70

LIMÓN, JOSÉ E. 1992 'Stereotyping and Chicano resistance: an historical dimension', in Chon A. Noriega (ed.), *Chicanos and Film: Representation and Resistance*, Minneapolis, MN: University of Minnesota Press, pp. 3–17

MAHOGANY, MARTHA 1995 'Segregation, whiteness, and transformation', *University of Pennsylvania Law Review*, vol. 143, no. 5, pp. 1659–84

MCGEE, PATRICK 1999 'Terrible beauties: messianic time and the image of social redemption in James Cameron's *Titanic'*, *Postmodern Culture*, vol. 10, no. 1

MIRANDÉ, ALFREDO 1997 *Hombres y Machos: Masculinity and Latino Culture*, Boulder, CO: Westview Press

MOLINA GUZMÁN, ISABEL 2006 'Competing discourses of community: ideological tensions between local general-market and Latino news media', *Journalism*, vol. 7, no. 3, pp. 281–98

MURJI, KARIM and SOLOMOS, JOHN 2005 'Racialization in theory and practice', in Karim Murji and John Solomos (eds), *Racialization: Studies in Theory and Practice*, New York: Oxford University Press

NEGRÓN-MUNTANER, FRANCES 2000 'Feeling pretty: *West Side Story* and Puerto Rican identity discourses', *Social Text*, vol. 18, no. 2, pp. 83–106

NEIBAUR, JAMES 1989 *The American Movie Macho*, Jefferson, NC: McFarland & Company

NORIEGA, CHON 1992 *Chicanos and Film*, Minneapolis, MN: University of Minnesota Press

RAMÍREZ BERG, CHARLES 1998 'From assimilation narrative to social problem', in Richard Delgado and Jean Stefanic (eds), *The Latino Condition: Critical Reading*, New York: New York University Press, pp. 215–22

—— 2002 *Latino Images in Film: Stereotypes, Subversion, Resistance*, Austin, TX: University of Texas Press

RODRIGUEZ, CLARA 1997 *Latin Looks: Images of Latinas and Latinos in the U.S. Media*, Boulder, CO: Westview Press, pp. 80–4, 180–4

—— 2002 *Heroes, Lovers, and Others: The Story of Latinos in Hollywood*, Washington, DC: Smithsonian Books

ROEDIGER, DAVID, R. 2006 *Working Toward Whiteness: How America's Immigrants Became White: The Strange Journey from Ellis Island to the Suburbs*, New York: Basic Books

ROSALDO RENATO and FLORES WILLIAM 1997 'Identity, conflict and evolving Latino communities: Cultural citizenship in San Jose' in William Flores and Rina Benmayor (eds.), *Latino Cultural Citizenship: Claiming Identity, Space and Rights*, pp. 57–96, Boston: Beacon Press

SANDOVAL SÁNCHEZ, ALBERTO 2002 'Paul Simon's The Capeman: staging Puerto Rican national identity as spectacle and commodity on Broadway', in Michelle Habell-Pallan and Mary Romero (eds), *Latino/a Popular Culture*, New York: New York University Press

TWINE, FRANCE WINDDANCE and GALLAGHER, CHARLES 2008 'The future of whiteness: a map of the "third wave"', *Ethnic and Racial Studies*, vol. 31, no. 1, pp. 4–24

VERA, HERNÁN and GORDON, ANDREW 2001 'Sincere fictions of the white self in the American cinema: the divided white self in Civil War films', in Daniel Lombardi (ed.), *Classic Hollywood Classic Whiteness*, Minneapolis, MN: University of Minnesota Press, pp. 263–80

—— 2003 '*Screen Saviors: Hollywood Fictions of Whiteness'*, Lanham, MD: Rowman & Littlefield

YANCEY, GEORGE 2003 *Who Is White? Latinos, Asians, and the New Black/Nonblack Divide*, Boulder, CO: Lynne Rienner

Contexts for bilingualism among US-born Latinos

April Linton and Tomás R. Jiménez

Abstract

This paper focuses on the contextual determinants of bilingualism among Latino adults who were born in the US or are members of the '1.5 generation' of Latinos who immigrated to the US when they were 10 or younger. We model the broader contexts reflecting contemporary developments that influence *change* in both the real and the perceived value of bilingualism. Using US census data for metropolitan areas in 1990 and 2000, we find that the replenishment of an immigrant population is a strong predictor of higher bilingualism among US-born Latinos. We draw on ethnographic data on later-generation Mexican Americans as well as field-work in dual-language immersion schools to explain our findings. The variables measuring the size and growth of the foreign-born Latino population in the MSA/PMSAs in our models capture the factors that encourage bilingualism that we identify in our ethnographic research: institutional contact with Spanish, labour-market rewards, cosmopolitanism.

Contexts for bilingualism among US-born Latinos

Historically, immigrants in the United States have been discouraged from using their native tongue and passing it on to their children. Immigration for most groups took place during a compressed period, and opportunities to speak the mother tongue of the immigrant generation dwindled after immigration ceased (Alba 1988; Massey 1995). The dominance of English in government, industry, education and popular culture has made language 'the single most important element in construction of national identity, both positively as a communicative instrument shared by members of the nation and as a boundary marker affirming their distinction from others' (Zolberg and Long 1999, p. 22). It is thus not surprising that the vast majority of sociological research on language in the United States focuses on English acquisition and use rather than other-language maintenance. The prevailing assumption is that bilingualism is a transitional state on the way to English monolingualism – maybe not for new immigrants, but definitely across generations.

Though the majority of third-generation Latinos are English monolinguals, Spanish has far greater generational longevity than other non-English languages in the United States (Rumbaut 2002; Alba 2004; Linton 2004a; Rumbaut, Massey and Bean 2006). Spanish speakers comprise over half of those who speak a language other than English at home. A continuous flow of Latin American immigrants makes it more practical for US Hispanics[1] to retain Spanish now than it was in the past, providing greater opportunities and incentives for bilingualism. A change in dominant ideology from a near-exclusive emphasis on Americanization to a rise in multiculturalism has elevated the status of Spanish relative to a previous time. Furthermore, globalizing economies and the emergence of communities that span national borders have altered the costs and benefits of English monolingualism and bilingualism (Levitt 2001; Smith 2005).

This paper models how contextual factors shape the level of bilingualism in a metropolitan area, focusing on bilingualism among Latino adults who were born in the US or are members of the '1.5 generation' – immigrants who were 10 or younger when they arrived. We ask: under what contextual circumstances does bilingualism thrive among US-born and 1.5-generation Hispanics? This research adds to micro-level explanations based on individual- and household-level circumstances (Alba *et al.* 2002; Bean and Stevens 2003) of bilingualism by putting forth a macro-level model of the contexts within which individuals and families make choices about language. We are interested in broader contexts that could influence the ease of Spanish maintenance as well as its cultural and/or economic utility because these contexts reflect contemporary developments that could influence *change* in both the real and perceived value of bilingualism.

We employ 1990 and 2000 US Census data to model how the dynamics of demographic, socio-cultural and economic change affect the level of bilingualism among US-born and 1.5-generation Latinos living in metropolitan areas. We also draw on in-depth interviews with later-generation Mexican Americans and interviews with parents and teachers affiliated with Spanish/English dual-immersion schools in Chicago, Los Angeles and five other Southern California school districts. We harness survey data and interviews in order to provide a complete analysis, one that specifies relationships between contextual factors and levels of bilingualism and that posits mechanisms that explain these relationships.

Bilingualism as a possible *endpoint* of linguistic assimilation

Bilingualism may not just be a transition stage prior to English monolingualism. It has the potential to be an endpoint of language change. Stevens (1985) suggests that bilingualism could be a stable outcome of linguistic assimilation among groups characterized by high rates of ethnic endogamy and non-English linguistic homogamy. One of her later studies establishes the importance of the demographic context in determining whether US-born adults with a non-English mother tongue continue to use that language alongside English (Stevens 1992).

The case for why bilingualism may become an endpoint of language shift becomes clear in recent research that measures the advantages of bilingualism for integration into American society. Portes and Rumbaut (2001) observed a high rate of shift away from the non-English mother tongue among children of immigrants in San Diego and Miami, but found that the fluently bilingual teenagers in their sample did better in school, had higher aspirations for the future, enjoyed better mental health, and family relations and were more likely to have friends from abroad. Second-generation Latino youths were more likely to belong to this group than youths from other backgrounds, especially if their parents used Spanish at home and they have co-ethnic friends (Portes and Rumbaut 2001, p. 141). Rumbaut's analysis of data from the third wave of the same survey, in which the respondents had reached adulthood, showed that Latinos' ability to speak and read Spanish 'did not atrophy but rather improved appreciably from their teen to their twenties' (2002, p. 67). About 25 per cent reported fluent bilingualism, and over 75 per cent of the respondents expressed the wish to raise their own children in Spanish and English.

Alba *et al.* (2003, p. 480) also find evidence for some 'staying power' for Spanish, especially in supportive familial and community contexts. They find that the rate of intergenerational language shift is lower for Spanish-speakers, compared to other immigrant groups or to Spanish-speakers in times past.

Recent research shows that later-generation Mexican Americans, who by virtue of their later-generation status would seem most likely to see their Spanish-language skills enter a twilight, are maintaining Spanish alongside English (Alba 2004). Jiménez's (2005) ethnographic research shows that the replenishment of a Mexican-immigrant population creates a linguistic context that maintains and in some cases resuscitates bilingualism among later-generation Mexican Americans. The large size of the Mexican immigrant population allows for frequent interpersonal interactions between Mexican Americans and their immigrant co-ethnics, facilitating the use of Spanish in Mexican

Americans' daily life, and marriages and romantic partnerships between Mexican Americans and immigrants bring the Spanish language close to home for Mexican Americans. The proliferation of Spanish-language media and the demand for bilingual employees further supports the use of Spanish alongside English. The opportunities for Spanish-language use for these later-generation Mexican Americans operate within a larger multicultural ideological context that, relative to an earlier era when Americanization dominated, tolerates and even supports bilingualism.

This multicultural context is also evident in Linton's (2004b) research on dual-language school programmes in which native English- and Spanish-speaking children are educated together, bilingually. Her qualitative case studies show that parents and education professionals choose the dual-language option not only because they believe it will improve students' academic performance and future college and employment options, but also because they highly value multiculturalism and want children to grow up knowing how to get along with people who are different from themselves. For parents this value holds regardless of race, ethnicity and Spanish or English ability.

Theorizing language choice

Sociologists have historically treated language shift as a central component of immigrant acculturation, Gordon's (1964) first sub-process of assimilation. The canonical theory of language shift is based on European-origin groups that came to US shores around the turn of the last century. It asserts that the first generation speaks primarily, if not exclusively, in a non-English mother tongue. The second generation maintains the use of their parents' native language, but adds to it English fluency. The third generation, born in the United States to US-born parents, speaks only English (Gordon 1964; Fishman 1965, 1972).

New theories of assimilation point to more nuanced patterns of acculturation, particularly between the first and second generations. In their research on the new second generation in the United States, Portes and Rumbaut (1996, 2001) develop three typologies of immigrant acculturation that in turn help determine the trajectory of assimilation. The first, consonant acculturation, involves both parents and children learning English and seeking to integrate into the American mainstream. With time, English becomes the dominant household language. The second generation adopts mainstream American customs, speaks mostly or only English, and is upwardly mobile. A second typology, dissonant acculturation, involves poorer, less-educated parents' near-exclusive use of their non-English mother tongue while their second-generation children make the transition to

English dominance and assimilate not into the mainstream, but to inner-city subcultures. In contrast to consonant acculturation, dissonant acculturation leads to poor educational and labour-market outcomes for the children of immigrants. But the linguistic outcome is the same in both cases: English monolingualism.

A third course is *selective acculturation.* In this process, ethnic networks and strong communities support children as they learn to deal with prejudice, navigate the education system and find a place in the labour market. The outcome is upward assimilation combined with bilingualism and biculturalism: 'While such a path may appear inimical to successful adaptation in the eyes of conventional assimilationists, in fact it can lead to better psychosocial and achievement outcomes because it preserves bonds across immigrant generations and gives children a clear reference point to guide their future lives' (Rumbaut and Portes 2001, p. 309). Selective acculturation offers a scenario in which maintaining a language other than English makes sense for Americans. In terms of contextual factors' influence on Spanish maintenance in the United States, one would expect that – to the extent that bilingualism among native-born Hispanics is a result of selective acculturation – there will be proportionally more bilinguals in places where Latino populations are concentrated and where Latinos have a visible, positive economic and social presence.

Other theories offer predictions about when and where the linguistic aspect of selective acculturation, bilingualism, will be maintained. Neoclassical economic (e.g. Pool 1991), human capital (e.g. Chiswick 1991; Chiswick and Miller 2002) and functionalist (Gellner 1983) theories posit that bilingualism will be practical or desirable only to the extent that it represents a significant labour-market advantage. In the first cases, the advantage is to individuals in society. In the last case it is to a particular society within a world of societies.[2]

Language choice also depends on the durability of language options. The theoretical canon of language shift (Gordon 1964; Fishman 1965) was built on the study of European-origin immigrant groups that came to the United States before and after the turn of the last century. As Waters and Jiménez (2005) point out, this wave of immigration took place during a temporally compressed period (roughly 1880–1920), and each new generation born in the US after the immigrant generation had less contact with a sizeable co-ethnic immigrant population (also see Massey 1995) and thus diminished opportunities to speak the mother-tongue of their immigrant ancestors (Alba 1988). Waters and Jiménez also point out that the forces that initiate and perpetuate migration appear to be well entrenched, making the continual replenishment of immigrants from particular countries, like Mexico, a feature of American immigration into the foreseeable future. Immigrant replenishment already has (Alba 2004) and will likely continue to increase the durability of non-English language options (most especially Spanish), and therefore bilingualism, by making opportunities to speak Spanish even more pervasive.

Modelling contexts for bilingualism

Drawing on the above discussion of theory and previous studies of language use and assimilation, we test the following hypotheses:

H1: There will be more Spanish-English bilingualism among US-born/1.5-generation Latinos in metro areas where there is a relatively large and geographically concentrated Latino population.

H2: The proportion of US-born/1.5-generation Latinos who maintain Spanish alongside English will be higher in metro areas where bilingualism is rewarded in the labour market.

H3: The proportion of US-born/1.5-generation Latinos who maintain Spanish alongside English will be higher in metro areas where there is a strong Spanish-language media presence.[3]

H4: Influxes of Spanish-speaking immigrants will positively influence the metro-area proportion of US-born/1.5-generation Latinos who maintain Spanish alongside English.

We also explore several other factors that may be related to the level of bilingualism among a metro area's US-born and 1.5-generation Latinos: the relative size of an area's foreign-born Latino population, whether or not Latino settlement is a new phenomenon in a metro area and a metro area's location within three states that have long and diverse histories of Latino immigration.

Data, variables and measures

Our units of analysis are metropolitan statistical areas [MSAs] or primary metropolitan statistical areas [PMSAs] and the native-born and 1.5-generation Hispanic adults (age 18–75) who live in them. Our analysis is limited to MSA/PMSAs that were at least 5 per cent Hispanic in 2000 and are represented in the 2000 Census 5-per cent Public Use Microdata Sample [PUMS]. Data about general characteristics of the Hispanic population come from the 1990 and 2000 censuses. Data about bilingualism or English monolingualism and some contextual variables come from the 1990 and 2000 PUMS (Ruggles et al. 1997). We gathered data on municipal government bilingual pay by phoning municipalities' human resource specialists and asking whether or not their city provides additional pay to bilingual employees. Data about the presence or absence of Spanish-language network television come from the *Television and Cable Factbook* (Warren 1991, 2001). Table 1 provides additional details about the variables; Appendix A shows Pearson correlations.

Dependent variable

The dependent variable is the 2000 proportion of native-born or 1.5-generation Hispanics, fluent in English, who retain Spanish. The Census asks respondents which language they speak at home, and how well they speak English. Here, Spanish-English bilinguals are those who report that they speak Spanish at home *and* speak English 'very well'. This measure by no means encompasses all bilinguals, and it does not provide information about a respondent's competency or literacy in Spanish. However, it is the best indicator available at the

Table 1. *Descriptive statistics for US metro areas*

	N	Minimum	Maximum	Mean	SD
US-born/1.5-gen. proportion bilingual 2000	119	0.17	0.94	0.59	0.16
US-born/1.5-gen. proportion bilingual 1990	117	0.17	0.91	0.61	0.16
proportion of Latinos foreign born, 2000	119	0.05	0.71	0.35	0.15
proportion of Latinos foreign born, 1990	117	0.03	0.73	0.28	0.14
1990–2000 change in proportion foreign-born	117	−0.08	0.41	0.08	0.09
Latino isolation index 2000	119	0.02	0.95	0.39	0.21
Latino isolation index 1990	119	0.02	0.95	0.30	0.21
1990–2000 change in isolation index	119	−0.44	0.22	0.08	0.07
proportion Latino 2000	119	0.05	0.94	0.20	0.19
proportion Latino 1990	116	0.01	0.94	0.16	0.18
new Latino destination	119	0.00	1.00	0.24	–
municipal gov't. pays a bilingual premium	119	0.00	1.00	0.41	–
network TV in Spanish, 2000	119	0.00	1.00	0.42	–
California	119	0.00	1.00	0.18	–
Florida	119	0.00	1.00	0.12	–
Texas	119	0.00	1.00	0.18	–

Sources: 1990 and 2000 Census and 5% PUMS; Television and Cable Factbook; municipal governments; Suro and Singer (2002)

macro-level, and well worth using (Bills 1989; Hart-Gonzalez and Feingold 1990; Solé 1990). Speaking Spanish at home reflects a preference for using the language, and – where applicable – a desire for one's children to know and use it.

Independent variables

We control for the proportion of a metro-area's Hispanic population that belong to the 1.5 generation since these individuals are most likely to have been raised in a Spanish-speaking home. We also control for the proportion of a metro area's Hispanics who are foreign-born. Foreign-born Hispanics – even those who speak English well – are likely to use Spanish in their daily lives. Thus, immigrants expand the community within which it is useful or desirable, and sometimes necessary, to speak Spanish. As Stevens (1992) points out, in such places Hispanics are more likely to marry other Hispanics, possibly increasing the prevalence of bilingual households (also see Qian and Lichter 2007).

Perhaps the most obvious factor to influence Spanish retention across generations is the presence of other speakers in one's area of residence (Stevens 1992; Schrauf 1999). Lacking a community of speakers – or at least of people for whom the Spanish language constitutes a part of a shared cultural heritage – it is improbable that many people who are fluent in English will actively maintain Spanish. To represent potential communities of speakers we employ a distance-decay isolation index (Morgan 1983): the probability that the next person a Hispanic individual encounters will also be Hispanic. The Hispanic isolation index is very highly correlated with a metro area's proportion Hispanic ($r = .868$), but in addition reflects the degree to which it is likely that Latinos interact with each other on a regular basis.

As Suro and Singer (2002) show, some metro areas in our study, such as Albuquerque, Chicago, Los Angeles, Miami and New York City, are 'established Latino metros' – places where Latinos have resided for quite some time and that still experience, in numeric terms, the largest increases in the Latino population. Others are 'new Latino destinations', where the growth rate of the Latino population is highest although the 1980 base population was quite low, such as Atlanta, Charlotte, Fort Lauderdale, Milwaukee and New Haven (2002, pp. 2–5, 15–16). We mark 'new Latino destinations' in order to explore ways in which this emergent demographic trend might influence Latino's language choices.

Bilingualism is often a benefit to workers in neighbourhoods, regions or occupational areas where more than one language is regularly spoken. The existence of this economic benefit and the good jobs and high incomes that accrue to it should positively influence the prevalence of bilingualism. To test our second hypothesis, we include a marker indicating that municipal governments within a MSA/PMSA pay a premium to bilingual workers.[4] Ideally we would have a way to measure the presence of a monetary reward for bilingualism in private-sector employment, but it is virtually impossible to survey all employers in each city within the MSA/PMSAs we study. We thus treat the pay provided to bilingual workers in municipal government jobs as a proxy for a premium on bilingualism in a given municipality.

Our third hypothesis posits that the presence of Spanish language media will encourage Spanish maintenance among Latino Americans. Spanish-language radio and television offer US-born and 1.5-generation Latinos access to Spanish and a way to reinforce their skills in the language even when they are not in direct contact with immigrants. To test this hypothesis we include the availability of Spanish-language network television in our models.[5]

In our final models we mark MSA/PMSAs in states where historical and/or political factors that we cannot directly measure might influence the level of bilingualism there. California and Texas were once part of Mexico and a long history of immigration means that a substantial number of Latinos in these states have histories that go back many generations. This could mean less bilingualism among the US-born because proportionally more of them will come from families that have been in the US for several generations. After the First World War and before civil rights legislation established some linguistic rights for non-English speakers, American schools discouraged or even forbade speaking anything but English. Civil rights legislation did not remove the stigma attached to speaking Spanish and high schools did not commonly offer it as a foreign language option until the 1980s. Yet Texas shares a large border with Mexico and border cities are largely populated by Latino Americans who feel equally at home on both sides.

Florida is unique because its primary Latino population is Cuban. Some Cubans migrated to avoid the Spanish regime, but those who disagreed with Castro (and expected to return to Cuba soon after leaving) and their descendants are still the dominant Latino group in Florida, where Cuban Americans' prosperity was never linked to Spanish language loss. Because the US government immediately recognized Cuban asylees as allies in opposition to Castro's regime, Cubans did not have to demonstrate their commitment to America by giving up Spanish (Crawford 1992). Later influxes of new Spanish-speaking immigrants (including the Mariel boatlift of 1980) probably promoted Spanish maintenance.

Finally, we test our fourth hypothesis, that immigrant replenishment – influxes of new immigrants from Latin America – will encourage bilingualism among US-born and 1.5-generation Latinos, by modelling changes in immigration and in levels of bilingualism between 1990 and 2000.

Analysis and findings

We report the OLS results of cross-sectional models using 2000 data (Table 2) as well as lagged models (Table 3) that incorporate 1990–2000 change.[6] Coefficients represent the effect of a one-unit change in the independent variable on the proportion of bilingual US-born and 1.5-generation Latinos in a metro area. As expected, the models in Table 2 show a robust, positive relationship between the proportion 1.5-generation Latinos in the dependent variable and the level of bilingualism we observe. Hispanic residential clustering (the isolation index) is also strongly associated with bilingualism. With spatial proximity accounted for, the proportion of Hispanics who are foreign-born exerts no significant effect on bilingualism among the US-born or 1.5 generation in these cross-sectional models. This is not surprising given that the isolation index does not differentiate between foreign- and US-born individuals, and a substantial proportion of individuals captured by the isolation index are likely to be foreign-born.

Model 2 indicates that the US-born and 1.5-generation Latinos in 'new destinations' are more likely to be bilingual than elsewhere. This is probably because there are very few later-generation Latinos in these places (Lichter and Johnson 2006); the 1.5 and second generations are more likely to be bilingual than third- or higher-generation individuals.

Models 3 and 4 show a negative relationship between bilingual pay premiums and the relative presence of bilinguals. We suspect that this finding can be explained by the fact that cities offer extra pay when the skill is in demand but in short supply. To explore this idea further, in Appendix D we report the logistic regression results of an analysis of pay premiums for bilingualism. The variables most importantly related to pay premiums by municipal governments are the Latino isolation index and location in California, where twenty-one of the twenty-two MSA/PMSAs pay bilingual premiums. We think this has to do with the sheer number of foreign-born Latinos in California – almost 5 million in 2000. The state with the second-highest number of foreign-born Latinos is Florida, with fewer than 1.5 million. In California, 53 per cent of 1.5-generation and US-born Latino adults reported bilingualism on the 2000 Census, compared to 72 per cent in Florida. In the California context, fluent Spanish-English bilingualism is in relatively short supply, as the public-sector labour market reflects. In other places, the presence of financial incentives for bilingualism may

Table 2. Coefficients for regression of the proportion bilingual among US-born and 1.5-generation Latino adults in US MSAs/PMSAs, 2000 (N = 118)

	Model 1	Model 2	Model 3	Model 4	Model 5	Model 6
Proportion 1.5-generation	0.898***	1.020***	0.931***	0.931***	0.981***	0.946***
	(.152)	(0.053)	(0.154)	(0.155)	(0.131)	(0.123)
Proportion Latinos foreign-born	−0.048	−0.106	−0.075	−0.076	−0.037	
	(.071)	(0.072)	(0.071)	(0.072)	(0.058)	
Latino isolation index (residential clustering)	0.497***	0.558***	0.584***	0.583***	0.506***	0.532***
	(.050)	(0.052)	(0.052)	(0.060)	(0.051)	(0.042)
New Latino destination		0.076**	0.067**	0.067**	0.066**	0.061**
		(0.026)	(0.026)	(0.026)	(0.022)	(0.021)
Municipal gov't pays a bilingual premium			−0.025	−0.051*	−0.007	
			(0.021)	(0.022)	(0.009)	
Network TV in Spanish				0.001	0.026	
				(0.025)	(0.021)	
California					−0.084**	−0.081***
					(0.027)	(0.023)
Florida					0.106***	0.111***
					(0.026)	(0.025)
Texas					0.110***	0.107***
					(0.024)	(0.024)
Constant	0.309***	0.273***	0.285***	0.286***	0.251***	0.241***
	(0.034)	(0.035)	(0.035)	(0.036)	(0.029)	(0.026)
Adjusted R2	0.505	0.537	0.556	0.552	0.718	0.720
F	41.132***	35.171***	30.501***	25.193***	34.326***	51.690***

*p <0.05.
**p <0.01.
***p <0.001.
Standard errors are shown in parentheses.

Table 3. *Lagged models: coefficients for regression of the 2000 proportion bilingual among US-born and 1.5-generation Latino adults in US MSAs/PMSAs on 1990 and 1990–2000 change variables (N = 116)*

	Model 1	Model 2	Model 3	Model 4	Model 5
Proportion bilingual, 1990	0.867***	0.873***	0.869***	0.809***	0.831***
	(0.043)	(0.043)	(0.042)	(0.051)	(0.044)
Proportion Latinos foreign-born, 1990	0.098**	0.131**	0.121**	0.114*	0.086*
	(0.036)	(0.042)	(0.041)	(0.044)	(0.036)
Latino isolation index, 1990	0.052†	0.060†	0.085**	0.113**	0.117***
	(0.030)	(0.031)	(0.032)	(0.0360)	(0.033)
1990–2000 change in proportion foreign born		0.141*	0.126†	0.150*	0.132*
		(0.066)	(0.064)	(0.165)	(0.061)
1990–2000 change in Latino isolation		−0.071	−0.071	−0.067	
		(0.086)	(0.084)	(0.084)	
New Latino destination			0.031*	0.031*	0.029*
			(0.012)	(0.013)	(0.012)
California				−0.001	
				(0.016)	
Florida				0.044*	0.042*
				(0.017)	(0.017)
Texas				0.017	
				−0.015	
Constant	0.015	−0.005	−0.014	0.005	−0.002
	(0.023)	(0.026)	(0.025)	(0.028)	(0.025)
Adjusted R2	0.877	0.880	0.886	0.890	0.891
F	277.677***	171.464***	150.61***	105.294***	159.282***

†p < .10.
*p < 0.05.
**p < 0.01.
***p < 0.001.
Standard errors are shown in parentheses.

simply be too new a phenomenon to create a significant response among employers or workers.

We do not observe a significant relationship between the presence of one or more Spanish-language network television stations in a metro area and the level of bilingualism among US-born or 1.5-generation Latinos there. In part this is because the availability of network TV in Spanish and the Latino isolation index are correlated ($r = 0.58$). Also, our measure of access to Spanish-language media is not as comprehensive as we would like.

Models 5 and 6 include markers for MSA/PMSAs within California, Florida and Texas. We find relatively less bilingualism among US-born and 1.5-generation Latinos in California and more bilingualism in Florida and Texas. Besides the reasons discussed in the previous section, high Latino political representation may be part of the explanation for the higher level of bilingualism in Texas. In 2000, there were 1,885 Latino elected officials in Texas – almost one for every 10,000 people – while in California there were 785 Latino elected officials, 0.2 for every 10,000 people (NALEO 2000).[7] This is relevant because, to the extent that they can, Hispanic voters glean information and discuss their concerns in two languages, and Hispanic politicians court voters in two languages.

Table 3 explores the 'replenishment' hypothesis that more US-born Latinos will be bilingual in places where there has been a relatively continuous and long-standing influx of Spanish-speaking immigrants. Here we look at relationships between metro-area characteristics in 1990 and bilingualism in 2000. We examine the degree to which bilingualism in 2000 can be predicted by its level in 1990, by 1990 measures of the variables that were significant in the final model of Table 2 and 1990–2000 change. Of course, the 1990 level of bilingualism in an MSA/PMSA is a robust predictor of bilingualism in 2000. More interestingly, the 1990 proportion of foreign-born Hispanics and *change* in that proportion are positively related to bilingualism among the US-born and 1.5 generation in 2000. This finding supports the 'replenishment' hypothesis and invites further exploration of how immigration trends relate to the language choices of Latinos who are not immigrants themselves. The California and Texas markers are not significant when we control for demographic dynamics, but a positive relationship remains between residence in Florida and Spanish maintenance. Characteristics of the Miami-Dade County area, such as its predominantly Cuban-origin Hispanic population, are undoubtedly driving this result. In addition, Spanish is a powerful language in the Miami business community (Anderson 1998). These factors 'have made it possible to abandon the majority description of Spanish as a *static characteristic* of a minority with a *problem*. Instead, the language minority has been able to engage the majority in viewing Spanish as a *negotiable* factor in a *relationship* that could be a *resource* for all' (García 1995: 154–5, italics in original).

Contexts for bilingualism: views from the ground floor

We now turn our attention to a 'ground-floor' view of the contextual determinants of bilingualism using ethnographic research among later-generation Mexican Americans in Kansas and California and ongoing research in dual-language immersion schools in southern California and Chicago. We use this ethnographic research to propose mechanisms that explain our quantitative findings.

Our first source of ethnographic data is 123 in-depth interviews with later-generation Mexican Americans and observation in Garden City, Kansas, and Santa Maria, California, in 2001 and 2002. All respondents' ancestors have been in the US since 1940 or earlier, are of Mexican descent on both their mother's and father's sides of the family and lived in their respective city for most of their lives. Both cities have a long history of Mexican immigration and a substantial number of residents who trace their immigrant roots in the United States to the early part of the twentieth century. Both cities have also seen a substantial increase in the number of Mexican immigrants between 1990 and 2000. In Finney County, where Garden City is the seat, the number of Mexican immigrants grew from 2,104, or 6.4 per cent of the total population in 1990, to 7,349, or 22.2 per cent of the population, in 2000. Santa Barbara County, where Santa Maria is located, experienced similarly dramatic growth. Mexican immigrants accounted for 34,157, or 9.2 per cent of all residents in 1990, but by 2000 the county's foreign-born Mexican population grew to 55,785, or 14 per cent of the total population. Garden City and Santa Maria are small cities whose size allows for frequent contact between Mexican immigrants and later-generation Mexican Americans.

It is important to note that these interviews were conducted with later-generation Mexican Americans who are most likely to be English monolinguals (Fishman 1965; Rumbaut, Massey and Bean 2006; Telles and Ortiz 2008). There are no 1.5-generation individuals in the sample, and the few second-generation individuals in the sample tend to be much older than the rest of the sample. It is, however, reasonable to expect that the processes influencing bilingualism among later-generation Mexican Americans are equally, if not more strongly, at work among 1.5- and second-generation individuals.

Our second source of ethnographic data is interviews with administrators, educators and parents involved with Spanish/English dual-language education (also called two-way immersion, dual-immersion and two-way bilingual immersion). The original purpose of this research was to learn why – given an anti-bilingual education political climate, increased standardized testing under No Child Left Behind and other challenges – dual-language education is a growing phenomenon. In other words, what (or who) is behind the dual-language movement?

Results from our analysis of census data represent an accumulation of the micro-processes. Our ethnographic data thus elucidate the micro-processes that are ultimately reflected in the proportion of US-born and 1.5-generation Latinos in a metropolitan area that is bilingual. We begin by explaining why the relative size of the foreign-born Hispanic population in 1990 and the 1990–2000 change in size increase the level of bilingualism among 1.5-generation and US-born Latinos ten years later. Recall that the lagged regression models in Table 3 indicate that immigrant replenishment – the continual influx of immigrants from the same country – exerts a positive effect on the level of bilingualism in metro areas. Our ethnographic data suggest that the increase in the foreign-born Latino population fuels opportunities for 1.5-generation and native-born Latinos to speak Spanish.

Findings from Garden City and Santa Maria show that the presence of a large immigrant population facilitates Spanish-language use even among those whose ancestors came to the United States three and four generations ago. Opportunities to speak Spanish come from interactions in public spaces, in the workplace, and through both romantic and platonic relationships. A 56-year-old retired salesman in Garden City, who is married to a foreign-born Mexican woman, explained:

[My wife's] dominant language is Spanish, so that's where I'm learning all of mine from. And her parents are from there too, so I speak to them in Spanish. I've gotten much better at it than I used to be. I'm just not totally fluent yet, but I'm getting there.

Interactions between Mexican Americans and their immigrant and second-generation friends often turn into *de facto* Spanish lessons where Mexican Americans receive informal tutoring from their bilingual peers.[8] The comments of a 16-year-old high school student in Santa Maria illustrate:

This girl in my algebra class, she was speaking it to me and I was like, "I don't understand Spanish." She's just like, "You don't?!" So now every time I see her and we talk, she talks to me in Spanish because she wants to help me learn. And she'll tell me what stuff means. And if I ask her a question about my Spanish homework she'll help me.

Interviews from Garden City and Santa Maria suggest that the opportunities for Spanish-language use depend not just on the size and growth of the immigrant population, but also on the frequency of contact that the native-born has with immigrants. Recall from our first regression model (Table 2, Model 1) that the proportion of foreign-born Latinos in a metro area exerts no statistically significant effect on the level of bilingualism when we control for Latino residential clustering, which has a strong, positive and statistically significant effect on the proportion of bilinguals in a metro area. Mexican Americans in Garden City and Santa Maria have frequent contact with immigrants partly because of the small size of each city. The frequency of contact between native-born Latinos and immigrants is probably more variable in large metro areas, where native-born Latinos may or may not live near Spanish-speaking immigrants. Interviews with Mexican Americans in these two small cities are thus likely to resemble the nature of contact between native-born and foreign-born Latinos in areas of high Latino concentration (Duarte 2008; Telles and Ortiz 2008).

Immigration also provides exposure to Spanish by infusing the use of the language into institutions that are part of daily life. Churches, restaurants, retail stores and the media serve as sites of Spanish immersion for later-generation Mexican Americans. For example, a 59-year-old retired teacher in Santa Maria said that he enjoys the Spanish-language masses because it allows him to maintain greater contact with the Spanish language, and hence his ethnicity:

> I like to go to the Spanish Mass even though I don't understand it as well as I do if I went to an English service. So it's one of my few connections to Spanish . . . . I guess I want to hang on to the fact that I am Mexican and that's one way to do it. I want to keep the language, even though I'm not anywhere [near] fluent. That helps to maintain some of the Spanish. I guess that's the reason, just hang on to the little Spanish that I do have, the little Mexican that I do have.

Others mentioned their use of Spanish language media as part of a larger context in which they are able to maintain use of both Spanish and English. In both cities, Spanish-language television and radio fill the airwaves, allowing later-generation Mexican Americans to access Spanish even when they are not in direct contact with immigrants. Although we did not find that the presence of bilingual media exerts an independent effect on the level of bilingualism, the presence of media is certainly part of the larger context that works in conjunction with direct contact with immigrants to facilitate bilingualism.

Likewise, dual-language programmes allow for regular access to both languages for Latino and non-Latino students alike. Spanish- and English-speaking pupils learn together, instructed by one or more teachers, from the time they begin school through at least the fifth grade. Programme objectives include high academic achievement, bilingual proficiency, bi-literacy and multicultural understanding (Christian 1994). Dual-language programmes are an example of schools institutionalizing the idea that newcomers to the United States are 'remaking the mainstream' (Alba and Nee 2003) and that immigrant acculturation is a two-way process that involves members of the receiving and sending societies.

Our qualitative research points to important factors shaping the desirability of bilingualism that the census data do not directly measure. Though the proliferation of Spanish instils fear about disunity in American society among some (Huntington 2004; Buchanan 2006), there is growing acceptance of bilingualism not just as a valuable aspect of human capital, but as part of a larger cosmopolitan identity. Interviews with educational professionals at dual-language schools reflect new, more cosmopolitan attitudes towards bilingualism. The initial impetus to begin a dual-language programme may come from parents or from education professionals in a school or district. Why do they make the effort? The quotes below, from California educators, illustrate three common reasons: dual-language education helps children excel; it is important to know Spanish; children should grow up in a multicultural environment (Linton 2007).

> Our Spanish language parents, I think for the most part they might not be empowered so to speak, but they are into what works. They are dedicated to the program. So I think we have that mix of a strong base of English-only parents who want this for their kids; they're advocates for bilingual education, and they've shown through history that they'll stick with the program.

> One of our parents is a reporter .... She's a fluent Spanish-speaker. Other parents in the program probably have a grandparent or a parent who speaks Spanish fluently, or maybe they've grown up in Los Angeles and speak Spanish and see the positive side of being bilingual and biliterate. Maybe some of the parents just speak Spanish but are not literate in Spanish. Or they might have a nanny who speaks Spanish. Or they might think it's a great thing for their kid to be bilingual and biliterate and nobody speaks Spanish. But they value language. They're making it a priority.

> [Diversity] was a really good selling point from the beginning. It was not just selling the fact that children would learn two languages but

would understand two cultures, and how important that is in a world where we need to have more cultures getting along.

While our variable measuring a bilingual pay premium in municipal government jobs showed no effect in the full model in Table 2, our ethnographic research suggests that there are informal labour-market rewards that encourage people to speak two languages. In areas with a large Spanish-speaking population, there is a 'common-sense' understanding that bilingualism is helpful for getting a job, According to a 17-year-old high school student in Garden City, his ability to communicate with Spanish-speaking customers made him an attractive job applicant at the grocery store where he now works:

> [Speaking Spanish is] one of the reasons I got a job at [the grocery store]. A lot of Hispanic people live on that side of town and they tend to shop at that store. And I put on my application that I was a good translator and sometimes people back in pharmacy or grocery department need me to translate for them and I do that.

Likewise, parents who choose dual-language education for their children see bilingualism as an advantageous skill in the twenty-first-century economy. A Long Beach, California parent expressed it this way: 'Your child can get out of school and go to the AAA and get a job. I work there, and we have a lot of people who call and ask for someone who speaks Spanish. And nobody does.' Similarly, the bilingual coordinator of a dual-language school in upscale Newport Hills, California, where (white) parents had asked for the programme, said that parents believed that Spanish was 'a good [economic] ticket to a good future'. The principal of a dual-language magnet school in Chicago noted that whites and African Americans often express economic reasons for wanting their children to be bilingual. Multicultural awareness, travel to Spanish-speaking countries and future academic advantages are on these parents' minds as well, but not nearly as much as the competitive advantage that bilingualism provides in a global economy.

Of course, Spanish-English bilingualism is primarily relevant because there is a sizeable Spanish-monolingual immigrant population that provides access to and creates a demand for Spanish-language use. Thus, the factors that encourage bilingualism that we identify in our ethnographic research – interpersonal and institutional contact with Spanish, cosmopolitanism, labour-market rewards – are probably captured by variables measuring the size and growth of the foreign-born Latino population in the MSAs and PMSAs in our statistical models.

Discussion and conclusion

This study has specified contextual circumstances under which bilingualism is most likely to be a stable feature of Hispanic American identity rather that a step along the way to English monolingualism. In doing so, it has demonstrated a strong relationship between macro-level incentives and individual choices. The United States is probably not moving towards a bilingual norm, but our findings provide evidence that, where the context is favourable, selective acculturation could persist into future generations. This is largely due to the fact that continuing immigration is replenishing US-born Latinos, making Spanish a more vibrant, accessible and desirable part of US-born Latinos' identity repertoire.

Our findings suggest that demographics matter: the influx of a large, Spanish-speaking immigrant population contributes to bilingualism among US-born Latinos and the 1.5 generation. In places where Latin American immigration is replenished, so too are the opportunities for Spanish-language use among US-born and 1.5-generation Latinos, and persons of other ethnicities as well. The mechanisms that account for how immigrant replenishment encourages bilingualism are highlighted in our research among later-generation Mexican Americans and in dual-language schools. As illustrated above, serendipitous encounters, friendships and even romantic relationships with Mexican immigrants provides later-generation Mexican Americans with ample opportunity to maintain and even re-learn Spanish, while at the same time schools in areas with substantial Latino immigrant populations are institutionalizing Spanish alongside English as an option for *all* students. We suspect these same opportunities account for the effect of the growth of Latino immigration on bilingualism among US-born and 1.5-generation Latinos in our quantitative study.

If a supply of Spanish language comes from immigration, there is also a demand that further supports the persistence of bilingualism reflected in both labour-market rewards and a positive evaluation of bilingualisms prevalent in American society. Employers increasingly seek out bilingual employees who can make goods and services more accessible to both Spanish monolinguals *and* an American-born English monolingual clientele. Employers incentivize available positions by expressing preference for bilingual job applicants and by remunerating bilingual employees. In 41 per cent of the metro areas we surveyed, city government workers are paid more if they are Spanish-English bilinguals.

The context that shapes bilingualism in the United States is not bounded by national borders. As others have shown (Levitt 2001; Smith 2005), transnational ties expand the context that facilitates bilingualism across national boundaries, facilitating bilingualism among US-born and 1.5 generation Latinos. Of course, return trips to the ethnic homeland can also reveal how migration and assimilation change the way people speak Spanish north of the border as compared to southern ethnic homelands. This linguistic 'dissimilation' (Fitzgerald 2008; Jiménez and Fitzgerald 2008) from sending communities is also at play in shaping bilingualism. Data limitations prevent us from modelling this transnational context, but its effects are no doubt helping to determine levels of bilingualism in the United States.

There are forces that work against bilingualism, reacting directly to the conditions that make bilingualism a more real and enduring possibility. Anti-immigrant groups, policies that aim to slow immigration, anti-bilingual-education measures and loudly voiced fears about non-English languages tearing at the American national fabric are important parts of the context that shapes language patterns. Yet our research shows that the forces that might work against bilingualism are counterbalanced by conditions that encourage bilingualism as a durable part of the American linguistic landscape.

Acknowledgements

We thank Diana Lewis, Joyce Lui and Jeff Lundy for research assistance, and an anonymous *ERS* reviewer for helpful comments.

Notes

1. We use the designations 'Hispanic' and 'Latino' interchangeably. We recognize the vast diversity within these categories. However, given our interest in Spanish-English bilingualism, the fact that the various subgroups (i.e. Cubans, Mexicans and Salvadorans) share a common language makes these categories quite relevant for the purposes of this paper.
2. Other scholars such as Hobsbawm (1990), Anderson (1991), Greenfeld (1992), Macias (2006) and Telles and Ortiz (2008) downplay economic incentives, instead pointing to ethnic identities and their meanings for members of various groups as the salient factors that inform official language policy and individual decisions about language acquisition and maintenance. We believe that these factors are important determinants of language choice, but the present analysis does not allow us adequately to incorporate hypotheses derived from theories of identity formation and maintenance.
3. In analyses not reported here, we tested the relationship between bilingualism and bilinguals' status in the community by looking at bilinguals' socioeconomic status [SES] relative to that of English monolinguals. Using 1990 data, Linton (2004a) found that there was more bilingualism among US-born/1.5-generation Latinos in places where bilinguals' SES was high compared to that of English monolinguals. We were not able to replicate this finding using 2000 data. This is probably because, in 2000, there was significantly less variation in bilinguals' and English monolinguals' SES. Here we reason that Spanish-language media reflect not only a metro area's demographics, but also the cultural and economic importance of the area's Latino population.
4. Two MSAs encompass cities that do and do not pay a premium for bilingualism: Charlotte/Gastonia/Rock Hill NC-SC-MS and Salt Lake City/Ogden UT. These are both coded '1' because there is a bilingual premium in the majority of the MSA.

5. The poor availability of data on the presence of Spanish-language radio for each of the metro areas we studied prevented us from including a variable for Spanish-language radio.
6. Appendices B and C show the final models in Tables 2 and 3 with MSA/PMSA proportion bilingual instead of the isolation index (Appendix B) and standardized regression coefficients (Appendix C).
7. This is at least in part due to the fact that, compared to other states, Texas has many more elected offices.
8. To be sure, language use can highlight boundaries which become apparent when later-generation Mexican Americans are deemed ethnically inauthentic by peers who are Spanish/English bilingual (also see Menchaca 1995; Ochoa 2004; Jiménez 2008).

References

ALBA, RICHARD D. 1988 'Cohorts and the dynamics of ethnic change', in Matilda White Riley (ed.), *Social Structure and Human Lives*, Newbury Park, CA: Sage, pp 211–28
—— 2004 *Language Assimilation Today: Bilingualism Persists More than in the Past, but English Still Dominates*, San Diego, CA: Center for Comparative Immigration Studies, University of California, San Diego
ALBA, RICHARD et al. 2002 'Only English by the third generation? Loss and preservation of the mother tongue among the grandchildren of contemporary immigrants', *Demography*, vol. 39, no. 3, pp. 467–84
ALBA, RICHARD and NEE, VICTOR 2003 *Remaking the American Mainstream: Assimilation and Contemporary Immigration*, Cambridge, MA: Harvard University Press
ANDERSON, BENEDICT 1991 *Imagined Communities: Reflections on the Origin and Spread of Nationalism*, New York: Verso
ANDERSON, NICK 1998 'A boomtown of bilingual education', *Los Angeles Times*, 25 May
BEAN, FRANK D. and STEVENS, GILLIAN 2003 *America's Newcomers and the Dynamics of Diversity*, New York: Russell Sage Foundation
BILLS, GARLAND 1989 'The US Census of 1980 and Spanish in the southwest', *International Journal of the Sociology of Language*, vol. 79, pp. 11–28
BUCHANAN, PATRICK J. 2006 *State of Emergency: The Third World Invasion and Conquest of America*, New York: Thomas Dunne
CHISWICK, BARRY R. 1991 'Speaking, reading, and earnings among low-skilled immigrants', *Journal of Labor Economics*, vol. 9, no. 2, pp. 149–70
CHISWICK, BARRY R. and MILLER, PAUL W. 2002 'Immigrant earnings: language skills, linguistic concentrations and the business cycle', *Journal of Population Economics*, vol. 15, no. 1, pp. 31–57
CHRISTIAN, DONNA 1994 *Two-Way Bilingual Education: Students Learning Through Two Languages*, Education Practice Report 12, Santa Cruz, CA, and Washington, DC: National Center for Research on Cultural Diversity and Second Language Learning
CRAWFORD, JAMES 1992 *Hold Your Tongue: Bilingualism and the Politics of 'English Only*, Reading, MA: Addison-Wesley
DUARTE, CYNTHIA 2008 'Negotiating 3rd+ generation Mexican American identity in Los Angeles, CA' PhD Dissertation, Sociology, New York, NY: Columbia University.
FISHMAN, JOSHUA A. 1965 'The status and prospects of bilingualism in the United States', *Modern Language Journal*, vol. 49, no. 3, pp. 143–55
—— 1972 *The Sociology of Language: An Interdisciplinary Social Science Approach to Language in Society*, Rowley, MA: Newbury House
FITZGERALD, DAVID 2008 *A Nation of Emigrants: How Mexico Manages its Migration*, Berkeley, CA: University of California Press
GARCÍA, OFELIA 1995 'Spanish language loss as a determinant of income among Latinos in the United States: implications for language policy in schools', in James Tollefson (ed.),

Power and Inequality in Language Education, Cambridge: Cambridge University Press, pp. 142–60

GELLNER, ERNEST 1983 *Nations and Nationalism*, Ithaca, NY: Cornell University Press

GORDON, MILTON M. 1964 *Assimilation in American Life: The Role of Race, Religion, and National Origins*, New York: Oxford University Press

GREENFELD, LIAH 1992 *Nationalism: Five Roads to Modernity*, Cambridge, MA: Harvard University Press

HART-GONZALEZ, LUCINDA and FEINGOLD, MARCIA 1990 'Retention of Spanish in the home', *US International Journal of Social Language*, vol. 84, pp. 5–34

HOBSBAWM, ERIC J. 1990 *Nations and Nationalism since 1780: Programme, Myth, Reality*, New York: Cambridge University Press

HUNTINGTON, SAMUEL P. 2004 *Who Are We? The Challenges to America's National Identity*, New York: Simon & Schuster

JIMÉNEZ, TOMÁS R. 2005 'Replenished Identities: Mexican Americans, Mexican immigrants and ethnic identity' PhD Thesis, Sociology, Cambridge, MA: Harvard University

JIMÉNEZ, TOMÁS R. 2008 'Mexican-immigrant replenishment and the continuing significance of ethnicity and race', *American Journal of Sociology*, vol. 113, no. 6, pp. 1527–67

JIMÉNEZ, TOMÁS R. and FITZGERALD, DAVID 2008 'Mexican assimilation: a temporal and spatial reorientation', *Du Bois Review*, vol. 4, no. 2, pp. 337–54

LEVITT, PEGGY 2001 *The Transnational Villagers*, Berkeley, CA: University of California Press

LICHTER, DANIEL T. and JOHNSON, KENNETH M. 2006 'Emerging rural settlement patterns and the geographic redistribution of America's new immigrants', *Rural Sociology*, vol. 71, no. 1, pp. 109–31

LINTON, APRIL 2004a 'A critical mass model of bilingualism among U.S.-born Hispanics', *Social Forces*, vol. 83, no. 1, pp. 279–314

—— 2004b 'Learning in two languages: Spanish-English immersion in US public schools', *International Journal of Sociology and Social Policy*, vol. 24, no. 7–8, pp. 46–74

—— 2007 'Spanish-English immersion in the wake of California Proposition 227: five cases', *Intercultural Education*, vol. 18, no. 2, pp. 111–28

MACIAS, THOMAS 2006 *Mestizo in America: Generations of Mexican Ethnicity in the Suburban Southwest*, Tucson, AZ: University of Arizona Press

MASSEY, DOUGLAS 1995 'The new immigration and ethnicity in the United States', *Population and Development Review*, vol. 21, no. 3, pp. 631–52

MENCHACA, MARTHA 1995 *The Mexican Outsiders: A Community History of Marginalization and Discrimination in California*, Austin, TX: University of Texas Press

MORGAN, BARRIE S. 1983 'An alternate approach to the development of a distance-based measure of racial segregation', *The American Journal of Sociology*, vol. 88, no. 6, pp. 1237–49

NALEO 2000 *2000 National Directory of Latino Elected Officials*, Los Angeles, CA: NALEO Education Fund

OCHOA, GILDA 2004 *Becoming Neighbors in a Mexican American Community: Power, Conflict and Solidarity*, Austin, TX: University of Texas Press

POOL, JONATHAN 1991 'The official language problem', *American Political Science Review*, vol. 85, no. 22, pp. 495–514

PORTES, ALEJANDRO and RUMBAUT, RUBÉN G. 1996 *Immigrant America: A Portrait*, Berkeley, CA: University of California Press

—— 2001 *Legacies: The Story of the Immigrant Second Generation*, Berkeley, CA: University of California Press; New York: Russell Sage Foundation

QIAN, ZHENCHAO and LICHTER, DANIEL T. 2007 'Social boundaries and marital assimilation: interpreting trends in racial and ethnic intermarriage', *American Sociological Review*, vol. 72, no. 1, pp. 68–94

RUGGIES, STEVEN et al., 2008 *'Integrated public use microdata series. Version 4.0'* [machine readable database] Minneapolis, MN: Minnesota Population Center

RUMBAUT, RUBÉN G. 2002 'Severed or sustained attachments? Language, identity, and imagined communities in the post-immigrant generation', in Peggy Levitt and Mary C. Waters (eds), *The Changing Face of Home: Transnational Lives of the Second Generation*, New York: Russell Sage Foundation, pp. 43–95
RUMBAUT, RUBÉN G. and PORTES, ALEJANDRO 2001 *Ethnicities: Children of Immigrants in America*, Berkeley, CA: University of California Press and Russell Sage Foundation
RUMBAUT, RUBÉN G., MASSEY, DOUGLAS S. and BEAN, FRANK D. 2006 'Linguistic life expectancies: immigrant language retention in Southern California', *Population and Development Review*, vol. 32, no. 3, pp. 447–60
SCHRAUF, ROBERT W. 1999 'Mother tongue maintenance among North American ethnic groups', *Cross-Cultural Research*, vol. 33, no. 2, pp. 175–92
SMITH, ROBERT C. 2005 *Mexican New York: The Transnational Lives of New Immigrants*, Berkeley, CA: University of California Press
SOLÉ, YOLANDA R. 1990 'Bilingualism: stable or transitional? The case of Spanish in the United States', *International Journal of the Sociology of Language*, vol. 84, pp. 35–80
STEVENS, GILLIAN 1985 'Nativity, intermarriage, and mother-tongue shift', *American Sociological Review*, vol. 50, no. 1, pp. 74–83
—— 1992 'The social and demographic context of language use in the United States', *American Sociological Review*, vol. 57, no. 2, pp. 171–85
SURO, ROBERTO and SINGER, AUDREY 2002 *Latino Growth in Metropolitan America: Changing Patterns, New Locations*, Washington, DC: The Brookings Institution
TELLES, EDWARD E. and ORTIZ, VILMA 2008 *Generations of Exclusion: Mexican Americans, Assimilation, and Race*, New York: Russell Sage Foundation
WARREN, ALBERT 1991 *Television and Cable Factbook: Stations Volume*, Washington, DC: Television Digest
—— 2001 *Television and Cable Factbook: Stations Volume*, Washington, DC: Television Digest
WATERS, MARY C. and JIMÉNEZ, TOMÁS R. 2005 'Assessing immigrant assimilation: new empirical and theoretical challenges', *Annual Review of Sociology*, vol. 31, pp. 105–25
ZOLBERG, ARISTIDE R. and LONG, LITT WOON 1999 'Why Islam is like Spanish: cultural incorporation in Europe and the United States', *Politics and Society*, vol. 27, no. 1, pp. 5–38

Appendix A. Pearson correlations

		US-born/1.5-gen. proportion bilingual 2000	US-born/1.5-gen. proportion bilingual 1990	proportion of Latinos foreign born, 2000	proportion of Latinos foreign born, 1990	1990-2000 change in proportion foreign-born	Latino isolation index 2000	Latino isolation index 1990
US-born/1.5-gen.proportion bilingual 2000		1	0.933 ***	0.091	0.257 **	−0.281 **	0.607 ***	0.636 ***
	N	119	117	119	117	117	119	119
US- born/1.5-gen. proportion bilingual 1990		0.933 ***	1	−0.020	0.184	−0.334 **	0.593 ***	0.639 ***
	N	117	117	117	117	117	117	117
proportion of Latinos foreign born, 2000		0.091	−0.020	1	0.818 ***	0.352 ***	0.057	−0.118
	N	119	117	119	117	117	119	119
proportion of Latinos foreign born, 1990		0.257 **	0.184	0.818 ***	1	−0.251 **	0.235 *	0.096
	N	117	117	117	117	117	117	117
1990-2000 change in proportion foreign-born		−0.281 **	−0.334 ***	0.352 ***	−0.251 **	1	−0.299 ***	−0.362 ***
	N	117	117	117	117	117	117	117
Latino isolation index 2000		0.607 ***	0.593 ***	0.057	0.235 *	−0.299 ***	1	0.944 ***
	N	119	117	119	117	117	119	119
Latino isolation index 1990		0.636 ***	0.639 ***	−0.118	0.096	−0.362 ***	0.944 ***	1
	N	119	117	119	117	117	119	119
1990–2000 change in isolation index		−0.170	−0.225 *	0.519 ***	0.390 ***	0.232 *	0.037	−0.296 ***
	N	119	117	119	117	117	119	119
proportion Latino 2000		0.530 ***	0.517 ***	−0.077	0.110	−0.317 ***	0.868 ***	0.871 ***
	N	119	117	119	117	117	119	119
proportion Latino 1990		0.516 ***	0.505 ***	−0.134	0.058	−0.320 ***	0.833 ***	0.857 ***
	N	116	116	116	116	116	116	116
new Latino destination		−0.125	−0.220 *	0.176 †	0.056	0.198 *	−0.341 ***	−0.386 ***
	N	119	117	119	117	117	119	119
municipal gov't. pays a bilingual premium		−0.050	−0.053	0.104	0.244 **	−0.224 *	0.300 **	0.239 **
	N	119	117	119	117	117	119	119
network TV in Spanish, 2000		0.292 ***	0.260 **	0.135	0.327 ***	−0.306 ***	0.580 ***	0.552 ***
	N	119	117	119	117	117	119	119
California		−0.178 †	−0.191 *	0.132	0.266 **	−0.200 *	0.249 **	0.207 *
	N	119	117	119	117	117	119	119

Appendix A (*Continued*)

		US-born/1.5-gen. pro portion bilingual 2000	US-born/1.5-gen. proportion bilingual 1990	proportion of Latinos foreign born, 2000	proportion of Latinos foreign born, 1990	1990-2000 change in proportion foreign-born	Latino isolation index 2000	Latino isolation index 1990
Florida		0.310 ***	0.259 **	0.156 †	0.261 **	−0.168 †	−0.084	−0.083
	N	119	117	119	117	117	119	119
Texas		0.349 ***	0.382 ***	−0.249 **	−0.169 †	−0.156 †	0.308 ***	0.323 ***
	N	119	117	119	117	117	119	119

† $p < .10$.
* $p < 0.05$.
** $p < 0.01$.
*** $p < 0.001$.

Appendix A (*Continued*).

		1990–2000 change in isolation index	proportion Latino 2000	proportion Latino 1990	new Latino destination	municipal gov't. pays a bilingual premium	network TV in Spanish, 2000	California	Florida	Texas
US-born/1.5-gen.proportion bilingual 2000		−0.170	0.530 ***	0.516 ***	−0.125	−0.050	0.292 ***	−0.178 †	0.310 ***	0.349
	N	119	119	116	119	119	119	119	119	119
US- born/1.5-gen.		−0.225 *	0.517 ***	0.505 ***	−0.220 *	−0.053	0.260 **	−0.191 *	0.259 **	0.382
	N	117	117	116	117	117	117	117	117	117
proportion bilingual 1990		0.519 ***	−0.077	−0.134	0.176 †	0.104	0.135	0.132	0.156 †	−0.249
	N	119	119	116	119	119	119	119	119	119
proportion of Latinos foreign born, 2000		0.390 ***	0.110	0.058	0.056	0.244 †	0.327 ***	0.266 **	0.261 **	−0.169
	N	117	117	116	117	117	117	117	117	117
proportion of Latinos foreign born, 1990		0.232 *	−0.317 ***	−0.320 ***	0.198 *	−0.224 *	−0.306 ***	−0.200 *	−0.168 †	−0.156
	N	117	117	116	117	117	117	117	117	117
1990–2000 change in proportion foreign-born Latino isolation index 2000		0.037	0.868 ***	0.833 ***	−0.341 ***	0.300 ***	0.580 ***	0.249 **	−0.084	0.308
	N	119	119	116	119	119	119	119	119	119
Latino isolation index 1990		−0.296 ***	0.871 ***	0.857 ***	−0.386 ***	0.239 **	0.552 ***	0.207 *	−0.083	0.323
	N	119	119	116	119	119	119	119	119	119
1990–2000 change in isolation index		1	−0.124	−0.193 *	0.183 *	0.146	0.008	0.093	0.006	−0.086
	N	119	119	116	119	119	119	119	119	119
proportion Latino 2000		−0.124	1	0.981 ***	−0.351 ***	0.265 **	0.532 ***	0.225 *	−0.006	0.373
	N	119	119	116	119	119	119	119	119	119
proportion Latino 1990		−0.193 *	0.981 ***	1	−0.334 ***	0.241 **	0.523 ***	0.160 †	0.026	0.390
	N	116	116	116	116	116	116	116	116	116
new Latino destination		0.183 *	−0.351 ***	−0.334 ***	1	−0.157 †	−0.245 **	−0.270 **	0.096	−0.263
	N	119	119	116	119	119	119	119	119	119
municipal gov't. pays a bilingual premium		0.146	0.265 **	0.241 **	−0.157 †	1	0.360 ***	0.525 ***	−0.147	0.016
	N	119	119	116	119	119	119	119	119	119
network TV in Spanish, 2000		0.008	0.532 ***	0.523 ***	−0.245 **	0.360 ***	1	0.428 ***	0.059	0.008
	N	119	119	116	119	119	119	119	119	119

Appendix A (*Continued*)

	1990–2000 change in isolation index	proportion Latino 2000	proportion Latino 1990	new Latino destination	municipal gov't. pays a bilingual premium	network TV in Spanish, 2000	California	Florida	Texas
California	0.093	0.225 *	0.160 †	−0.270 **	0.525 ***	0.428 ***	1	−0.174 †	−0.220
N	119	119	116	119	119	119	119	119	119
Florida	0.006	−0.006	0.026	0.096	−0.147	0.059	−0.174 †	1	−0.101
N	119	119	116	119	119	119	119	119	119
Texas	−0.086	0.373 ***	0.390 ***	−0.263 **	0.016	0.008	−0.220 *	−0.101	1
N	119	119	116	119	119	119	119	119	119

† p < .10.
* p < 0.05.
** p < 0.01.
*** p < 0.001.

Appendix B. *Best models of bilingualism among US-born and 1.5-generation Latinos, proportion Latino substituted for Latino Isolation Index*

	2000	1990–2000
Proportion US-born/1.5-generation bilingual, 1990		0.882*** (0.039)
Proportion 1.5-generation, 2000	1.071*** (0.047)	
Proportion Latinos foreign-born, 1990		0.093* (0.037)
Proportion Latino	0.522*** (0.057)	
Proportion Latino, 1990		0.093** (0.033)
New Latino destination	0.061* −0.025	0.025* −0.012
California	−0.072** (0.027)	
Florida	0.079** (0.030)	0.027† (0.016)
Texas	0.105*** −0.029	
constant	0.328*** (0.028)	−0.011 (0.026)
Adjusted R2	0.612	0.884
F	32.003***	147.765***

†p <.10.
*p <0.05.
**p <0.01.
***p <0.001.
Standard errors are shown in parentheses.

Appendix C. *Standardized regression coefficients for best models of bilingualism among US-born and 1.5-generation Latinos*

	2000	1990–2000
Proportion US-born/1.5-generation bilingual, 1990		0.835***
Proportion 1.5-generation, 2000	0.420***	
Proportion Latinos foreign-born. 1990		0.079*
Latino isolation index, 2000	0.700***	
Latino isolation index, 1990		0.162**
1990–2000 change in proportion foreign born		0.074*
New Latino destination	0.168*	0.082*
California	−0.203***	
Florida	0.231**	0.088*
Texas	0.263***	
Adjusted R2	0.720	0.891

*p < 0.05.
**p <0.01.
*** p <0.001.
Standard errors are shown in parentheses.

Appendix D. *Log odds for regression of pay premiums for Spanish-English bilingualism in US MSAs/PMSAs, 2000 (N = 118)*

	Model 1	Model 2	Model 3
Latino isolation index	23.407**	682.593***	56.234*
Proportion Latinos foreign-born	3.967	9.756	3.303
Proportion US-born/1.5-generation bilingual		0.001***	0.154†
California			28.753**
constant	0.124**	1.047	0.337
−2 log likelihood	149.206	135.945	117.630
Percentage correct	67.2	72.3	73.1

†p <.10.
*p <0.05.
**p <0.01.
***p <0.001.
Standard errors are shown in parentheses.

'I am somebody': barrio Pentecostalism and gendered acculturation among Chicano ex-gang members

Edward Flores

Abstract

Segmented assimilation theorists posit that second-generation immigrants today are at risk of downward acculturation and socio-economic mobility, and that dense co-ethnic communities provide the greatest resistance. Drawing upon data from ethnographic interviews and non-participant observation at a Pentecostal church, this paper will suggest that American-origin religious institutions may provide shelter against downward mobility through 'religious optimism'. Using a race-gender framework to explain exit from gang lifestyle and acculturation into a group promoting mainstream American values, this paper will suggest that religious optimism may sometimes be infused with traditions from the black Protestant church, as well as inner-city stylistic expressions. Therefore, the first suggestion in this paper is that the segmented assimilation paradigm should not dichotomize the values of immigrant groups against those of native-born blacks and Latinos. The second suggestion in this paper is that segmented assimilation theorists should take into consideration that trajectories may shift in adulthood.

Introduction

This paper is an ethnography of what most would consider a contradiction: ex-gang member male Latinos who still look like gang members, but seek the American dream. These men have ambitions to fulfil the social and economic responsibilities of fatherhood: to work a well-paying job and provide emotional support for their families. To understand how Latino ex-gang members reach for such a dream, not just in spite of but perhaps even due to Mexican-American subculture, we need to understand how religious participation underpins their everyday lives. This paper will look at Latinos' interactions in an urban-American religious institution, a site previously ignored in assimilation scholars' portraits of immigrant neighbourhoods.

I will begin by briefly reviewing literature relevant to one of the dominant theoretical paradigms in immigration studies: segmented assimilation theory. Then, I will describe the methods by which I collected my data: non-participant observation and semi-structured interviews. In my findings, I will first illustrate the continuity in masculine identities between Latino gang members and Latino ex-gang members now in Victory Outreach. I will coin the term *reformed barrio masculinity* to describe Latinos who once endorsed and engaged in illegal activities such as gang membership and drug use, but who now condemn such behaviours, despite donning an oppositional style. Second, I will shed light on how Victory Outreach members use American-origin religious worship to contest dominant society's implicitly racist/sexist claims about inner-city ex- gang members and drug addicts. Third, I will analyse how engagement in Victory Outreach activities re-orients men towards the household and ultimately transforms members' gendered socio-economic behaviour, from downwardly mobile deviant barrio masculinity to reformed barrio masculinity. I will finish with two recommendations for segmented assimilation theory. First, native-born blacks and Latinos should not be used as a homogenous baseline for measuring second-generation immigrants' socio-economic outcomes. Second, segmented assimilation theory needs to account for acculturation and socio-economic mobility throughout adulthood.

Literature review

Contemporary assimilation theorists argue that modern-day second-generation immigrants are exposed to cultural values and practices not present during European immigration of the early twentieth century. Today, immigrants tend to settle in hyper-segregated urban neighbourhoods disproportionately affected by declining wages and employment in manufacturing and an hourglass economy; some scholars suggest a web of social pathologies emerges in these neighbourhoods (Wilson 1987). Furthermore, Fordham and Ogbu (1986) claim that native-born minority youth encourage their racially similar peers to reject the dominant values of a historically racist nation, through an 'oppositional culture'. As a result, segmented assimilation theorists claim that contemporary first-generation immigrants must draw upon ethnic community resources to protect their children from the anti-education/

anti-occupational attainment message projected by native-born lower-income blacks and Latinos or risk losing their children to that class (Portes and Zhou 1993; Portes and Rumbaut 2001). Segmented assimilation theorists posit three general trajectories for second-generation immigrants.

One is classical assimilation into a white mainstream. In immigrant families, this occurs through 'consonant acculturation', or the same-rate acculturation of first-generation immigrants and their children. The romanticized myth of the American 'melting pot' and early twentieth-century European immigrant assimilation best fits this concept. This type of assimilation is complicated by racial difference for black and Latino second-generation immigrants in urban, low-income neighbourhoods, as barriers often block the assimilation of these immigrants into mainstream America.

On a second path, black and Latino immigrants begin to realize their grim prospects in an economically and racially stratified society, and they acculturate into black American and US-Latino 'oppositional' groups. This occurs through 'dissonant acculturation', the more rapid acculturation of second-generation immigrant children than of their first-generation parents. According to Portes and Rumbaut (2001), 'oppositional groups' are best illustrated by native-born Mexican-Americans who identify as 'Chicanos'. Such groups may reject the means of upward mobility provided by mainstream America, such as the educational system, instead engaging in gang activity and drug use. Using data from the Children of Immigrants Longitudinal Survey (CILS), Portes and Rumbaut (2006 [1990]) reveal that, by 2003, one in five male second-generation Latinos in Southern California had been incarcerated. The average age of respondents in the CILS is only 24, and Portes and Rumbaut call this 'the most tangible evidence of downward assimilation available to date' (2006[1990], p. 280).

In the third trajectory, the immigrant co-ethnic community provides a protective influence. This is guided by 'selective acculturation', which involves acculturation only insofar as it is necessary to succeed in America. Margaret Gibson's (1988) study best illustrates this trajectory; Punjabi Sikhs in a central California high school acculturated to practices necessary for educational attainment in America, but did not acculturate into the peer-group cultures surrounding them at school. In sum, immigrant parents must draw upon their own capital, or social capital from an immigrant co-ethnic community, in order to protect their children from the negative influence of native-born black and Latino cultures.

Segmented assimilation theorists contend that the ethnic church is a major site where immigrants can build co-ethnic communities, sheltering their children from the influence of an 'oppositional culture'. Scholars of religion and immigration have long debated whether churches which intensify ethnic identification have beneficial effects upon the lives of their congregants (i.e. Greeley 1972; Barton 1975; Smith 1978). Bankston and Zhou (1996) responded to this debate by portraying the Vietnamese Catholic church as a site sheltering second-generation youths from assimilating into American 'oppositional culture'. Further research on immigration and religion also suggested this, though focusing on middle-class Asian-Americans (i.e. Chai 1998; Chong 1998; Busto 1999; Yang 1999). Most recently, Cao (2005) investigated such processes among working-class Chinese immigrant youth in New York, and found that such religious participation re-oriented immigrant youth from a culture oppositional to mainstream America.

In sum, segmented assimilation scholars dichotomize traditional ethnic churches and inner-city, native-born minority cultures. My work, however, will focus on an evangelical church which *draws upon* style associated with 'oppositional culture'. Whereas other authors have argued that adoption of symbols from an oppositional culture may largely be symbolic (Kasinitz, Mollenkopf and Waters 2004), I will explore how shifts in socio-economic trajectories may actually hinge upon the continuity of a style deemed 'oppositional'. Necker-man, Lee and Carter (1999) have argued that minority cultures do indeed provide upward socio-economic trajectories, though this research focused on the middle class. My research is situated at a church associated with the 'urban underclass', Victory Outreach.

Victory Outreach is a Pentecostal sect of Christianity, founded in 1967 by a charismatic leader, Sonny Arguinzoni. By 2007, the organization had expanded to over 600 churches and ministries worldwide. At Victory Outreach, members preach the idea that 'all things are possible with God' (Leon 1998). Victory Outreach members are overwhelmingly Latina/o, many of them ex-gang members or ex-drug addicts with incarceration records, who believe that Christian conversion is the key to spiritual change and material wealth. Victory Outreach's evangelist efforts are at the crossroads of what scholars call 'the borderlands', settings where raced/gendered identities are highly in flux (Leon 1998). Rather than being an extension of the immigrant Latino community, Victory Outreach members wear clothes and speak slang characteristic of a US-origin Mexican-American style, 'Chicano' style. In this paper I will explore how Victory Outreach members endorse mainstream American values, through the guise of a Chicano style which Portes and Rumbaut (2001) have deemed 'oppositional'. In this paper, I will use the word 'style' to refer to the aesthetic characteristics, such as dress or speech, which identify someone or something with Chicano culture. I will use the word 'values' to refer to the moral codes which guide Pentecostal asceticism, such as abstention from substance abuse or extra-marital affairs.

Second-generation immigrant mobility is a gendered process. Second-generation Latina and black women generally have higher average educational attainment and socio-economic prestige than second-generation men (Kao and Tienda 1995; Fuligni 1997; Rumbaut 1997; Feliciano and Rumbaut 2005). Some scholars (i.e. Lopez 2003; Tafoya-Estrada 2004) claim that the gender gap in second-generation immigrants' educational outcomes is partly the result of parenting practices that expose males and females to different barriers and opportunities. While immigrant parents are more likely to police their daughters and confine them to the house, immigrant parents' lack of regulation of second-generation boys' behaviour leaves those boys prone to acculturate into the low-income neighbourhood (Waters 2001; Portes and Rumbaut 2001; Smith 2006). Masculine behaviour, among lower-income adolescents, is often tied to displays of defiance towards authority that often lead to educational under-performance (Willis 1977; Gibson 1991; Macleod 1995). Robert Courtney Smith (2006), in his ethnography of a transnational Mexican-American community in New York, found that some second-generation Mexican-American males experienced downward mobility by being socialized into an urban American 'rapper masculinity'. Conversely, they were sheltered by a co-ethnic community that facilitated return visits to Mexico and socialization into 'ranchero masculinity'.

This characterization of competing masculinities, among racial minority second-generation males, dovetails with Alfredo Mirandé's (1997) and Elizabeth Brusco's (1995) distinction between *machismo* (or the person who acts it out, who is a *machista*) and *macho*. Mirandé's research (1997) suggests that both foreign-born and US-born Latinos perceive *macho* and *machismo* as different masculinities; machismo is egoistic behaviour, while being macho requires abiding by codes of honour, as well as being openly affectionate to women and children. Although Brusco (1995) focuses on evangelical conversion among Colombians, she too defines machismo as different from male dominance or patriarchy; the fundamental attribute of machismo is non-domestic involvement, often characterized by drinking, smoking and romantic affairs. However, Brusco (1995) found that the values of Pentecostal Christianity reformed Colombian men's masculine behaviour from machismo to macho. Evangelical Pentecostalism's:

> Ascetic codes forbid much of the behavior associated with the machismo complex: men can no longer drink, smoke, or have women outside of their marriage. A man's social world becomes

transformed also, from the male public world to a redefined private world where the family is the central focus. (Brusco 1995, p. 125)

Brusco claims that such a shift in gendered practices re-orients the flow of capital back towards the house, with the effect of stimulating consumption habits that influence the likelihood of upward mobility.

Household consumption can include income-generating purchases, such as real estate (houses or land, urban and rural), live-stock, a car or truck, and of course education for children. It is important to note that such investment is distinct from individual entrepreneurship because it is strategically linked to consumption and it is household based. (Brusco 1995, p. 125)

Although Brusco focuses on the Colombian case, I will base my analysis on Brusco's framework, as Mirandé did not touch upon the concepts of socio-economic mobility or religious participation.

The topic of second-generation immigrants' experiences as adults has recently entered the segmented assimilation debate. Herbert Gans (2007) argued that segmented assimilation theorists examined the concept of 'second generation decline' by focusing their research disproportionately on adolescence, when acculturation and assimilation are processes that occur throughout the life course. Gans (2007) claims that, for example, a manual labourer who is downsized at a manufacturing plant experiences a type of acculturation. Rumbaut (2005) uncovered quantitative evidence from the CILS suggesting that education, incarceration and early child-bearing have negative consequences for adult second-generation immigrants' socio-economic trajectories. In early adulthood, such processes accumulate to make upward mobility more difficult. However, this does not mean such mobility is impossible. I would like to explore the adult acculturation of Chicano men who were previously downwardly mobile, but no longer wish to be.

In sum, I would like to point out two caveats which come between segmented assimilation theory, as popularly used, and the way I will use segmented assimilation theory to frame my study of ex-transitioning gang members. First, second-generation immigrants' acculturation and socio-economic trajectories are gendered. Second, acculturation occurs throughout the life course. In this study, I will seek to answer four questions: 'How are Victory Outreach symbols and messages received by ex-/transitioning gang members?'; 'How are these symbols and messages meaningful?'; 'How do former and transitioning gang members in Victory Outreach explain and narrate their departure from gang life?'; 'How do ex-/transitioning gang members use the outreach activities to transition out of gang life?'

Data and methods

Interviews and non-participant observation at Victory Outreach events, at two sites in the eastern Los Angeles metropolitan area, constitute the data for this study. Victory Outreach-Dos Robles offered services to anywhere between 150–230 persons. About four-fifths were adults and half men. Victory Outreach-El Valle offered services to anywhere from forty to eighty persons. About half were adults, and half were also men. Both churches were both composed predominantly of third-plus-generation Latinos, although, in my estimates, about two-fifths of Victory Outreach-Dos Robles' congregation were second generation and one-fourth of Victory Outreach-El Valle's congregation. Among males, pastors anecdotally mentioned that many, but not all, had been prior gang members. Those who were not prior gang members were often ex-drug addicts, although I focused only on ex-gang members for the sake of conceptual clarity.

Non-participant observation was a key component of this project. I spent fifty-five hours at field sites taking notes. I took notes of social interactions as members worshipped, as well as during religious activities and fellowship events. I observed at weekly worship services, 'street evangelism' rallies, bible studies in members' homes, a car wash and a Dodgers game. I explained the purpose of this project as one in which I sought to learn more about the meaning of faith-based outreach to transitioning gang members, and I asked some subjects if they were willing to be interviewed. I conducted and recorded semi-structured interviews with twenty male Latino ex-/transitioning gang members.

Regarding the origins of my respondents, eight of my respondents were born in the US to immigrant parents (second-generation immigrants), while two were brought to the US at an age of six months; of these ten, eight were of Mexican descent and two of Salvadoran descent. In addition, one of my respondents could reasonably be classified as one-and-a-half generation: Mario who joined a transnational street gang in El Salvador and was then brought to the US at the age of 13. Nine of my subjects were third-generation-plus Mexican-Americans. The men ranged in age from 19 to 72, but only four were older than 43. Lastly, most had criminal records and had previously been incarcerated. However, despite the fact that I am not an ex-drug addict or gang member, there was little discomfort for either subjects or myself when interviews were carried out. Victory Outreach is an evangelist organization. Members dedicate much of their free time to meeting new persons, sharing their stories and trying to foster relationships with new persons. After interviews, many respondents smiled and said a few positive words about the experience.

I followed the extended case method in the process of collecting data and writing analyses (Burawoy *et al.* 1991). I sought to integrate anomalous cases of Latinos who promote mainstream values through a barrio style into segmented assimilation theory, which tends to conflate socio-economic trajectories with cultural influences. I also sought to integrate the experiences of my previously downwardly mobile subjects into segmented assimilation theory, which assumes adolescent acculturation is a significant predictor of socio-economic mobility in adulthood.

I will draw upon my sample of one-and-a-half- and second-generation immigrant Latinos, which I will refer to from here on as 'second-generation', in order to best illustrate the concepts I use in relation to segmented assimilation theory. However, the processes I will describe affected third-generation-plus respondents in a way indistinguishable from second-generation immigrant respondents. This falls in line with Gans' (2007) suggested re-conceptualization of acculturation and mobility, in the segmented assimilation paradigm, as processes not limited to first- and second-generation immigrants.

Findings

Values, style and masculinity

I found that the codes of ex-gang members who had converted to Pentecostal evangelicalism through Victory Outreach contrasted with those of their past. These ex-gang members once condoned drug use, violence, marital affairs and lack of emotional support to family members. However, as Pentecostal evangelicals, ex-/transitioning gang members now condemned such behaviours. At a Sunday worship service at Victory Outreach-El Valle, Pastor David said, 'Now, a lot of people might think, yeah, but they used to be smokin' dope and tryin' to get with each other. But we ain't the same any more'. Members in the congregation validated the statement with 'Amen'. This resonates with Brusco's (1995) work on masculinity and reformed behaviour among Colombian men. However, members had reformed from a non-household masculinity that was slightly different from that of Brusco's male Colombian subjects.

Barrio symbols were visible on flyers that were handed out at Victory Outreach, with air-brush artwork and low-riders promoting church events. Many if not all male members groomed themselves and wore clothes according to what was popular in the barrio. Such a style included thick moustaches, shaved heads, old gang tattoos, plaid shirts, white shirts, Raiders and USC jerseys, loose-fitting jeans or pleated khakis with white sneakers. Men in Victory Outreach also spoke using East Los Angeles barrio slang, such as *heina* (girlfriend), *homeboy* (close male friend) or *ranking out* (deciding to not participate in something after committing to it). The cultural symbols and institutionalized social relations giving life to such barrio masculinity had been planted deep in the roots of East Los Angeles since Depression-era zoot suit culture. For this reason, I will conceptualize East Los Angeles male Latino gang lifestyle as a US-based masculine identity, rather than a continuation of the cultural patterns found in my second-generation respondents' countries of origin. I will label US-Latino gang masculinity *deviant barrio masculinity*, due to the types of neighbourhoods such behaviour flourishes in (lower-income Latino neighbourhoods, or *barrios*) and the pronounced oppositional nature that characterizes it.

In contrast, men who express what I term *reformed barrio masculinity* still fashion much of the style from deviant barrio masculinity but now promote mainstream values. These men value non-criminal behaviour, legitimate employment and being emotionally supportive of family members. These men express reformed barrio masculinity, as opposed to a mainstream masculinity, because barrio cultural style, such as clothing and speech, still colour the expressions of their behaviour. Male members spread the message of God to gang members on the street by speaking with local language familiar to gang members and drug addicts from such neighbourhoods. Aside from informal social interactions, flyers and church decorations, pastors commonly drew upon life in the barrio to illustrate examples in their sermons. A pastor once used the examples of helping out during weight-lifting, serving burritos to visitors in one's house and taking *chiles rellenos* to a church function in order to deliver a sermon concerning the importance of thoughtfulness in practicing Christian servitude. During another sermon a member talked about early days in Victory Outreach when he would run from a pastor 'like a probation officer'. And on another occasion, a reverend talked about trials that build character. He said, 'We need a crisis, we need a trial. I hear someone in the back saying, "we're done with trials". But this is a different form of trial, not the type in front of a judge.' In all examples, persons in the congregation laughed at jokes, a sign that church leaders reached the congregation by reference to life in East Los Angeles barrios.

The continuity between deviant barrio masculinity and reformed barrio masculinity provides a bridge for youth who have acculturated into gangs but now seek to achieve the American dream: to maintain a stable job, get married and have kids. This goal implicitly requires avoiding confrontations with the legal system. Jaime, a 32-year-old second-generation Mexican-American, recalls the first time he tried to look for change in his life, away from gangs. Jaime saw gang members on a flyer advertising a Victory Outreach performance and attended without knowing it was a spiritual event.

> My role model was a gang member, all tattoos, coming out of prison, being buff, having all kinds of women, that's what I wanted to grow up to be. So I seen all that in the play, I see nothing but homeys with big ole' whips, tattoos, in the play talking about God, and that they're not using drugs, and they're not in prison no more, and I say, "ey, cool".

Jaime's attitude, and that of other Victory Outreach members, suggests that reformed barrio masculinity challenges segmented assimilation's conflation of oppositional style and values; an oppositional style is not necessarily synonymous with anti-mainstream values. Mario, a 28-year-old El Salvadoran immigrant who came to the US at the age of 13, had joined a major transnational gang in El Salvador. Despite being from a different country, Mario's perceptions of and relations with Victory Outreach ex-gang members were almost identical to Jaime's.

> I was messing with them too, like, "Man, you're Spider, the one from [the Mexican-American movie] Blood in/ Blood out"... [T]hey get along with me because I came from their background ... we relate, you know? I know exactly what they were talking about, their words, and the meaning of the words, and then they start talking to me about God.

Thus, the segmented assimilation model (i.e. Portes and Rumbaut 2001; Zhou and Bankston 1998) should take into consideration that Chicano identity and American-based religious institutions can also attempt to shelter second-generation immigrants against downward mobility. Other scholars have noted that Victory Outreach makes use of cultural styles found among low-income urban Latinos in order to gain and maintain membership (Sanchez-Walsh 2003; Leon 2004). I also found this to be true in my research. In such a setting, 'oppositional' identity was not merely symbolic, as Kasinitz, Mollenkopf and Waters (2004) suggest, but instrumental. The following section will describe how members use Chicano identity, together with an institutionalized form of worship influenced by the black Protestant church, to challenge stereotypes and inspire hope in upward mobility.

Religious optimism

> My fiancée came to me one day and said, "They were like ... [Mario's] not gonna change" ... [W]hen she said that, right away, a scripture came to my mind. It's gonna be a lot of people talking about you ... don't worry about it because they hate [God] first ... we believe in what we believe. We believe in God. And that's it. (Mario)

The quote above reveals how Mario used biblical scripture to combat the dominant belief that inner-city, male gang members cannot change. Victory Outreach is a space where raced/gendered stereotypes in dominant society are challenged. During worship services at Victory Outreach, members' personal relationships with God are 'magnified and exalted'. Loud, well-rehearsed music is played while some persons move to the music in their seats or standing up. Some simply clap, and yet others hardly move – focused deeply in a profound prayer. It is at this point that one can look around and see many men with plaid shirts, oversized clothes, pleated khakis and white sneakers or shaved heads. Worship styles are diffuse; as one member raises his/her hand high to pray, another might be holding both hands with palms out and yet another may be doing nothing at all. Here, one may notice hands and arms, among the crowd, still revealing the tattoo of an old gang. A karaoke screen guides the congregation with song lyrics, and after a few songs to start off a worship service the pastor begins his sermon.

Sermons are often powerful and sensational. At the climax of any given sermon is pronounced participation from the part of the congregation, very much like 'call-and-response' as described by Patricia Hill Collins (1990). Call-and-response, in its strict definition, is a form of congregation participation in black Protestant churches. However, Collins (1990) describes call-and-response as more than simply a form of spiritual worship; call-and-response validates knowledge claims rooted in the local knowledge of black churches. I find that, just as a black-oriented world view is dialogued and expressed through interactions within a black church, so too is a Latino-oriented world view dialogued and expressed through interactions in Victory Outreach churches. Victory Outreach congregation members used call-and-response reactions to help shape the intensity of messages sent by Pastors during services, although not to the same degree one might expect in a very participatory black Protestant church. Messages from the Gospel are embedded in stream-of-thought prayers, songs and sermons, challenging dominant perceptions of barrio gang members and drug addicts as lacking compassion and lacking the ability to change.

Reverend Ernest at Victory Outreach-Dos Robles once gave a sermon which referenced his own prior gang affiliation, in order to deliver a message about using spirituality in order to forgive and receive forgiveness. Ernest asked, 'How many of us have partners that are impossible?' Several people said, 'Amen'. Ernest said, 'But that was once us'. The woman next to me nodded her head and said, 'uh-huh, Amen'. Ernest said, 'When I first got saved I was scaring everyone away'. A few people in the audience laughed. Ernest said:

> But I still didn't trust nobody. It wasn't until I built relationship with God. You need to learn to forgive, because you've been forgiven. I have heart for everyone now, and that's how it started with me. I don't deserve it, I should be 6 feet under, like many of you here, but somebody saw something in me.

Many in the congregation clapped and cheered loudly, validating his claim that one can change from expressing a deviant barrio masculinity to a reformed barrio masculinity.

Members contest dominant perceptions of gang members and drug addicts in more staunch terms as well. The following occurred at a Victory Outreach-El Valle service. Pastor David said, 'I want you to turn to somebody and say, "I *am* somebody!"' The congregation replied, 'I am somebody'. The pastor followed with, 'Yes I am! Yes I am! You *are* somebody! You've been washed in his blood! You've been smothered in his love! You are a child of the most high king!'

After every phrase members in the congregation repeated the pastor. A minute later the pastor said, 'Whether you're Latino ... or you're black ... or you're white ... or you're Indian ... or you're from El Valle and your name is Shotgun'. A couple of members in the congregation exuberantly responded with 'Amen'. Pastor David shortly thereafter brought the congregation's emotions down to a relaxed tone, calmly, slowly stating, 'I am worth more than who I am on the outside'. One person quietly said, 'Amen'. The rest of the congregation sat in complete silence. Pastor David then continued his sermon with more call-and-response interactions.

The participatory-oriented nature of formal worship services creates a sense of belonging for members. This is not new. Black Protestant churches have had a long history of resisting racial oppression in America, through socially cohesive and highly personal religious ceremonies. Church leaders drew upon traditions from the black Protestant church, such as Reverend Jesse Jackson's phrase ('I *am* somebody') and call-and-response, in order to proclaim the quintessential characteristic of mainstream America: an optimistic belief in free will. Pentecostalism generally promotes Protestant America's 'health and wealth gospel' (Miller and Yamamori 2007). To the extent that Victory Outreach uses black Protestant traditions to sponsor the optimistic American belief in free will, we can say that second-generation Latino immigrants in Victory Outreach are acculturating into a segment of American society influenced by black Protestantism and religious optimism. Where immigration scholars, such as Kao and Tienda (1995), have used the term *immigrant optimism* to describe immigrants with third world origins, a disciplined work ethic and lofty goals, I will coin the term *religious optimism* to describe both low-income non-immigrants and second-generation immigrants with disadvantaged origins, a disciplined work ethic and lofty goals. The following characterizes the nature of religious optimism,

> I know it's something that's gonna seem impossible. Sometimes we might be, "Man, I'm gonna go out there, get my big house".... We might be going out there for one, two, three, four years, and we might still be living in an apartment.... But I know we still got that communication with God.... I mean, what else is gonna happen? You know? (Mario)

Thus, persons who survive the most negative aspects of a disadvantaged upbringing, such as growing up in the inner-city, may actually later feel hope in becoming upwardly mobile. In the next section I will discuss how members' gendered behaviours were reformed in such a way as to maximize their contributions to the household, sheltering them against downward mobility and influencing the probability of upward mobility for them and their families.

Reformed barrio masculine acculturation and upward mobility
Christian asceticism in Victory Outreach

I measured socio-economic mobility by two criteria: did my respondents quit illegal economic activity and were they now formally employed? Prior to Christian conversion, all my respondents were either unemployed or engaged in an illegal economy. However, at the time of my research none was engaging in illegal economic activity, and most were employed.

One might argue that the illegal economy offers greater opportunities than the formal economy. I found no evidence to validate this idea. Respondents who had been involved in the illegal economy either already experienced, or mentioned, the downsides of illegal economies: potential risk of being arrested and spending many years in prison, as well as the unstable and dangerous aspects that caused stress to them and their family members. In this section I illustrate how four respondents, Rudy, Gustavo, Marcelo and Arturo, experienced upward mobility through a shift to reformed barrio masculinity. Just as in

Brusco's (1995) study, the values of Pentecostal evangelicalism redirected masculine behaviour towards household needs, and induced upward mobility for members and their families.

Household relationships
Established members role modelled appropriate behaviour for newer members. For example, Pastor Steve taught Rudy, a third-plus-generation Mexican-American in his late 20s, not to have extra-marital affairs. The gospel reference for this lesson was the classic 'do unto others as you would have them do unto you'. Rudy said:

> When I came into the church ... my wife was pregnant and I was still being with other women ... the leadership of this church, Pastor Ben ... told me that ..."What if she was to do that to you? How would you feel?" I wouldn't like it, you see? You know, do to others what you would like done to you.

To the degree that this lesson was imparted successfully to Rudy, the time and money that normally would have been spent on extra-marital affairs could hypothetically be redirected towards the household. Arturo, a second-generation Mexican-American in his late 30s, also shared a similar story of following in the footsteps of another member.

> I remember one of the pastors that came to speak at our church ... [H]is son came and testified ... how his dad was very affectionate to him, how his dad never missed one of his games or practices, and that influenced me too when I started having kids ....[T]here's very few times that me as a father hasn't been to his practices or been to one of [my son's] games.

Members' influence upon children was not limited to parenting. In immigrant households, older siblings often fulfil capacities traditionally associated with adult parenting (Thorne *et al.* 2003). Gustavo, a 19-year-old second-generation El Salvadoran, quit selling drugs in order to set a better example for his younger siblings. 'I did not wanna go to jail for twenty years, just for doing something stupid.... Just doing nothing and being a bad habit to your mom. To your brothers. They're trying to follow in your footsteps and, it's, it's, just not right.'

Gustavo, desiring a positive influence that he can pass down to his siblings, now participates in church activities as opposed to gang activity. Marcelo, a 20-year-old second-generation Mexican-American had lost privileges to see his son years ago. This was tied to Marcelo's two-year addiction to crystal methamphetamine, the eighteen months he spent in juvenile hall for selling drugs and the under-employment he experienced up until recently. However, he has been clean for about four years now, and has become more and more involved in church activities. Marcelo also landed a new job with higher pay and more hours, influencing the courts to grant him custody of his son on weekends.

Work

Two Victory Outreach members I interviewed, Gustavo and Marcelo, landed new jobs during the last month of my fieldwork. Gustavo landed a new job at a hotel, through in-laws that once attended Victory Outreach. This job was at a hotel in downtown Los Angeles, and paid above a living wage and offered benefits. Marcelo landed a $10/hour fulltime job as a driver. In addition, due to his involvement in activities, Marcelo earned a free van from the church. After packing up from a tiny 'street evangelism' rally, Marcelo made the comment to Veronica, 'that's one of the reasons why I believe God gave me this free van'. The following week, at nearby housing development, Marcelo told me how Paul, a mid-30s second-generation Mexican-American member of Victory Outreach, helped to get him hired. Paul was also going to try to get one more church member another job in the same company. Although Gustavo and Marcelo both made use of social networks at Victory Outreach for employment, Marcelo's experience best exemplifies the manner by which Christian ascetic codes can reform machista males' behaviour towards the household, leading to capital accumulation and upward mobility. Once a drug-user and absent from his son's life, Marcelo now is drug-free, owns a van, holds a full-time job and is part of his son's life, due to his participation with church.

Rudy also experienced a shift from deviant barrio masculinity to reformed barrio masculinity, through labour market participation. Rudy was approached by male members of the church, during a time when he was selling drugs, and was told that he needed to make responsible economic contributions to his household. In a machista-oriented relationship, a male frequently has little regard for others in his household, but this type of relationship is strongly contested by men in Victory Outreach.

> Here comes Pastor Steve and the leadership of the church and they're trying to help me to direct me and to say, "You need to get a job to support your family. You can't just get responsibilities and then run from it, like you used to.... You are the man and you need to go get a job. It doesn't matter if you start off at McDonald's."

Arturo spent most of his time between the ages of 16 and 25 incarcerated. Arturo now works a white-collar job in 'purchasing' at a large corporation, and claims that he learned a particular work ethic from social interactions at Victory Outreach. He said:

> Another principle that was taught to me was the principle of working, working a full-time job. I would go to work sites not wanting to work.... Today I'm able to hold a job, I'm able to work for eight hours plus, without being tempted to leave. Without you know, arguing with my boss, that I don't wanna do the work that I'm being asked to do.

The work ethic that established Victory Outreach members seek to impart to newer members has positive effects upon their occupational and earnings attainment. Rudy, Arturo, Gustavo and Paul all now work jobs that pay above a living wage, and Marcelo comes close. However, even in Marcelo's case, participation in Victory Outreach activities prevented him from relapsing into street life, exposed him to social networks that facilitated a new employment opportunity and offered him the resources necessary to meet the obligations of his new job. In relation to literature on segmented assimilation, these subjects do not appear to be truly upwardly mobile in the same way that other second-generation immigrants, such as the educated children of Indian doctors or Cuban businessmen, are. In fact, possessing few educational qualifications and an incarceration record, in an economy with a bi-furcating labour market, may prove to be a stagnant socio-economic trajectory in the long run (Western 2002). However, the fact that Victory Outreach ex-gang members are now heavily sheltered against downward mobility, and groomed to contribute socially and economically to their households, suggests that the socio-economic effect of conversion may resemble a gradual ripple effect, such as that described by Brusco (1995). For this reason, I focused on the effect that reformed barrio masculinity had upon male, adult Latino ex-gang members' broader household participation, as opposed to a gender-free analysis of individual experiences as segmented assimilation would have.

Muscular Christianity

Victory Outreach's reformation of male behaviour is not the same as that which has occurred with other Christian-based men's movements. Historically, Christian-based American men's movements, such as the Promise Keepers, have targeted feminism and the feminization of social spheres as responsible for emergent social problems (Messner 1997). During my research on Victory Outreach I found no such indications. For example, at a Victory Outreach carwash, male members were excessively cheerful and humorous while working, despite the fact that a woman was responsible for collecting money and keeping track of members' duties. This is not to say that progressive understandings of sex and gender existed at Victory Outreach. The division of labour between Victory Outreach male and female members, with male pastors, female ushers and male security guards, reflects the sexual division of labour that feminists have so widely protested against in mainstream society. Arlene Sanchez-Walsh (2003) corroborates this facet of Victory Outreach. However, Victory Outreach is a patriarchal institution in which male leaders encourage male members to reflect upon the way in which their behaviour can be reformed for the social and economic benefit of themselves and their families. For example, Mario said:

> Sometimes [women] go off, like, "Naw! You don't do nothing!" ... [Victory Outreach leaders] teach us to humble ourselves, to be quiet. Between all the words that they're throwing out, you're gonna be able to hear their need. You know, and you're gonna be able to capture what the problem is. And then you're gonna have to work on it, to fix the problem. Not bring more problems.

After Mario talked about the changes he is ready to make in his life to be ready for domestic responsibilities, I asked what he expects from his wife. Mario said, 'What I'm expecting from her? To be the way she is, all the way through.' Whereas 'muscular Christianity' leaders sought to masculinize men and feared the feminization of social spheres, Victory Outreach leaders sought to shape hyper-masculine men into persons more sensitive to social interactions – in a manner which brought them in line with broader American conventions of sex and gender.

Conclusion

Chicano style was not synonymous with values that lead to downward mobility. Such a style did facilitate downwardly mobile values among my respondents in adolescence. However, all my respondents reported being drawn to the cultural style of Victory Outreach due to the sense of belonging it offered. An intense, spiritual relationship with God, cloaked in an urban, masculine, barrio style, replaced the sense of belonging members once experienced with gangs. Through social interactions with established male members, new male members' commitment to Christian asceticism deepened. As with Brusco's (1995) research on Colombian males, Christian asceticism among second-generation immigrant males redirected their gendered behaviour away from substance abuse and extra-marital affairs and towards the household. This induced the likelihood of upward mobility among my respondents and their families. Thus, Victory Outreach members drew upon a gendered cultural style to create a bridge between distinct socio-economic trajectories; as adults, members went from an oppositional, downwardly mobile socio-economic trajectory, embodied in deviant barrio masculinity, to a newer pathway emphasizing domestic responsibilities and a work ethic, embodied in reformed barrio masculinity. This corroborates recent scholars' claims that acculturation and assimilation are gendered processes (Lopez 2003; Smith 2006), as well as Gans' (2007) claim that acculturation and assimilation occur throughout the life course.

Although the material resources for upward mobility were not apparent to members of Victory Outreach, hope in upward mobility became pronounced through spiritual worship. Call-and-response social interactions, drawn from the historically resilient black church and community, were used to challenge dominant society's racist/sexist perceptions of minorities, magnifying religious optimism. Thus, Victory Outreach's institutionalization of interactions fell into a broader religious tradition influenced by the black Protestant church. This has implications for segmented assimilation's depiction of socio-economic paths among native-born groups.

Segmented assimilation scholars have conceptualized traditional ethnic religion as one mechanism sheltering second-generation immigrants from downward mobility, assuming that exposure to such co-ethnic networks protects immigrants from assimilating into a native-born black and Latino-influenced oppositional culture (Zhou and Bankston 1998; Cao 2005). However, as this article suggested, there is not simply a homogeneous and downwardly mobile native-born minority culture into which second-generation immigrants may acculturate. Second-generation immigrants in densely populated native-born black and Latino neighbourhoods are exposed not just to a strand of urban culture which experiences marginalization and expresses frustration, but another strand which experiences gradual improvement and/or expresses hope. Non-immigrants and second-generation blacks and Latinos can be sheltered from downward mobility by drawing upon black-influenced religious worship and barrio culture. To the extent that this is facilitated by religious institutions, we should term such a pathway 'religious optimism'. Zhou and Bankston's (1998) research on a community of Versailles residents, in a seminal piece of segmented assimilation research, suggested this; the southern black church has historically had very strong membership, and in Zhou and Bankston's (1998) research, Versailles' blacks actually outperformed Vietnamese in educational attainment. The findings in this paper suggest a reformulation of segmented assimilation's conceptualization of the socio-economic pathways available to second-generation immigrants, so as to include the beneficial effects of black American and US-Latino cultures. In contrast to segmented assimilation theory's homogeneous depiction of the detrimental influences of Chicano and black 'reactive ethnicity', this study suggests that Chicano and black cultures may have positive effects upon the socio-economic well-being of second-generation immigrants.

Acknowledgements

I thank Pierrette Hondagneu-Sotelo, Amon Emeka, Glenda Flores, Natasha Warikoo and two anonymous reviewers from this journal for helpful comments on earlier drafts. I thank Min Zhou, discussant at the University of California-Los Angeles (UCLA) migration conference, 'Waves, Flows, Streams and Floods', at which this was first presented. I also thank the University of Southern California-College of Letters, Arts and Sciences for a diversity grant that enabled some of the data collection for this project.

References

BANKSTON III, CARL L. and ZHOU, MIN 1996 'The ethnic church, ethnic identification, and the social adjustment of Vietnamese adolescents', *Review of Religious Research*, vol. 38, no. 1, pp. 18–37

BARTON, JOSEF L 1975 *Peasants and Strangers: Italians, Rumanians, and Slovaks in an American City, 1890–1950*, Cambridge, MA: Harvard University Press

BRUSCO, ELIZABETH 1995 *The Reformation of Machismo: Evangelical Conversion and Gender in Colombia*, Austin, TX: University of Texas Press

BURAWOY, MICHAEL, BURTON, ALICE, FERGUSON, ANN ARNETT, FOX, KATHRYN J., GAMSON, JOSHUA, GARTRELL, NADINE, HURST, LESLIE, KURZMAN, CHARLES, SALZINGER, LESLIE, SCHIFFMAN, JOSEPHA and UI, SHIORI 1991 *Ethnography Unbound: Power and Resistance in the Modern Metropolis*, Berkeley, CA: University of California Press

BUSTO, RUDY V. 1999 'The gospel according to model minority? Hazarding an interpretation of Asian American evangelical college students', in D. K. Yoo (ed.), *New Spiritual Homes: Religion and Asian Americans*, Honolulu, HI: University of Hawaii Press

CAO, NANLAI 2005 'The church as a surrogate family for working class immigrant Chinese youth: an ethnography of segmented assimilation', *Sociology of Religion*, vol. 66, no. 2, pp. 183–200

CHAI, K. 1998 'Competing for the second generation: English-language ministry at a Korean Protestant church', in R. Stephen Warner and Judith G. Wittner (eds), *Gatherings in Diaspora: Religious Communities and the New Migration*, Philadelphia, PA: Temple University Press

CHONG, KELLY H. 1998 'What it means to be Christian: the role of religion in the construction of ethnic identity and boundary among second generation Korean Americans', *Sociology of Religion*, vol. 59, no. 3, pp. 259–86

COLLINS, PATRICIA HILL 1990 *Black Feminist Thought: Knowledge, Consciousness, and the Politics of Empowerment*, Boston, MA: Unwin Hyman

FELICIANO, CYNTHIA and RUMBAUT, RUBÉN G. 2005 'Gendered paths: educational and occupational expectations and outcomes among adult children of immigrants', *Ethnic and Racial Studies*, vol. 28, no. 6, pp. 1087–118

FORDHAM, SIGNITHIA and OGBU, JOHN 1986 'Black students' school success: coping with the burden of acting white', *Urban Review*, vol. 18, no. 3, pp. 176–206

FULIGNI, ANDREW J. 1997 'The academic achievement of adolescents from immigrant families: the roles of family background, attitudes, and behavior', *Child Development*, vol. 68, no. 2.

GANS, HERBERT, J. 2007 'Acculturation, assimilation and mobility', *Ethnic and Racial Studies*, vol. 30, no. 1, pp. 152–64

GIBSON, MARGARET A. 1988 *Accommodation without Assimilation: Sikh Immigrants in an American High School*, Ithaca, NY: Cornell University Press.

—— 1991 'Ethnicity, gender and social class: the school adaptation patterns of West Indian youths', in Margaret A. Gibson and John U. Ogbu (eds), *Minority Status and Schooling: A Comparative Study of Immigrant and Involuntary Minorities*, New York: Garland

GREELEY, ANDREW M. 1972 *The Denominational Society: A Sociological Approach to Religion*, Glenview, IL: Scott, Foresman

KAO, GRACE and TIENDA, MARTA 1995 'Optimism and achievement: the educational performance of immigrant youth', *Social Science Quarterly*, vol. 76, pp. 1–19

KASINITZ, PHILIP, MOLLENKOPF, JOHN H. and WATERS, MARY C. 2004 'Worlds of the second generation', in Philip Kasinitz, John H. Mollenkopf and Mary C. Waters (eds), *Becoming New Yorkers: Ethnographies of the New Second Generation*, New York: Russell Sage

LEON, LUIS 1998 'Born again in East L.A.: the congregation as border space', in R. Stephen Warner and Judith G. Wittner (eds), *Gatherings in Diaspora: Religious Communities and the New Migration*, Philadelphia, PA: Temple University Press

—— 2004 *La Llorona's Children: Religion, Life and Death in the U.S.-Mexican Borderlands*, Berkeley, CA: University of California Press

LOPEZ, NANCY 2003 *Hopeful Girls, Troubled Boys: Race and Gender Disparity in Urban Education*, New York: Routledge

MACLEOD, JAY 1995 *Ain't No Makin' It: Aspirations and Attainment in a Low-Income Neighborhood*, Boulder, CO: Westview Press

MESSNER, MICHAEL A 1997 *Politics of Masculinities: Men in Movements*, Thousand Oaks, CA: Sage

MILLER, DONALD E. and YAMAMORI, TETSUNAO 2007 *Global Pentecostalism: The New Face of Christian Social Engagement*, Berkeley, CA: University of California Press

MIRANDÉ, ALFREDO 1997 *Hombres y Machos: Masculinity and Latino Cultura*, Boulder, CO: Westview Press

NECKERMAN, KATHRYN, LEE, JENNIFER and CARTER, PRUDENCE 1999 'Segmented assimilation and minority cultures of mobility', *Ethnic and Racial Studies*, vol. 22, no. 6, pp. 945–65

PORTES, ALEJANDRO and RUMBAUT, RUBEN G. 2001 *Legacies: The Story of the Immigrant Second Generation*, Berkeley, CA: University of California Press

—— 2006 [1990] *Immigrant America: A Portrait*, Berkeley, CA: University of California Press

PORTES, ALEJANDRO and ZHOU, MIN 1993 'The new second generation: segmented assimilation and its variants', *Annals of the American Academy of Political and Social Science*, vol. 530, pp. 74–96

RUMBAUT, RUBÉN G. 1997 'Ties that bind: immigration and immigrant families in the United States', in Alan Booth, Ann C. Crouter and Nancy Landale (eds), *Immigration and the Family: Research and Policy on U.S. Immigrants*, Mahwah, NJ: Lawrence Erlbaum Associates

—— 2005 'Turning points in the transition to adulthood: determinants of educational attainment, incarceration, and early childbearing among children of immigrants', *Ethnic and Racial Studies*, vol. 28, no. 6, pp. 1041–86

SANCHEZ-WALSH, ARLENE 2003 *Latino Evangelical Identity: Evangelical Faith, Society, and Self*, New York: Columbia University Press
SMITH, ROBERT C. 2006 *Mexican New York: Transnational Lives of New Immigrants*, Berkeley, CA: University of California Press
SMITH, TIMOTHY L. 1978 'Religion and ethnicity in America', *American Historical Review*, vol. 83, pp. 1115-85
TAFOYA-ESTRADA, ROSAURA 2004 'The unintended consequences of patriarchy: Mexican immigrant culture and education among the second generation', Master's thesis, Sociology Department, University of California, Irvine
THORNE, BARRIE, ORELLANA, MARJORIE FAULSTICH, LAM, WAN SHUN EVA and CHEE, ANNA 2003 'Raising children, and growing up, across national borders: comparative perspectives on age, gender and migration', in Pierrette Hondagneu-Sotelo (ed.), *Gender and U.S. Immigration: Contemporary Trends*, Berkeley, CA: University of California Press
WATERS, MARY C. 1999 *Black Identities: West Indian Immigrant Dreams and American Realities*, Cambridge, MA: Harvard University Press
WESTERN, BRUCE 2002 'The impact of incarceration on wage mobility and inequality', *American Sociological Review*, vol. 67, pp. 1-21
WILLIS, PAUL E. 1977 *Learning to Labour: How Working Class Kids Get Working Class Jobs*, Farnborough: Saxon House
WILSON, WILLIAM J. 1987 *The Truly Disadvantaged: The Inner City, the Underclass, and Public Policy*, Chicago, IL: University of Chicago Press
YANG, FENGGANG 1999 'ABC and XYZ: religious, ethnic and racial identities of the new second generation Chinese in Christian churches', *Amerasia Journal*, vol. 25, no. 1, pp. 89-115
ZHOU, MIN and BANKSTON, CARL L. 1998 *Growing Up American: How Vietnamese Children Adapt to Life in the United States*, New York: Russell Sage

'It is their nature to do menial labour': the racialization of 'Latino/a workers' by agricultural employers

Marta Maria Maldonado

Abstract

Latino/as[1] constitute the largest ethno-racial minority group in the United States, and a significant and growing proportion of the US labour force. Nevertheless, they remain at the bottom of the US economy, concentrated and overrepresented in 'bad jobs'. Using a case study from agricultural work, this paper examines how racialization is implicated in such positioning of Latino/as within the labour market. Based on data from in-depth interviews, I explore *how* agricultural employers articulate racial meanings about and in relation to Latino/a workers. While employers espouse colour-blindness, they routinely invoke racial meanings in their assessment of workers and everyday practices. They use race as proxy for worker quality, making racialized distinctions between recent immigrants and second+-generation Latino/as. A dual frame of reference serves as an ideological tool to de-problematize exploitative work conditions in the United States. I explore the theoretical and political implications of these findings.

Introduction

Latino/as constitute the largest, fastest growing ethno-racial minority group in the United States. Historically, the incorporation of Latino/as into the US has been tied to employers' need for labour. Jobs have been and continue to be an important 'pull factor' for Latino/a immigration. Latino/as were 13 per cent of the total US labour force in 2005, and will constitute about a quarter of the total US labour force by 2050 (Toossi 2006). Despite their growing presence in the labour force, Latino/as remain on the bottom rungs of the US economy.

Further, they tend to be concentrated and overrepresented in 'bad jobs' associated with low wages, instability, lack of benefits and poor prospects for advancement (Canales 2007).

The growing presence of Latino/as in such jobs cannot be fully explained by 'supply-side' or human capital factors such as workers' education and training alone (Canales 2007). Recent analyses have called attention to the role of 'demand-side' factors, such as employer recruitment, as impetus for immigration and for the growing presence of Latino/a workers in various industries. In fact, employer recruitment and State-led economic development initiatives are major driving forces for Latino/a immigration into various regions of the United States. Although not the only factor driving continued Latino/a immigration, recruitment by employers is largely responsible for channelling Latino/a workers into low-wage jobs in various industries, including farm work, forestry, domestic work, meatpacking and construction (e.g. Heffernan 2000; Johnson-Webb 2002; Kandel and Parrado 2005; Krissman 2005).

Employer recruitment practices are directly related to employers' sense of the ability and suitability of various groups of workers for particular work. Existing research from various work contexts suggests that, for employers, race often serves as proxy for worker skills and marker for the desirability of workers. Racial meanings inform and affect employers' perceptions and evaluations of workers, their judgement regarding which workers are fit for different jobs, their assessments of who are good and bad workers, the production of notions of skill, the connection of skills to specific jobs and the production of meanings about jobs themselves (Kennelly 1999; Moss and Tilly 2001; Shih 2002; Waldinger and Lichter 2003). Given the racialized history and contemporary structure of the United States, racialization[2] affects the way workplaces operate day-to-day. Race has informed and shaped employers' practices historically, including recruitment and hiring, thereby structuring access to the US labour system and becoming an axis along which that system is routinely organized. As Waldinger and Lichter state: 'In a racialized society like the United States, entire ethnic groups are ranked according to sets of socially meaningful but arbitrary traits; these rankings determine fitness for broad categories of jobs' (2003, p. 8).

Understanding how Latino/as get inserted and shuffled within the US occupational structure necessitates analysing the everyday production of racial meanings, *how* such meanings emerge, are deployed and become embedded in everyday institutional discourse and practice.[3] Historically, racialized (and gendered) discourses about Latinos/as in the United States have entailed their representation as particular kinds of worker. Such representations have furnished the ideological underpinning for guest worker and labour recruitment programmes, and for policies that have opened or closed US 'doors' to Latino/as. This paper explores how employers articulate racial meanings about Latino/a workers[4] and how such meanings help inform and justify practices and arrangements in workplaces.

The racialization of Latino/as in the United States: theoretical considerations

Recent sociological scholarship has moved away from a focus on race as a static category of membership or identity, towards a focus on racialization, or race as fluid, dynamic, historically specific and geographically contingent relation and process. Theorizing and documenting empirically *how* racialization occurs is a central task in contemporary sociological scholarship (see Darder and Torres 2004; Murji and Solomos 2005; Bonilla-Silva 2006). While the racialization of Latino/as (mostly Mexicans and Puerto Ricans) at their time of incorporation into the United States has been examined extensively (Almaguer 1994; Guerin-Gonzalez 1994; Menchaca 2001; Whalen 2001) *contemporary* processes of Latino/a racialization have seldom been explored (notable exceptions include Naples (2000) and De Genova and Ramos-Zayas (2003)).

Since the mid-1960s, most immigration to the United States has come from Latin America. US Latino/a populations have grown and become increasingly diverse in national origin, ethnicity, race and class. Also, Latino/as have dispersed geographically, with the most dramatic population growth occurring in 'new destinations'. Multiple questions regarding these demographic changes necessitate theoretically anchored analysis and empirical investigation. How have these changes altered the racial stories told about Latino/as? How have they reconfigured racial representations and racialized social relations and conditions? Given continuous replenishment of Latin American immigrant populations, how are various cohorts racialized? How do the racial stories told about second-generation Latino/as compare with those about the newly arrived? Is there a racial ordering of generations of Latino/a immigrants?

Different racializations and multiple racisms

Historically, analyses of racial matters in the United States have emphasized a white-black binary, with Latino/as (among other racialized populations) becoming 'invisible minorities' whose experiences are understood only in relation to that binary. Recent scholarship has begun to examine the racialized experiences of 'invisible' groups, revealing different processes of racialization, demonstrating the limitations of unidimensional conceptions of racism and documenting multiple and different racisms.

Jung (2002), for example, shows how analyses that homogenize 'the Asian worker experience' obscure the distinct ways in which Filipino and Japanese agricultural workers were racialized in pre-Second World War Hawaii. He demonstrates that the racisms these two groups faced varied in intensity and form. Racist discourses against Filipinos emphasized their purported racial inferiority, while racism against the Japanese entailed fear that they were *not* racially inferior and questioned their loyalty to 'America'. Kim (1999)'s work also reveals the multidimensionality of racialization and racisms. She introduces the concept *racial triangulation* to explain the valorization of Asian groups *vis-à-vis* one another and relative to whites and blacks. She proposes that such valorization occurs along an axis of superiority/inferiority and also along cultural lines, Similarly, De Genova and Ramos-Zayas (2003) document how Mexicans and Puerto Ricans are differently racialized – and participate in the construction of their own racialized differences – all within a larger structure of racial inequality and oppression.

This essay contributes to this burgeoning literature by examining the ways in which Latino/as are racialized in a specific context of contemporary US class relations. Using a case study from agricultural work, I examine how Latino/as are racialized by employers. I analyse agricultural employers' discourse as it reflects larger ideological forces that sustain and reproduce structural racism (Bonilla-Silva 1997, 2006) by normalizing and de-problematizing racially unequal arrangements and making them invisible. My interpretation of the discourse of employers scrutinizes the social significance and social consequences of their racialized accounts. I identify racial stories, describe discursive patterns and place employers' accounts of race systemically, within the larger realm of power relations.

The case study

This research draws from in-depth interviews with white[5] and Latino/a (Mexican and Mexican American) employers[6] in the tree-fruit and vegetable industries in Washington. These industries present an interesting case for analysing the production of racial meanings about Latino/as in US workplaces. Despite increasing mechanization, they remain among the most labour-intensive industries in the United States. Also, since the *Bracero Program*, they have relied heavily on Latino/a (primarily Mexican) labour for filling low-end jobs (Gamboa 1990).[7] Finally, the personnel practices that agricultural employers in Washington rely on (which enable and foster continuous recruitment of new Latino/a immigrant workers) are increasingly used *across* the

United States, within other agricultural industries (e.g. meatpacking), and outside the agricultural sector (Krissman 2000; Johnson-Webb 2002; Kandel and Parrado 2005).

The sample included forty employers[8] from twenty-six farm operations and firms (packers/shippers, equipment and input suppliers, warehouses) representing the various sizes[9] and types of agricultural operations in Washington (see Table 1).

Since the perceived race of the interviewer might affect interviewees' willingness to speak frankly about their racial views (Reese *et al.* 1986), white employers were matched with a white interviewer and Latino/a employers were matched with a Latina interviewer.[10] Access to agricultural employers was obtained through contacts from Washington State University (WSU)'s Cooperative Extension, the Washington State Department of Agriculture and WSU faculty and their contacts in growers' groups. Most employers were introduced to the study by these individuals, who explained that they would be asked questions about their workforce, day-to-day practices and views on the dynamics and challenges facing the industry. Contacts reached employers at grower group meetings or via phone or email and furnished the lead investigator (the author) with names and contact information for willing study participants. An interviewer followed up with employers via phone or email. The sample was expanded in a snowball fashion.

Interviews lasted between one and two hours, and were audio-taped and transcribed verbatim. To preserve confidentiality, employers were given pseudonyms. Coding of the interview data initially involved identifying situations when employers spoke directly and explicitly about race/ethnicity. A subsequent stage of analysis involved identifying implicit references to race and subtle racialized meanings. Analysis aimed at identifying the breadth of employers' responses. I identified cross-cutting and recurrent themes and divergent themes, and drew comparisons between the responses of white and Latino/a employers.

The ethno-racial division of agricultural work

To contextualize employers' discourse on race/ethnicity, it is useful to have a sense of the demographic make-up of the workplaces they

Table 1. *Sample description*

	Males	Females	Total
White	26	2	28
Mexican	10	1	11
Mexican American	1	0	1
Total	37	3	40

operate. Early in each interview, employers were asked to describe the ethno-racial and gender composition of workplaces and particular jobs (what percentage of the workforce was comprised of which groups). They were asked to explain how they thought such a composition came to be, and what factors they thought might account for it. Without exception, employers' described workplaces that were highly segregated and hierarchically organized by race/ethnicity and gender.

White employers (typically involved in mid-to-large operations) described workplaces where most low-wage jobs (field jobs, like pickers, irrigators, tree trainers, and warehouse jobs, like packers, sorters and label machine operators), direct supervisory and lower management positions (foremen, crew bosses and line supervisors) were occupied by *Hispanics* (employers' term). The overwhelming majority of office, managerial, professional and ownership positions were occupied by w*hites/Anglos/ Caucasians* (employers' terms), with women occupying mostly the office jobs, and men dominating the others. Employers in orchard operations described their workforce as mostly Hispanic and male, except during peak harvest, when many Hispanic women also work. In warehouses, employers described a workforce primarily Hispanic and female, except for some supervisory positions and for jobs as mechanics, forklift drivers, and palletizers, which tend to be occupied by (Hispanic and white) men. All Latino/a employers who *owned* and managed small agricultural operations (ten out of twelve) described a workforce comprised mostly of *mexicanos* or *hispanos* (their terms), and claimed never to have had white workers.[11]

'I don't care if you're black, white, pink, or whatever': colour-blindness in agricultural workplaces

Despite their own accounts of a markedly racialized division of labour and of racialized hierarchies in their workplaces, all (both white *and* Latino/a) employers minimized the importance of race/ethnicity. In effect, employers' discourse suggests that an ideology of colour-blindness[12] is pervasive and dominant in agricultural workplaces, and that the minimization of racism is one of its central frames (Bonilla-Silva 2006). However, there were some differences in the ways in which Latino/a and white employers adhered to a colour-blind framework.

The majority of white agricultural employers explicitly claimed to 'not see race.' For example, Alex, a white manager at a large operation stated:

> Well, I don't really know, I don't really notice trends like that because, I try to keep an open mind. I mean .... I'm not a real [laughs] racial type .... I don't look at, whether they're black, white,

pink or, whatever....I look at what they have to offer, and if they have something to offer, we try to, bring 'em on. But, I would say we're pretty fair with the way we do, we have some people... Hispanic...that are lead people, our seconds, basically.

Several white employers declined to answer direct questions about race. One such employer remarked that such questions were not necessary. Further, the explicit mention of race/ethnicity seemed inflammatory to several white (but to none of the Latino/a) employers. Mike, a white assistant manager at a large operation, expressed frustration at being asked to talk about the ethno-racial composition of jobs in his workplace:

I, it just [laughs] I could, I could go into a whole soapbox in my opinion .... Race, race is an issue in this country mainly because those populations want to keep it an issue in this country. When you really get to the hiring and, and firing and who's on your team type situation...it's based, as far as I'm concerned, on performance. I don't care if you're from Mars; if you can do the job and you can communicate with me ... and do it effectively, hey, you're hired. You know, I could care less .... But there – excuse my, my opinion here ... there are people out there that want to make it an issue constantly. And ... it just, it just, it irritates me [laughs]. I mean, it just flat-out irritates me, that it even has to be a question. And, I take it to the point of, for instance, on my own census deal that comes out every you know, four years or ten years .... You know, it just, completely whizzes me off, that they sit there ... 'what race are you?' I scratch it out and put 'American'. You know? [Raises voice] To hell with you! I mean, you know? We're all under the same flag and, by God, we fought in the same wars! We're all Americans here! Yes, it's neat that you have an ethnic background. I mean, I like to say that, you know, my family's origins are from Scotland, and I like, bagpipe music, and stuff like that. Um, but I don't make an, you know, I [laughs] I don't run around going, 'God, we're getting whizzed on all the time.' You know, Scotchmen are always getting whizzed on. Oh, and we've gotta be sensitive, you know, because, you know, don't call us 'kilt walla, wearers.' I mean .... Come on, you know? I got, I got better things to do with my time than that. (Interviewer: Do you feel like race is an issue in terms of, the work that you're doing or ...) Is it an issue? Not as far as I'm concerned [laughs]. And not as far as, as [name of business] is concerned .... We're an equal-opportunity employer, and [pause]. You know, I think that ... I guess what I'm trying to say is that ... one, I'm, I'm a little irritated in even kinda going there with the question, and, two, you know, if the folks were there and they were go, you know, have the degree background and yadda-yadda and they were here in the work pool in [town], then they'd be working here. You know, by virtue of the fact that they're not here doesn't mean that, anything other than that they're not available .... And that's all I was, I guess, in a circuitous way trying to get – you know, it's just, 'geez, Louise'. Absolutely, you know? If somebody wants to make race an issue, then I don't have time to talk to 'em.

Mike's and Alex's statements display a *rhetorical incoherence* which, as Bonilla-Silva (2006) argues, reflects the tension associated with talking about race in a world that insists that race does not matter. For these employers, race is evidently an uncomfortable subject. What is significant about these statements is that, in both style and substance, they mirror the views of most white Americans (Gallup 1997; Krysan 2002). Mike frames race in terms of ethnicity (culture), and ethnicity as ultimately optional and voluntary. A growing literature documents that, in contrast with people of colour,[13] whites often do not think of themselves as members of a racial or ethnic group, seeing ethnicity as situational, as something they may or may not choose to embrace (Waters 1990; Feagin, Vera and Batur 2001). Viewed in this way, race is no longer an organizing principle of social life. In effect, constructing race solely as a cultural marker is tantamount to stripping it of its structural implications.

White employers also engaged in what Bonilla-Silva (2006) has termed the *naturalization of racism*, providing seemingly non-racial or race-neutral explanations for the ethno-racial division of labour and hierarchies in their workplaces, most often attributing them to 'supply and demand.' As one employer noted:

[T]he workers are one hundred per cent Hispanic .... [O]n all the ranches that I run ... we have no Caucasian people at all .... And the reason being is that we don't get anybody applying for it. It's mostly been just Hispanic people were applying. (Interviewer: How do you think it became that way?) Supply and demand, you know. Basic economics.

Latino/a employers did not make explicit claims about not noticing race, but also used race-neutral explanations for the ethno-racial composition of jobs. Two recurrent explanations provided by Latino/a employers emphasized the high concentration of Latino/as in their worksites' vicinity, and maintained that Latino/as are 'who looks for this kind of work'. Vicente, a Mexican male, owner-operator of a small orchard said: 'That's who is around here, Mexicans. No American has ever helped me, they've never stopped by to ask for work' (author's translation).

Employers explicitly invoked market dynamics and demographic processes – specifically, the growth and concentration of Latino/as in the region – as if they were un-racialized phenomena. Such framing of market dynamics as 'natural' filters out the active role that employers have played and continue to play in attracting Latino/a workers to the region, and how employers' day-to-day practices are implicated in producing and reproducing a predominantly Latino/a labour force in the bottom jobs. For example, employers indicated they rely on Latino/a workers' networks for filling low-end jobs, and, if/when they need to advertise for jobs, their hiring agents target Latino/a areas and neighbourhoods, newspapers in Spanish and Latino/a radio stations. When hiring managers, employers in mid-size and large operations rely on their own personal networks of family and friends. Tony, manager at a large operation and owner of a small orchard, explained: 'This industry, in the white-collar positions, the management positions in this industry, last names stay the same, first names change.' The last names to which Tony is referring are those of the white families (some of which are 'corporate families') that own and manage the vast majority and the largest operations in the state. Tony's description points to the industry as a closed system where control and ownership rest persistently with whites. This same manager later described how his business goes about finding managers:

> [T]here's not a lot of white people [in the industry], so to speak, so you need to pay attention to names, and so ... if you're looking [to fill] a position, you find out who wants it, you need to find out who's available, and then you call that individual, and say, "Are you interested? Would you come in for an interview? Gimme a resume." A lot of it is just word of mouth.

Statements by white *and* Latino/a employers suggest widespread adherence across employers' race/ethnicity to the belief that 'race is not an issue'. However, only white employers claimed they 'do not see race'. Some white employers expressed frustration and anger at the mention of race and ethnicity. Latino/a employers did not display such emotions, but, like white employers, adhered to a colour-blind framework by offering race-neutral explanations for the division of labour and the hierarchies in workplaces.

Culture as explanation for subordination in the labour market

Ten out of twenty-eight white employers (but none of the Latino/a employers) alluded to culture – typically, a monolithic 'Hispanic culture' – as explanation for the overwhelming presence of Latino/as in low-end jobs. For example, a white male, owner-operator of a mid-size orchard offered the following explanation: 'From a labour-standpoint you [white] folks don't work at the same pace as those .... Hispanic folks. It's not that [whites] are physically not able, it's just not culturally within them, I guess.' Russ, a white owner-operator of a mid-size orchard said:

> [T]here are cultural differences ... the Hispanic people, they tend to be a hard-working group of people. Their nature is to ... do menial-type labour. They're ... not ashamed to be labourers. There's no shame in that for them. Typically, [for] Caucasians, typical white society, that's a negative. If you're a ditch digger or a fruit picker, that's a low-end job and that's just ... something that, the young folks aren't seeking to be, I guess.

Cultural explanations were also used by several white employers to explain the near absence of Latino/as in managerial, professional and ownership positions. Larry, manager at a large operation noted:

> These people, Hispanics particularly, are very reluctant to ... be bosses of ... their peers ... they're very reluctant to do this. So, you'll find that exceptional guy that can get past that cultural thing, and, really be able to interact with the people, and be cordial and yet get the job done.

Similarly, several white employers used culture to explain gender hierarchies in their workplaces. When asked why there are few Latinas in supervisory or management positions, Jim, part-owner of a mid-size orchard, said:

> The Hispanics – a woman probably wouldn't get along real good with being the boss over the Hispanics, because of their culture. They don't listen to women as they do in the United States .... [A] woman in charge wouldn't ... get the respect there .... Hispanics just don't respect women the same way as the Americans do.

Scott, manager at a large operation argued similarly:

> The Hispanic men do not like taking direction from females, a number of the Hispanic females are not comfortable with – they make decisions all the time, but telling somebody to do something is

difficult for them, not part of what they do. Now, my suspicion is that they do that at home all the time, but not in public, it's not something that they are as comfortable doing and yet they're very good at what they do and can be very effective.

White employers' emphasis on culture as explanation for the overwhelming presence of Latino/as in low-end jobs, and for their scarce presence in positions of power is symptomatic of the re-articulation of inequality in the United States within a colour-blind framework. Rather than being anchored in open claims about biological superiority or inferiority of groups, contemporary racism entails the coding of race in the language of 'difference' and 'culture'. Cultural difference is assumed to have grounding that is essentially biological, and as such it is treated as ultimately inevitable and unchangeable. Bonilla Silva (2006) has called this the *biologization of culture*.

By alluding to natural tendencies of 'Hispanic culture' and ascribing to 'Hispanics' as a group a propensity to perform well in menial jobs and to not want to be bosses, white employers normalize and de-problematize the systematic pegging of Latino/as to low-end jobs. As Sayer and Walker (1992) argue, skills and jobs are defined and redefined according to their bearers. Back-breaking, low-wage jobs become 'Hispanic jobs', and a class of predominantly white owners and managers accrues the profits generated by such competent and cheap labour, and the public and psychological wage that DuBois (1969) identified as the principal benefit of whiteness.

The relative valorization of Latino/a workers

Agricultural employers' racialized assessments of Latino/a workers frequently involved comparisons between Latino/as and other ethno-racial groups. This is not surprising because racialization is always relational: the meanings associated with one group and the positioning of one group in a racial order are determined and defined in relation to those of other groups. Further, employers in various work contexts routinely evaluate workers of different ethno-racial groups in relation to one another (e.g. Griffith 1993; Hossfeld 1993; Moss and Tilly 2001; Shih 2002). What is remarkable is how agricultural employers place and evaluate Latino/as in relation to whites and other ethno-racial minorities, and also various Latino/a groups *vis-à-vis one another*.

When discussing why Latino/as constitute the overwhelming majority of farm workers and entry-level workers in warehouses and packing operations, both white and Latino/a employers routinely cited the strong work ethic and performance of Latino/as, comparing it with the purportedly poor work ethic and performance of whites Such perceived differences lead to employers' preference for Latino/as for filling low-end jobs. Employers also alluded to such differences to explain why there are few, if any, whites in such jobs. The following quotes by white employers illustrate these findings:

> Most white people are not gonna work as hard as most Hispanic people.... I don't know why. I could speculate: they don't wanna work for the wage. Physical labour is becoming beneath a lot of people. (Roy, manager at mid-size operation)

> We ... have to have more productive people, and white people are not productive at all in the orchards. Cuz we have rarely hired some white people, and they'll be lucky if they last a day, just because they cannot, productively, stay up with the Hispanics. (Randy, part-owner of mid-size operation)

Most Latino employers also characterized whites as uninterested in manual labour, lazy, and unwilling to work hard, and described Mexicans as dependable and willing hard workers. Lupe, owner-operator of a small orchard spoke of whites' lack of dependability: 'White people, Americans, show up. But they don't stay very long, they leave' (author's translation).

Several white employers contrasted the work ethic of Latino/as with the alleged poor work ethic of other ethno-racial minority groups. Tony, white male, manager at a large operation and owner of a small orchard, stated: '[T]he Mexican population is, bar none, one of the hardest working people that I have ever seen in my life. And I have had experience with Native American, Orientals, Filipino, or Vietnamese, Africans – African-Americans.'

Another practice of relative valorization employers used involved assessing Latino/a workers in terms of perceived degree of assimilation and legal status. Both white and Latino/a employers distinguished between the work ethic of recently arrived and second+-generation Latino/as. White employers emphasized that the longer Latino/as live in the United States, the more Americanized they become, and the 'lazier' they get. The following quotes illustrate this recurrent theme:

> I've seen the worth – work ethic deteriorate over the ... last twenty years. People don't want to work as hard. They want more money. And they want shorter hours. They want weekends off. I'm just seeing that gradually go that way. And, it's a simple excuse for it, they're becoming more American .... The Hispanic people traditionally are very hard, hard workers .... When I was a child, my dad hired people. They worked hard ... and didn't complain, and ... just worked, from sunup to sundown ... cuz that's what they were

used to. But now that most of ... our workers, workforce is half-ass Americanized – a lot of 'em are fully Americanized – they are becoming more lazy as far as the work ethic .... Sure, we need to pay a fair price ... fair wage for a fair job. But just their attitude is changing. (Joe, manager of mid-size orchard, owner of small orchard)

[T]he generation that is coming into the workforce now, is ... typically second or possibly third generation of being here in the United States ... who's actually been brought upon amongst the culture of the United States is – today's younger Hispanic workforce has come up in, is more in tune with our culture rather than the Hispanic culture of what we've dealt with in the past .... I guess that leaves open to debate ... is our culture better or is their culture better? I don't know, but ... there is a recognizable difference in, in those who are brought up within our culture ... versus those who weren't. (Troy, manager at mid-size orchard, owner of small orchard)

Several Latino/a employers also distinguished between the work ethic of newly arrived Latino/as and that of those who have settled in the United States. Tomás, Mexican owner-operator of a small orchard stated:

There are [Latino/a] people who have been here for years and they don't do good work, and there are people who are recently arrived, but ... they put a lot of effort into their work and quickly learn what you want them to, and there are people that, because they are already here, they already know, and they know English, and their work is so much worse than the work of those who just arrived. I have heard them saying, 'Fire me, if you're gonna fire me, go ahead, who cares.' And almost always it is people who have been here for a long time. The majority of them are more problematic.

Legal status was routinely identified by employers as an important predictor of worker quality and as an indicator of the desirability or undesirability of workers. Employers identified undocumented workers as ideal workers, because the economic, social, cultural and political vulnerabilities they face leave them no choice but to work hard and go 'the extra mile' without complaint. One employer stated:

I've heard from foremen that they say that illegals, those guys sometimes work harder than the legal guys. Because the illegal guys evidently have a harder time finding work ... they're hungrier, they work harder just to keep their job, and then hopefully stay here longer. Because if they lose their job, it's pretty much dire straits. As where if they're American citizens, they have opportunity for maybe a better education or if they get fired down the road to get a job somewhere else, too....I guess the threat of getting fired is just not as severe on American citizens than to illegals. (Henry, manager, small operation)

In discussing workers' economic vulnerability, agricultural employers invoked what Waldinger and Lichter (2003) have called a *dual frame of reference*. They de-problematized the conditions facing Latino/a immigrant workers in the United States by comparing them to the conditions workers would presumably face in their countries of origin. In the words of one white employer:

We have a very, very nice, life here in the United States, okay? Compared to other countries. If you get a chance to visit around and see how they live, and ... what their culture is like, you can understand why the Hispanics wanna be here. I mean, this, to them getting a seven-dollar job in a farm is, fantastic. Even though they work hard, but they work hard at home, for pennies, and so, that's never been a problem. (Larry, manager at large operation)

Larry's admission that 'that's never been a problem' bespeaks a shared understanding among agricultural employers, and documented by scholars in other work contexts including high-tech manufacturing (Hossfeld 1993) and textiles (Chapkis and Enloe 1983). Such understanding is that immigrants from poor countries are more willingly exploitable, more willing than other workers to take on the hardest jobs and put up with unfavourable work conditions for the lowest pay. They are assumed not just to be okay with working hard for little money, but to be *content* to do so.

When asked to identify problems affecting the agricultural labour force, several white employers expressed concern about the potential disappearance of the worker vulnerabilities described above. One such employer stated:

What we're seeing is ... a shift in who is out there; instead of being the lean, mean, hungry guy ... what we're finding ... is that ... instead of the guys who really want to, get out there and do the job for ya and please ya, we're ending up ... with folks that ... can take it or leave it basically. (Mike, assistant manager at large operation)

Several white employers expressed concern about labour shortages due to tougher immigration controls. Two such employers indicated they were beginning to look in the direction of immigrant groups other than Latino/as, which would not only be plentiful, but a cheaper and more manageable labour force.

> I've heard Thailand, they're very productive people....the productivity of the people that we have now is getting worse, and we feel that it's because they've become more strict on the borders, and they're getting less of the people that really want to get over here and work, and they're doing more of the people that've kinda found out how to work the system ... they're getting less and less productive. ... [O]ur costs are getting more expensive, and it's getting hard. (Randy, part-owner of mid-size operation)

Several employers (both white and Latino/a), saw length of stay in the United States as related to Latino/as' ability to become social insiders and manipulate the system to their advantage. Such insider knowledge, employers claim, spoils the quality of Latino/a workers. As Russ, owner-operator of a mid-size orchard put it:

> [A] person that's been here settled in the United States a long time, they've learned the system, they've learned ... how they can take advantage of unemployment or state industrial insurance ... they've become pretty savvy in terms of what they can get away with, and that's human nature. People are going to learn how to settle in and how to just become a cog in the factory.

Roy, manager at a mid-size operation made a similar point:

> [W]ithin the Hispanic community, there's some change in those that have lived in the country a long time. Maybe they've lived in California, and they kinda migrate somewhat with the crops.... There's a group, and it's within every ethnic group, but we see it mostly because we're hiring Hispanics, some of them ... they're in the system. They know what unemployment is, they know their Medicaid benefits, they know Food Stamps, those sorts of things. And they're only gonna work a certain amount of hours or dollars, where it won't ... disrupt their ability to get some of these services .... As that population assimilates into our culture a bit, gets to know ... bills and switch to our governmental services, many of them don't work hard as they once did.

This finding supports Waldinger and Lichter's (2003, p. 227) point that, at the bottom of the labour market, social insiders are unwanted. Outsider status keeps recent Latino/a immigrants vulnerable, thereby making them ideal workers.

Discussion and implications

The research discussed here reveals that speaking monolithically of the racialized experience of 'Latino/a workers' obscures the multiple and distinct ways that an increasingly diverse Latino/a population is racialized in the United States. The racial stories told about Latino/a workers differ based on generation, length of stay in the United States, apparent degree of assimilation, legal status and gender. Such stories place recent Latino/a immigrants and second+-generation Latino/as differently in the field of racial positions. The former are at the bottom as the most vulnerable and exploitable, but second+-generation Latino/as are also racially subordinated, framed as lazy abusers of the system.

Both white and Latino/a employers use colour-blind discourse to ignore, erase and minimize structural racism and race and ethnicity as sociocultural factors. Among white employers, a colour-blind discourse relies on cultural myths to reinforce systemic racism as a non-issue, hiding and allowing it to continue unabated. By claiming not to see race, and by framing market dynamics as devoid of racial content, agricultural employers act as if race does not matter, creating an illusion of fairness and progressive politics, while reproducing the subordination of Latino/as, and safeguarding white privilege in workplaces. However, adherence to a colour-blind ideology does not preclude the racialized assessment of workers by employers. In everyday business decisions, most employers used race/ethnicity, citizenship, legal status and gender as proxies for worker quality and as markers for the desirability of workers. The racialized assessment of workers was coupled with hiring and recruitment practices that relied on Latino/a worker networks to fill low-end jobs, and on white employer networks to fill management positions.

Culture was used by white employers to frame Latino/as as ideal labourers, and to explain why they tend not to occupy ownership and management positions. The use of the 'soft' language of cultural difference normalized and de-problematized the segmentation of jobs and racial hierarchies in workplaces. As Winant (2001) argues, these forces justify exclusionary politics and policy better than traditional white supremacist arguments can do.

Waldinger and Lichter (2003) posit that immigrant workers are more willing to accept precarious wages and job conditions because they use a dual frame of reference; they remain attached to the communities they left behind, planning to return or remembering the impoverished conditions they faced there. White and Latino/a) agricultural employers also routinely used such a dual frame of reference to de-problematize the exploitative conditions facing Latino/a workers, relative to conditions they would presumably face in their countries of origin. This finding suggests that improving the conditions facing Latino/a workers in US workplaces necessitates evaluating wages and work conditions relative to those of others *within* a US context. Similarly, the continuous replenishment of immigrant workers from Latin America enables the maintenance of an underclass of undocumented workers who, by virtue of their multiple vulnerabilities, are identified and sought by employers as the most desirable workforce.

The identification of Thai workers as a promising alternative to Latino/a labour by several employers points to how the positioning of ethno-racial groups within the US labour queue is relational and dynamic. It responds to and reflects historically specific articulations of race, gender, class and state formation processes shaped by both local and global forces. The seasonal agricultural labour force in the Pacific Northwest has been comprised of various ethno-racial and national groups at different historical junctures: agricultural employers have relied on Chinese, Japanese, Native American, Filipino and white (immigrant and native) workers for filling low-end jobs. The ethno-racial composition of jobs has changed and will probably change again. While US employers have constructed new immigrants from Latin America as ideal workers since the turn of the twentieth century, the toughening of immigration controls, increased surveillance of Latino/a workspaces and communities and the imperatives of competition and expansion facing US agribusiness might force employers to replace Latino/as with labourers from other parts of the world, thereby changing the racialized structure of agricultural work. As the ethno-racial composition of jobs changes, we might expect the ideological terrain to change as well.

The evidence discussed here suggests that the racial division of labour and the hierarchies that exist in agricultural workplaces are not accidental, but produced from day to day by employers through the mobilization of racial ideologies and through practices enabled and sustained by such ideologies. Racial meanings influence employers' perceptions and assessments of workers, and employer practices serve as the mechanism through which racist ideologies become institutionalized and invisible. To contest the social and economic subordination Latino/as continue to face effectively, analyses and political praxis must attend to how racist ideologies become entrenched and invisible in institutional contexts like work. This involves identifying how racial meanings about Latino/as (and other groups) emerge, and are how they are used day-to-day by powerful institutional actors.

The research discussed here also highlights the relational and global dimensions of the racial politics of labour. The racial politics that subordinate Latino/a workers in the United States are bound within a system of *global apartheid* (Amin 2001, cited in Winant 2004, p. 88) and a racialized global political economy. Those from the global south and east are subordinated in the world-systemic racial order, and their racialization is implicated in their super-exploitation in the global economy. In the context of globalization, if Latino/a workers become scarce or too demanding, agricultural employers have the competitive imperative and the flexibility to tap a cheaper and more readily exploitable labour force, in the US or abroad (e.g. Thai workers). Exploitation is aided by racialization, independently of who is racialized as subordinate. This highlights the need for a coalitional politics of labour, not just among Latino/as, but beyond pan-ethnic boundaries.

Acknowledgements

Thanks to Anastasia Prokos, Sharon Bird, Carmen R. Lugo, and to anonymous *Ethnic and Racial Studies* reviewers for their helpful comments on earlier drafts of this paper.

Notes

1. Pan-ethnic labels such as Latino/a or Hispanic are problematic because they obscure vast differences in national origin, mode of incorporation, citizenship, race and class, for example. I use the label *Latino/a*, however, to highlight the shared dimensions of the experiences of these groups and their similar structural location (for illuminating discussions of the origins and political content of the labels Hispanic and Latino, see Gimenez 1998; Alcoff 2005).
2. Racialization refers to the production, reproduction of and contest over racial meanings and the social structures in which such meanings become embedded. Racial meanings involve essentializing on the basis of biology or culture.
3. Racial meanings are also resisted and contested. This paper focuses on how those in power articulate and use racial meanings.
4. Racialization entails the *relational* production of meanings, and the hierarchical placement of racial groups *relative to* one another. Racial stories about non-dominant groups (explicitly or implicitly) entail the production of racial stories about dominant groups, and are implicated in the reproduction of disadvantage for racially subordinated populations, and also in the maintenance of power and privilege for dominant groups. The meanings that circulate about Latino/as in agricultural workplaces need to be examined in relation to meanings that circulate about other groups (including whites).
5. Those identified by the US Census as non-Hispanic white.
6. In 2003, 97.3 per cent of owner-operators in Washington identified their race as white. The second largest group of employers (5.1 per cent) identified their ethnicity as 'Spanish, Hispanic, or Latino'.
7. The vast majority of agricultural production workers in Washington in non-managerial occupations are of Mexican origin (Stromsdorfer 2006).
8. Farm owners/operators, CEOs of agricultural firms and others who occupy supervisory or management positions and have the power to make hiring and personnel decisions, including, crew bosses, foremen, line supervisors, human resources directors.
9. Size is measured as number of employees. The sample included operations between six and 6,000 employees. Businesses with fewer than 100 employees are labelled as small; those

between 100 and 800 employees are mid-size; and those with more than 800 are labelled as large.
10. Differences among Latino/as might not be apparent to non-Latino/as, but are immediately discernible among Latino/as. The author, who is Puerto Rican, conducted the interviews with Mexican employers, and was always 'read' by respondents as non-Mexican given her accent and word usage.
11. The operations owned by Latino/as tended to be small. Seven out of ten Latino/a *owners* worked as foremen or supervisors in larger operations owned and managed by whites, and worked on their own businesses 'on the side'.
12. Colour-blindness revolves around the claim that one does not notice or think in terms of race, and the minimization or denial of racism as a factor that affects the lives of racial minorities (Bonilla-Silva 2006).
13. Macías (2006) shows that for second+-generation Mexican Americans, especially those with mixed ancestry, ethnicity also tends to be situational or optional.

References

ALCOFF, LINDA MARTIN 2005 'Latino vs. Hispanic: the politics of ethnic names', *Philosophy & Social Criticism*, vol. 31, no. 4, pp. 395–407
BONILLA-SILVA, E.DUARDO 1997 'Rethinking racism: toward a structural interpretation', *American Sociological Review*, vol. 62, pp. 465–80
―― 2006 *Racism without Racists: Color Blind Racism and the Persistence of Racial Inequality in the United States*, 2nd edn, New York: Rowman & Littlefield.
CANALES, ALEJANDRO L. 2007 'Inclusion and segregation: the incorporation of Latin American immigrants into the U.S. labor market', *Latin American Perspectives*, vol. 34, no. 1, pp. 73–82
CHAPKIS, WENDY and ENLOE, CYNTHIA (eds), 1983 *Of Common Cloth: Women in the Global Textile Industry*, Amsterdam: Transnational Institute; Washington, DC: Institute for Policy Studies
DE GENOVA, NICHOLAS and RAMOS-ZAYAS, ANA Y. 2003 *Latino Crossings: Mexicans, Puerto Ricans, and the Politics of Race and Citizenship*, New York: Routledge
DUBOIS, W. E. B. 1969 *Black Reconstruction in America, 1860–1880*, New York: Atheneum
FEAGIN, JOE R., VERA, HERNÁN and BATUR, PINAR 2001 *White Racism: The Basics*, 2nd edn, New York: Routledge
GALLUP ORGANIZATION 1997 *Black/White Relations in the U.S.*, June
GAMBOA, ERASMO 2000 *Mexican Labor and World War II: Braceros in the Pacific Northwest, 1942–1947*, Seattle, WA: University of Washington Press
GIMENEZ, MARTHA E. 1998 'Latinos/Hispanics...what next! Some reflections on the politics of identity in the U.S.', *Cultural Logic*, vol.1, no. 2, http://eserver.org/clogic/1-2/gimenez.html
GRIFFITH, DAVID C. 1993 *Jones's Minimal: Low-Wage Labor in the United States*, Albany, NY: SUNY Press
HEFFERNAN, WILLIAM D. 2000 'Concentration of ownership and control in agriculture', in Fred Magdoff, John Bellamy Foster and Frederick H. Buttel (eds), *Hungry for Profit: The Agribusiness Threat to Farmers, Food and the Environment*, New York: Monthly Review Press, pp. 61–75
HOSSFELD, KAREN 1993 'Hiring immigrant women: Silicon Valley's simple formula', in Maxine Baca Zinn and Bonnie Thornton Dill (eds), *Women of Color in US Society*, Philadelphia, PA: Temple University Press, pp. 65–94
JOHNSON-WEBB, KAREN D. 2002 'Employer recruitment and Hispanic labor migration: North Carolina urban areas at the end of the millennium', *The Professional Geographer*, vol. 54, no. 3, pp. 406–21

JUNG, MOON-KIE 2002 'Different racisms and the differences they make: race and "Asian workers" in pre-war Hawaii', *Critical Sociology*, vol. 28, no. 1–2, pp. 77–100

KANDEL, WILLIAM and PARRADO, EMILIO A. 2005 'Industrial restructuring and new rural Hispanic migration: the case of the U.S. meat processing industry', *Population and Development Review*, vol. 31, no. 3, pp. 447–71

KENNELLY, IVY 1999 '"That single-mother element": how white employers typify black women', *Gender & Society*, vol. 13, no. 2, pp. 168–92

KRISSMAN, FRED 2000 'Immigrant labor recruitment: US agribusiness and undocumented immigrants from Mexico', in Nancy Foner, Rubén G. Rumbaut and Steven J. Gold (eds), *Immigration Research for a New Century: Multidisciplinary Perspectives*, New York: Russell Sage Foundation

—— 2005 '"Sin coyote ni patron": Why the "migrant network" fails to explain international migration', *International Migration Review*, vol. 39, no. 1, pp. 4–44

KRYSAN, MARIA 2002 'Recent trends in racial attitudes: a 2002 data update for Howard Schuman, Charlotte Steeh, Lawrence Bobo, and Maria Krysan 1997 *Racial Attitudes in America: Trends and Interpretations*, revised edn, Cambridge, MA: Harvard University Press', http://tigger.uic.edu/~krysan/racialattitudes.htm (accessed 14 January 2008)

MACÍAS, THOMAS 2006 *Mestizo in America: Generations of Mexican Ethnicity in the Suburban Southwest*, Tucson, AZ: University of Arizona Press

MOSS, PHILIP and TILLY, CHRIS 2001 *Stories Employers Tell: Race, Skill, and Hiring in America*, New York: Russell Sage Foundation

REESE, S. D., et al. 1986 'Ethnicity of interviewer effects among Mexican Americans and Anglos', *Public Opinion Quarterly*, vol. 50, pp. 563–72

SAYER, RANDREW and WALKER, RICHARD 1992 *The New Social Economy: Reworking the Division of Labor*, Cambridge, MA: Blackwell

SHIH, JOHANNA 2002 '"...Yeah, I could hire this one, but I know it's gonna be a problem": how race, nativity and gender affect employers' perceptions of the manageability of job seekers', *Ethnic and Racial Studies*, vol. 25, no. 1, pp. 99–119

STROMSDORFER, ERNST W. 2006 *Agricultural Workforce in Washington State*, Washington State Employment Security Department

TOOSSI, MITRA 2006 'A new look at long-term labor force projections to 2050', *Monthly Labor Review*, Washington, DC: US Department of Labor, Bureau of Labor Statistics, pp. 19–39

WALDINGER, ROGER and LICHTER, MICHAEL L. 2003 *How the Other Half Works: Immigration and the Social Organization of Labor*, Berkeley, CA: University of California Press

WATERS, MARY C. 1990 *Ethnic Options: Choosing Identities in America*, Berkeley, CA: University of California Press

WINANT, HOWARD 2001 *The World Is a Ghetto: Race and Democracy since World War II*, New York: Basic Books

—— 2004 *The New Politics of Race*, Minneapolis, MN: University of Minnesota Press

New immigrant destinations and the American colour line

Helen B. Marrow

Abstract
I analyse how Hispanic newcomers are becoming incorporated into the rural southern racial hierarchy during an early stage of immigration. I examine patterns in newcomers' (1) racial/ethnic identifications and (2) social interactions with whites and blacks, showing how and why they lend preliminary support to a black/nonblack colour line model, in which the central distinction separates the positions of people with African ancestry from all others. Hispanic newcomers, including many who are dark-skinned, poor, and undocumented, have come to perceive the social distance separating themselves from whites as more permeable than that separating themselves from blacks, and are engaging in distancing strategies that may reinforce this distinction.

Scholars are engaged in a dynamic debate about how contemporary immigrants are becoming incorporated into the American racial hierarchy. Most studies have been quantitative analyses at the national level or qualitative analyses in major immigrant gateways. Yet the phenomenal geographic dispersion of immigrants since the 1980s, led primarily by Mexicans, raises critical questions about how newcomers will be incorporated into the racial fabric of 'new destinations'.

Such questions take on special significance in the 'traditional' American south. Not only have natives of this region, especially ones living in rural areas, been most isolated from historical and contemporary immigration, but African Americans are also present in larger numbers and the American racial 'binary' remains strongest here (McClain et al. 2006, 2007). These features magnify the boundaries separating the region's two dominant groups from each other and from immigrants. Thus, I ask: how will Hispanic newcomers'[1] identities affect their incorporation into this largely binary region; will racial discrimination prevent their incorporation; and how might southern notions of race be ultimately reformulated by their incorporation?

I take strategic advantage of the recent increase in immigration into the rural American south to examine these questions during an early stage of immigration. I examine patterns in newcomers' (1) racial/ ethnic identifications and (2) social interactions with whites and blacks, showing how and why they lend preliminary support to a black/nonblack colour line model, in which the central distinction separates the positions of people with African ancestry from all others. Hispanic newcomers, including many who are dark-skinned, poor, and undocumented, have come to perceive the social distance separating themselves from whites as more permeable than that separating themselves from blacks, and are engaging in distancing strategies that may reinforce this distinction.

Models of the American colour line

The historic black/white binary is being challenged by rising immigration, and three models describe new configurations that may replace it. The first predicts a white/nonwhite colour line in which the central distinction divides the positions of whites from all others. Here Asians and Hispanics/Latinos are 'nonwhites' due to common experiences of colonialism, oppression, exploitation, and racialization – something that has arguably been furthered by their inclusion in civil rights policies as 'racial minorities' and common language as 'people of color' (Skrentny 2002; Lee and Bean 2007, pp. 5–6). Scholars and activists who see a white/nonwhite divide point to persisting material gaps between whites and all other groups, and to persisting feelings of racialization among all nonwhites. Here we expect Hispanic newcomers in the south to exhibit greater material, subjective, and behavioural distance from whites than blacks, and such distance to stay stable or increase over time. While we may observe distinctions between Hispanics and blacks, we expect them to be less salient overall.

The second model also predicts a binary colour line, yet one in which the central distinction divides the positions of blacks (defined as people with African ancestry in the American context) from all others. Lee and Bean (2007) summarize how in the 1990s scholars began noticing the uniquely enduring separation of blacks while simultaneously documenting how several formerly 'nonwhite' European and Asian immigrant groups had distanced themselves from blackness and achieved upward socioeconomic mobility over time (Perlmann and Waldinger 1997; Yancey 2003). Here Asians and Hispanics are 'nonblacks' who have achieved 'whiteness' or 'honorary whiteness' with upward mobility, while African Americans remain the 'exception' who have not (Gans 1999).

Scholars who see a black/nonblack divide point to growing material and behavioural gaps between blacks and all other groups, and to more quickly loosening feelings of racialization among Asians and Hispanics than blacks. For example, segregation in residential (Wilkes and Iceland 2004) and adolescent friendship (Quillian and Campbell 2003) patterns is higher among blacks and black Hispanics than among Asians and other Hispanics. Not only are white-Hispanic and white-Asian intermarriage rates rising more rapidly than white–black ones (Lee and Bean 2007; Qian and Lichter 2007), but identity among multiracials with Hispanic and Asian heritage is more fluid and symbolic than that among multiracials with black heritage (Lee and Bean 2007). And it is specifically *blackness* that influences how nonwhite children of immigrants in New York City experience racial discrimination (Kasinitz et al. 2008).

While some scholars argue that Asians and Hispanics may become 'whites' (Warren and Twine 1997), eventually reconstituting the white/black divide, the black/nonblack model only requires that they be located meaningfully closer to whites than blacks. Here we expect Hispanic newcomers in the south to exhibit greater material, subjective, and behavioural distance from blacks than from whites, and such distance to stay stable or increase over time. While we may observe distinctions between Hispanics and whites, we expect them to be less salient than those between either Hispanics and blacks or whites and blacks. We also expect Hispanic newcomers to engage in distancing strategies from blacks, and whites to express preferences for Hispanics over blacks. Finally, we expect to see central differences between the experiences of Hispanic newcomers with versus without African ancestry.

The third model predicts a triracial colour line similar to those in Latin American countries which emphasize national unity and organize social hierarchies more in terms of class and skin colour than racial ancestry (Bonilla-Silva 2002; Massey 2007). Here two central distinctions divide the positions of three groups, as whites allow some newcomers to become 'whites', create an intermediate racial group of 'honorary whites' to buffer racial conflict, and incorporate most immigrants into a 'collective black' stratum. While some Hispanics may become 'whites' or 'honorary whites', most Mexicans, Puerto Ricans, Dominicans, and Central Americans are 'collective blacks' due to their racialized incorporation as colonial subjects, refugees from wars, or illegal migrant workers (Bonilla-Silva 2002, pp. 8–9).

Scholars who see a triracial divide point to growing material, subjective, and behavioural gaps both *between* and *within* contemporary racial groups, driven primarily by class and skin colour. For instance, skin colour influences: rates of intermarriage with whites among Asians and Latinos (Qian 2002), attitudes toward blacks among Puerto Ricans and Cubans (Forman, Goar, and Lewis 2002), and indicators of integration among Mexicans (Murguia and Saenz 2002). Class and skin colour influence identity choices among black–white multiracials, with a few middle-class and light-skinned ones constructing themselves as 'culturally white' despite their African ancestry (Rockquemore and Arend 2002). Still, some evidence points to a black/nonblack divide. Regardless of skin colour Latinos (especially Mexicans) are closer to non-Hispanic whites than blacks in their attitudes toward blacks (Forman, Goar, and Lewis 2002), suggesting that many do not see themselves as 'collective blacks' (Lee and Bean 2007, p. 9). 'Cultural whiteness' among black–white biracials is still an exception; most identify as biracial or black, underscoring enduring constraints on people with African ancestry (Rockquemore and Arend 2002, p. 59). While steeper socioeconomic gaps in intermarriage rates with whites have emerged between more- and less-educated Asians and Hispanics, intermarriage remains persistently low even among better-educated blacks (Qian and Lichter 2007). And Murguia and Saenz (2002) point out that a three-tier racial system has always existed in the United States, yet many middle-tier groups have moved up into the top tier over time instead of remaining 'secondary' and unequal to whites, as the triracial model predicts (Bonilla-Silva 2002, p. 13).

Nonetheless, here we expect Hispanic newcomers in the south to exhibit varying degrees of material, subjective, and behavioural distance from whites and blacks depending on class and skin colour. We expect those who are lightest-skinned and highest-class to exhibit greater distance from blacks than from whites, yet still meaningful distance from whites. Vice versa, we expect those who are darkest-skinned and lowest-class to exhibit greater distance from whites than from blacks. Finally, we expect variation in both anti-black distancing behaviour among Hispanics (ranging from strongest among 'whites' to weakest among 'collective blacks') and whites' preferences for Hispanics (ranging from strongest toward 'whites' to weakest toward 'collective blacks').

Site selection and methods

Data come from 129 individual semi-structured interviews and additional ethnographic research that I conducted between June 2003 and June 2004 in Bedford and Wilcox counties, pseudonyms for two nonmetropolitan 'new immigrant destination' counties in eastern North Carolina. North Carolina was the premier new destination state in the 1990s, posting the highest growth rates in its Hispanic/Latino (394 per cent) and immigrant (274 per cent) populations among all states. Bedford and Wilcox are located in the rural eastern part of the state, where poverty is acute and the black–white binary extremely sharp.

Slightly over half of the 129 interviews (N = 70, 54 per cent) were conducted with Latin American immigrants of varying nationalities, in either Spanish or English. These foreign-born respondents hail primarily from Mexico (N = 39), but also from South America (N = 16), Central America (N = 14), and Cuba (N = 1). Approximately one-seventh of the interviews (N = 18, 14 per cent) were conducted with US-born Hispanics, mostly Mexican and Puerto Rican Americans, in either Spanish or English. Finally, approximately one-third of the interviews (N = 41, 32 per cent) were conducted with white (N = 27) and black (N = 14) 'key native informants', in English, and serve to triangulate my findings among Hispanic respondents. The high proportions of Mexican- followed by Central and South American-origin respondents reflect their dominance among North Carolina's Hispanic population, which was 65.1 per cent Mexican, 8.2 per cent Puerto Rican, 1.9 per cent Cuban, and 24.8 per cent 'other' Hispanic in the 2000 Census.

Interview respondents were located by combining theoretical and snowball sampling designs across four institutional arenas in both counties: workplaces, elementary school systems, courts and law enforcement systems, and politics. Interviews ranged from thirty minutes to three hours, and respondents were asked a battery of questions regarding their migration history; family background; racial/ethnic identification; employment history; views on race, immigration, and life in the rural south; and political participation. Employers, school and legal personnel, and political leaders were asked additional questions about their experiences with the local Hispanic community. I supplemented these interviews with various forms of participant-observation research over the course of the year (see Marrow 2008). To ensure anonymity, all names and identifying characteristics of respondents and places have been changed.

There is variation among Hispanic respondents' skin colours, class statuses, and legal statuses. Their skin colours range from very light to very dark, although most dark-skinned respondents come from countries with relatively weak histories of African presence and thus have mixed indigenous ancestry (Forman, Goar, and Lewis 2002). Their educational levels range from primary school to professional degrees, and while most work in low-wage jobs at the bottom of the regional labour market, others work in skilled blue- and white-collar occupations. Their citizenship and immigration statuses range from US citizens by birth (N = 18) or naturalization (n = 12) to legal permanent residents (N = 12) to temporary nonimmigrant visa or work permit holders (N = 7) to undocumented immigrants (N = 33).[2] The latter group comprises 47 per cent of foreign-born Hispanics in the sample, originating from Mexico, Guatemala, El Salvador, Honduras, Colombia, Ecuador, Peru, and Chile.

The strong binary context is evident in Bedford and Wilcox counties in several ways. First, minority groups other than African Americans have little historical presence in either county, with Hispanics arriving since the 1980s. Second, the population of African Americans is large in both counties (58 per cent in Bedford and 29 per cent in Wilcox in the 2000 Census). Third, the separation of blacks from whites runs deep in both counties. Whites are internally divided along several lines, especially class status, belonging either to the middle or to the poor and working classes. In contrast, blacks' socioeconomic position is weaker; most belong to the poor and working classes, while only a few belong to the middle class. In this way, Hispanic newcomers enter local contexts heavily influenced by the racial binary and its resulting inequalities. They encounter a native population starkly divided by both race and class, including a black population that is almost entirely poor and working-class.

Yet they also enter rural contexts where population sizes are small enough that 'everybody knows everybody' and complete racial isolation is not possible (Jiménez 2005, p. 31). That is, tensions between groups exist, blacks are socioeconomically disadvantaged compared to whites, and there is visible residential and social segregation in both counties (which Hispanic respondents saw and remarked on). Still, unlike the situation in many highly segregated gateway cities, rural areas' 'limits of space, resources, and opportunities for segregation' (Erwin 2003, p. 67) force residents to interact in workplaces, neighbourhoods, public spaces, and public schools. Consequently, almost all respondents reported having come into contact with someone outside their own group, usually in these spaces. Plus, even if they did not know many out-group members personally, the nonmetropolitan character of these places meant that they at least knew something about one another (Jiménez 2005, p. 165). The one exception could be contracted seasonal farmworkers, who were often isolated on farms with little interaction with other residents. However, even agricultural worker respondents had some contact with whites and blacks within their workplaces.

Hispanic newcomers' racial/ethnic identifications

Hispanic respondents both self-identified and reported external identification by southern natives most strongly as something other than whites or blacks – particularly as Hispanics, Latinos, or people of some 'other race'. This includes respondents who self-identified as Hispanic, *hispano*, or Latino (37.5 per cent), respondents who were not asked how they self-identified but who nonetheless employed these terms (25.0 per cent), and respondents who self-identified secondarily as such even when their primary identifications were by national origin (9.1 per cent).

As illustrated by Ricardo and Noélia, a working-class immigrant couple from Veracruz, Mexico, foreign-born respondents in this group have picked these terms up after migration as available language with which to make sense of their new place as minorities in the rural south's racial hierarchy. Ricardo and Noélia explained how Latin American-origin newcomers from a variety of countries get aggregated into a larger 'Hispanic' or 'Spanish' (and sometimes reduced simply to 'Mexican') grouping – one portrayed as racially distinct from whites, blacks, and Asians (i.e., 'Chinese') alike:

Interviewer:	How do you define yourself in terms of race or ethnicity?
Ricardo:	Well, in Mexico, we are Mexicans. And here, for everyone we are Hispanics. That's what they call people from Colombia, Paraguay, Uruguay, wherever ... every one of them same.
Noélia:	It's the only thing that they have on forms for race or ethnicity.
Ricardo:	'Hispanic.'
Noélia:	Hispanic, black, white, and sometimes they say 'Chinese'.
Ricardo:	Or sometimes to play with us, and they say 'Spanish' instead.

Yet some respondents either self-identified or reported external identification by southern natives as whites. A few (approximately 3 per cent) self-identified as whites, adamantly resisting both the Hispanic/Latino and black labels even when natives see them as such. Others (approximately 8 per cent) either self-identified ethnically as Hispanics/Latinos yet racially as whites (as did Davíd, a lower-middle-class immigrant from Medellín, Colombia), or thought that natives perceive them to be whites because of their individual light skin or hair colours (as did Isabel García, a lower-middle-class immigrant from Buenos Aires, Argentina). Consistent with the triracial model, white racial identification emerged more strongly among light-skinned and middle-class respondents from South America and the Caribbean, while 'other' or 'Hispanic' racial identification emerged more strongly among dark-skinned and lower-class respondents from Mexico and Central America.[3]

In contrast, very few respondents identified or reported external identification by southern natives as blacks.[4] Consistent with the black/nonblack model, only one self-identified as black (Carmen, a dark-skinned, lower-middle-class woman who has African ancestry), and only two others reported ever being identified as black, with both changing over time. One – Lidia, a dark-skinned, upper-working-class immigrant from Oaxaca, Mexico – even reported being discriminated against by whites and called 'black' when she first migrated to North Carolina in 1980, but said this has changed as immigration into the area has increased and natives have become more familiar with and willing to acknowledge 'Hispanics' as a distinct group.

Therefore, consistent with the triracial model, respondents' strongest internal and external identifications as Hispanics, Latinos, or people of some 'other race' denote an early pattern of incorporation that exhibits some collective social distance from both whiteness and blackness. Yet consistent with the black/nonblack model, respondents' stronger internal and external identifications as 'others' and 'whites' than as 'blacks' denote an early pattern of incorporation that also exhibits greater collective social distance from blackness than from whiteness. While class and skin colour do influence respondents' racial identifications, they generally do so within a 'nonblack' zone. Even dark-skinned, poor, and undocumented Mexican and Central Americans tend neither to self-identify nor perceive external identification as 'collective blacks'.

Social interactions with whites and blacks

What factors lie behind these patterns of 'nonblack' identification? Undoubtedly, they are at least partially based on the way race is organized in Latin America, where distancing from blackness is frequently encouraged. In contrast to how the legacy of the 'one-drop rule' encourages many Americans to identify as 'blacker' than their phenotypes might suggest, legacies of white superiority encourage many Latin Americans to identify as 'whiter'. Upon migrating to the United States, many Latin Americans find that they are viewed as 'darker' here, yet continue to maintain their previous identifications (Rodríguez 2000, pp. 106–25).

My data also show that anti-black stereotypes play a role (Mindiola, Niemann, and Rodríguez 2002; Kim 2004; McClain et al. 2006). While it is unclear whether these stereotypes originated abroad or after migration or both, many (though certainly not all) Hispanic respondents expressed them toward blacks. Antonia, a medium-skinned, college-educated, legal permanent resident from Veracruz, Mexico, and Nadia, a poor, dark-skinned, undocumented immigrant from Mexico City, illustrated stereotypical views of blacks as loud, violent, lazy, uneducated, dependent, or lacking in family values:

Antonia: In my work I have seen that the blacks are louder, feistier. Whites are like, quieter. I think it's a question of education, or culture.

Nadia: The blacks are sometimes pretty dirty. They don't do things right, or they don't want to work. They don't want to be responsible or work. They don't do what people tell them to. They drink a lot. Their worst traits are that they are very rude. They say ugly words.

As Nina, a dark-skinned, lower-middle-class, naturalized citizen from Cali, Colombia, explained, many Hispanics, including those likely to become 'collective blacks', learn to devalue blackness and make efforts to dissociate from it, since whiteness is privileged over blackness in both their home countries and here (Dzidzienyo and Oboler 2005):

Nina: Some Hispanics come here to this country and they want nothing to do with blacks. Even in our own countries we learn this. We learn we don't want to be a part of their community.

Yet these patterns are also based on Hispanics' social interactions with whites and blacks, through which they develop a sense of how they are viewed and of where the strongest intergroup boundaries lie. Within the complex range of intergroup relations that I documented, intriguing patterns emerge. Overall Hispanic respondents perceived better interpersonal relations with whites than blacks; they perceived that whites treat Hispanics better than whites treat blacks, and many also perceived that Hispanics are 'discriminated' against more by blacks than whites. Thus, many Hispanic newcomers have come to perceive that the boundaries separating themselves from whites, although existent, are more permeable than those separating themselves from blacks or whites from blacks.

Whites' preferences for Hispanics over African Americans

Hispanic respondents' perception that whites treat them better than whites treat blacks is consistent with the literature on past European and Asian immigrants who, while not initially viewed as 'whites', were also not viewed equally to 'blacks' but rather more like 'almost blacks' or 'in-betweens' who were preferred as cheap and docile labour and eventually afforded greater opportunity to 'move up' into full or honorary whiteness (Loewen 1988; Roediger 2005). Importantly, while light-skinned and higher-class Hispanic respondents perceived preferences for Hispanics over blacks, so did dark-skinned and lower-class ones. Paco, a poor, dark-skinned farmworker from Jalisco, Mexico, who is now a legal permanent resident but used to be undocumented, saw whites in both Florida and North Carolina erecting a stronger residential boundary against blacks than against Hispanics. Likewise, Armando, a medium-skinned, upper-working-class, naturalized citizen from Monterrey, Mexico, saw them erecting a stronger interpersonal boundary:

Paco: With the white people that I know, they like Hispanics here more than blacks. You see, over where I live [in Lake Placid, Florida] there are lots of [white] American people and only about four Hispanics there living with them. Like, it's not an issue – everything is fine and there aren't any problems between us. But if a black person moves in there, the whites will start to sell their houses. Because they will become cheaper. So whites don't like the blacks. Why? I don't know.

Armando: I've heard it from several friends who are white that they would rather see their children go out with a Hispanic than with a black.
Interviewer: Do you know of a lot of interracial dating around here?
Armando: Oh yes. [It's] mostly between whites and Hispanics. It's very rare to see a black person married to Hispanics.

Indeed, I confirm that whites express strong preferences for Hispanics. In workplaces, employers viewed them as having a better work ethic and being more pliant and loyal workers than 'lazy' and 'entitled' blacks (Kirschenman and Neckerman 1991; Johnson-Webb 2003, pp. 114–15; Waldinger and Lichter 2003; Griffith 2005, p. 66). In daily life, neighbourhoods, and interpersonal relationships, whites exhibited greater ambivalence toward Hispanics (including undocumented immigrants) than blacks, frequently juxtaposing negative stereotypes of Hispanics with positive evaluations of their 'desire to work hard', 'better themselves', and 'support their families'. One upper-working-class white native remarked that she would prefer to have Hispanics' 'pretty' brown hair than blacks' 'ugly' black hair. Another upper-class one remarked that the Burger King 'is just nicer now' with Hispanic employees, whereas blacks did not care enough to 'keep it up'. Even the few notable examples I documented of whites separating themselves from Hispanics in neighbourhoods and schools could not rival the strong distaste they exhibited toward living among blacks.

John Doherty, a bilingual white attorney in Bedford county, nicely summarized this crucial difference between how whites view blacks – their true 'other' in the rural south – versus Hispanics. He distinguished between the strong and hostile *racial hatred* many whites feel toward African Americans, versus the more ambivalent *cultural xenophobia* they feel toward Hispanics, whom they know less well:

John Doherty: And there is that [white] bias against the Mexicans here, too, but it's not the hostile 'You oughta send all the niggers back to Africa.' But it is a cultural, sort of xenophobic reaction.

This distinction frames white–Hispanic relations as comparatively more positive than white–black ones. It also signals to Hispanics that the privileges of whiteness are ultimately closer within their reach than that of blacks, providing them with enormous incentives to distance themselves away from blackness to gain upward mobility, which can exacerbate any anti-black stereotypes among them.

Hispanic newcomers' responses to perceived discrimination by blacks

Many (though certainly not all[5]) Hispanic respondents also perceived that Hispanics are more 'discriminated' against by blacks than whites (Griffith 2005, p. 66; Rich and Miranda 2005, p. 204). Delmira, a medium-skinned, lower-working-class immigrant from Mexico City, who is now a legal permanent resident but used to be undocumented, and Ricky, a medium-skinned, college-educated Mexican American from McAllen, Texas, illustrated this:

Delmira: Blacks still have that 'For years we've been discriminated and discriminated' [mentality]. And sometimes it's the opposite sometimes. They discriminate against others [Hispanics].

Ricky: Blacks feel threatened, they think that Hispanics going to take something away from them ... and they have tendency to treat Hispanics a little bit wrong.

To be sure, Hispanic respondents acknowledged some discrimination from rural southern whites. Yet in many cases what they had expected to encounter from whites, based on their knowledge of American immigration policy or their interpersonal relations with whites elsewhere in the United States, was worse than what actually transpired in eastern North Carolina. Furthermore, Hispanic respondents tended to report a balance in their interactions with whites – noting that while some display prejudice and discrimination, others do not, and still others display friendliness, acceptance, and a surprising degree of cultural cosmopolitanism that helps to counter other negative white voices. Álvaro, a medium-skinned, college-educated immigrant from Coahuila, Mexico, who is now a legal permanent resident but used to be undocumented, described this common perception of a bifurcated '50–50' response from whites, compared to more negative '25–75' treatment by blacks:

Álvaro: I see more white people, Caucasians, doing positive things to the Hispanic community versus the African American people. With a better attitude and approach. They are being more kind. I can't say [the relationship between Hispanics and blacks] is good. Because my opinion is that a big part of the African American population, they really don't accept the Hispanic community. We are intruders. Just a small part, one probably quarter, are the ones who can see us as allies.

This distinction may seem surprising, given the legacy of white-on-nonwhite discrimination in the rural south, the larger gap separating the current material positions of Hispanic newcomers from whites than from blacks, and the lack of resources with which rural black southerners can truly 'discriminate' against other groups. Yet Hispanic newcomers were interpreting 'discrimination' from blacks in two key ways. First, Hispanic newcomers perceived that education and class strongly structure natives' responses, with better-educated and higher-class natives responding most positively (Mindiola, Niemann, and Rodríguez 2002; Hernández-León and Zúñiga 2005; Vallas and Zimmerman 2007; Fennelly 2008; Marrow 2008). Since blacks in eastern North Carolina are poorer than whites, at both the group and individual levels, Hispanics likewise perceived that blacks' reactions to newcomers are more negative, as they respond to greater fears of being displaced or 'leapfrogged' by Hispanics, not only economically in low-wage workplaces but also socially in lower-class neighbourhoods and public schools. As expressed by Alicia, a medium-skinned, lower-middle-class immigrant from Chile who is currently in the process of naturalization through her white American husband, discrimination comes mostly from black Americans 'and the white people that here you call "rednecks". It's social class that accounts for it.'

In this way, the structural conditions affecting Hispanic newcomers and blacks in the rural south create a context in which Hispanics' interpersonal relations with blacks are more heavily shaped by symbolic – even if not actual – economic competition (Dunn, Aragonés, and Shivers 2005; Rich and Miranda 2005; McClain et al. 2007; Marrow 2008). Hispanic and white respondents signalled this as a main reason why blacks are responding poorly to Hispanics:

Nina: There is a lot of black–Hispanic tension, and I've heard a lot about it. There's some bad feelings on the part of African American students when Hispanic students start doing very well, which a lot of them already are …
Interviewer: Jealousy, you mean?
Nina: Yes. Like I know one little [Hispanic] girl who was doing really well in school, and she was beaten up by a black student in school. I really do think there is some jealousy. Of African American students feeling that these people are not even from here, they are only recently arrived, they don't even speak the language. And here they are, and doing better only after a little bit of time. They are doing well. And that's hard on African Americans. And I kind of see the same tension with the adults. The feeling of jealousy of having these people be new, being undocumented, not being from this country, and having their jobs.

In such competitive situations, negative tensions between minority groups carry great potential for misinterpretation as group rejection (Rockquemore 2002), or even discrimination (Kasinitz et al. 2008), such as when a light-skinned, college-educated, undocumented Colombian respondent working in a textile mill in Bedford county said, 'I feel the blacks don't like us. And that it is worse than with the whites', or when a poor, dark-skinned, undocumented Guatemalan respondent working in a food processing plant in Wilcox county said that 'the black race does not like Hispanics very much because they think that we are taking away their jobs', reporting that this thing 'you could even call racism, right?' made him feel 'humiliated' and 'made fun of' by some blacks. In turn, these perceptions of competition-induced 'discrimination' can foster resentment, stereotyping, and distancing against blacks.

Second, Hispanic newcomers perceived 'discrimination' most strongly in terms of what Kim (1999) calls a *horizontal (non)citizenship axis*, along which *both white and black natives* can mark and ostracize them as undeserving civic and cultural 'outsiders', and secondarily in terms of a *vertical skin colour axis*, along which *white natives* can mark them as racially inferior. That is, when Hispanic respondents spoke of prejudice and discrimination, they did so mostly in terms of nonracial exclusion (along lines such as English language ability, class status, personal appearance, nativity, real or presumed legal status, and so forth), and secondarily in terms of racial exclusion. Often respondents even identified their physical features or skin colours as significant insofar as they serve to denote civic and cultural outsiderness. For example, many reported being stopped by law enforcement officials for 'driving while Mexican'; they understood that these officials identify them as 'Hispanic' according to their physical appearance, yet this is because their 'Hispanic' features have been racialized *in association with* probable undocumented status, which ostracizes them as undeserving 'foreigners'. As Jiménez (2008) argues, in an era of unprecedented Latin American immigration, race is significant in Hispanic newcomers' lives partially due to the direct (for immigrants) and indirect (for later generations) effects of nativism.

Furthermore, Hispanic respondents often perceived blacks to be worse perpetrators of this horizontal exclusion. Merced and Octavio, a medium-skinned, working-class, undocumented immigrant couple from Sinaloa, Mexico, expressed frustration with blacks who 'ignore' them when they attempt to speak English, relative to whites who 'help' more:

Merced: Even though some blacks do understand you, they say they don't. Sometimes I go up to our English teacher, and I'll ask him, 'How do you say X thing?' And he says, 'You say it like this.' And then I say it back to him like he said it to me, and he tells me, 'Yes, you've got it!' So I ask him, 'How come some black people tell me they don't understand what I am saying to them?'

Octavio: Almost the majority of *gringos* ask me to talk, and they will try to understand me. And they help me. However, there are other people who make fun of you. There is some difference [between whites and blacks] there.

Like Merced and Octavio, other Hispanic respondents perceived that whites are more 'open-minded' toward them and their 'foreign' cultures than blacks, whom they perceived as 'staying more separate' and excluding Hispanics more strongly. Raquel, a poor, medium-skinned, 1.5-generation undocumented immigrant from Tegucigalpa, Honduras, who dropped out of her high school in Tennessee after the tenth grade, recalled severe rejection by black schoolmates who ostracized her for her 'foreign' dress and personal appearance, compared to whites, who came to form her close circle of friends. Laura, a medium-skinned, lower-working-class immigrant from Chihuahua, Mexico, thought that there is 'more communication and common interests' between Hispanics and whites than blacks, because 'whites try to strike up more conversation with Hispanics' in order to get to know more about them and their backgrounds, while 'blacks, well, not as much'. Even when Hispanics did not perceive whites as 'open-minded', they did not necessarily see blacks as more so. Eugenio, a poor, dark-skinned, 1.5-generation undocumented immigrant from Oaxaca, Mexico, thought that while whites ostracize Hispanics as 'dirty' and undeserving foreigners, blacks do so even more strongly. Here Eugenio tapped not only into the acute threat of socioeconomic disenfranchisement that lower-class African Americans feel in the face of rising immigration, but also into their sense that they, like whites, are the kind of real 'Americans' that Hispanics are not:

Eugenio: They always look at you and say, 'He doesn't speak English.' Because I've been in restaurants and had black people sitting next to me, or white people. And they just keep on yapping ... 'Look at that. He's dirty. And all these Hispanics come and steal our jobs.' They'll sit there and keep on talking trash about you.

Interviewer: This talking trash – do you think Hispanics get it mostly from white or black Americans?

Eugenio: They get it mostly from blacks. Honestly, I don't know why. Like one time, during Hurricane Floyd, all the lights went out. And the Salvation Army, or the soldiers would come over here to Bedford Mobile Home Park with dump trucks. And they would drop clothes off here, or water, or canned foods. And I overheard a conversation that a black lady had. She said, 'You know, look at 'em. They come over here to our country, to our land, steal our jobs, steal our money. And now they even want to steal our needs [i.e. donated relief items]. Those needs are for us, the Americans.' They were saying this and that about us.

Why these Hispanic respondents perceived greater horizontal exclusion, sometimes interpreted as 'discrimination', from blacks than from whites is still unclear. Opinion data show lifelong southern blacks supporting *less* restrictive immigration policies and *less* exclusionary policies toward undocumented immigrants than lifelong southern whites; however, they also show lifelong southern blacks espousing more particularistic ideas about what it takes to be American than lifelong southern whites (Griffin and McFarland 2007, p. 13), and blacks exhibiting greater concern about undocumented immigrants than whites in Virginia (Vallas and Zimmerman 2007). Opinion data from Durham, North Carolina also show that blacks exhibit *fewer* negative stereotypes of Hispanic immigrants than vice versa (McClain et al. 2006), which may be consistent with my observation that blacks in eastern North Carolina were not aware of how exclusively Hispanics perceived them to be acting. Perhaps blacks are unaware of how they are treating Hispanics poorly along nonracial lines – particularly if the characteristics associated with noncitizenship, rather than aligning Hispanics and blacks together as 'collective blacks' at the bottom of the regional racial hierarchy, exacerbate feelings of competition instead? Or perhaps Hispanics' anti-black stereotypes or observations of whites' stigmatization of blacks are flavouring their interpretations of whites and blacks' behaviours, leading them to judge those of blacks as more harsh?

Regardless, Hispanic newcomers perceived negative treatment from blacks in 2003–4 and described it as 'unexpected', in contrast to perceiving more 'surprisingly' pleasant relations with whites, especially when they were prepared to encounter significant discrimination from them. Something that surprised Inés, a light-skinned, middle-class, undocumented immigrant from Medellín, Colombia, was discrimination by blacks against Hispanics, not by whites against either blacks or Hispanics. And despite having heard about the KKK and anti-immigrant vigilante activity on the US–Mexico border before migrating, Mauro, a poor, dark-skinned undocumented immigrant from Guatemala City, reported being most surprised by a black coworker who refused to return his smiles and greetings each morning at work. In contrast, 'From what I have gotten to know of white Americans, they have always been very friendly. I have never felt any discrimination from them.' These perceptions of horizontal exclusion by African Americans can, like those arising from economically induced competition, foster resentment, stereotyping, and distancing in return.

Conclusion

This analysis lends preliminary support to a black/nonblack colour line model in the region where African American populations are the largest and the racial binary has reigned supreme. To be clear, my data do not show that Hispanic newcomers' interactions with blacks in the rural south are always conflict-ridden, nor those with whites always smooth. My data also do not show that Hispanics have yet become 'whites'. Strong linguistic, cultural, and racial boundaries continue to separate the two groups, and discrimination by whites is indeed harming Hispanics' wellbeing in fundamental ways. What my data do show, however, is how and why a subjective black/nonblack colour line might emerge *despite* persisting gaps between the material positions of whites and Hispanics. Despite them, Hispanics, including many poor, dark-skinned, and undocumented Mexican and Central American labour migrants, are neither self-identifying as nor perceiving that they are treated equally to 'collective blacks' in everyday lived experience. Moreover, through a combination of factors – their own anti-black stereotypes, observations of whites' unique stigmatization of blacks, and (mis)perceptions of 'discrimination' by blacks – many Hispanics have come to perceive the social distance separating themselves from whites as more permeable than that separating themselves from blacks, and are engaging in distancing strategies that may reinforce this distinction.

Thus, my findings offer weakest support, at least during this early stage, for a white/nonwhite colour line model in which distinctions among nonwhites appear less salient than those between whites and all nonwhites. They also offer tentatively weak support for a triracial colour line model in which dark-skinned, poor, and undocumented Hispanic newcomers all become 'collective blacks', perceiving greater distance from whites than blacks irrespective of African ancestry. Clearly skin colour, class, and noncitizenship do matter to Hispanic newcomers' racial incorporation in the rural south. Nonetheless, their influences still operate within a 'nonblack' zone that exhibits greater overall distance from blackness than from whiteness, suggesting that African ancestry may continue to play the dominant role in determining where the most salient boundary in rural southern society lies, as the black/nonblack model predicts.

Of course, I have painted a picture of racial incorporation during an early stage of immigration, and appropriate caution is needed when moving the research agenda forward. Racialization processes depend on a multitude of factors, and intergroup relations stemming from them have been shown to vary across both place and time (Montejano 1987). Thus, more research is needed to determine how stable the patterns that I have uncovered in eastern North Carolina are and how applicable they may be to places elsewhere in the south. This will be especially important in places which have larger middle-class African American and Hispanic communities, since poverty and lower-class status are central in fueling black–Hispanic tensions, and in places which have smaller black populations, since the boundary separating whites from all other groups may appear more salient in places with smaller minority populations.

More research is also needed to understand how the patterns that I have uncovered in eastern North Carolina might develop over time, particularly as immigration continues and anti-immigrant sentiments sharpen. Perhaps these trends will lead first-generation Hispanic immigrants (especially ones who are dark-skinned, poor, or undocumented) to perceive greater discrimination from whites – particularly if they perceive blacks to begin exhibiting more solidarity and empathy rather than exclusion in the context of everyday interactions (and not just in elite coalition-building projects) than they did in 2003–4. But perhaps these trends may also exacerbate tensions between first-generation Hispanic immigrants and blacks, by increasing perceptions of economic and symbolic threat and the salience of noncitizenship more generally.

Future research can also examine how US-born Hispanics in the region identify and perceive their relations with whites and blacks. Evidence suggests that 'second-generation' children of Latin American immigrants come to view 'race' and race relations differently than their first-generation parents, generally exhibiting greater perceptions of discrimination by whites and more favourable attitudes toward blacks. In my research, all of the eighteen US-born Hispanic respondents (with the exception of one who has African ancestry) identified as something 'nonblack', and few reported significantly better relations with blacks than did foreign-born respondents. Furthermore, the 1.5-generation Hispanic youth I interviewed expressed acute perceptions of discrimination from blacks, often in the context of negative experiences attending American middle and high schools. Therefore, 1.5- and second-generation status did not appear to significantly blur the boundary separating blacks and Hispanics, at least in 2003–4. However, further research on the experiences of Hispanic youth coming of age in a context of greater anti-immigrant sentiment will help contextualize these findings. And further research comparing the experiences of US-born Hispanics *with* versus *without African ancestry* will help clarify the specific role that African ancestry, relative to skin colour, class, and legal status, may come to play in the long-term racial incorporation of Hispanics in the rural south.

Notes

1. The US Census defines Hispanics/Latinos as all 'persons of Mexican, Puerto Rican, Cuban, Central or South American, or other Spanish culture or origin, regardless of race' or where they were born.
2. Legal status for $N=6$ foreign-born respondents was unspecified.
3. The former also identified more strongly as whites in 2000 Census data than the latter, at the national and state levels (weighted IPUMS data, author's analysis).
4. In the 2000 Census members of *all* Latin American immigrant groups in North Carolina identified more strongly as whites and 'other race' than blacks. The only two groups with high rates of black identification (Panamanians at 19.0 per cent and Dominicans at 10.5 per cent) make up a small portion of North Carolina's Hispanic population (weighted IPUMS data, author's analysis).
5. Some Hispanic respondents reported that blacks do *not* discriminate against Hispanics as strongly as whites do, saying that blacks empathize with discrimination and harbour their resentment toward whites, not Hispanics. Here I focus on Hispanic respondents who did

report discrimination by blacks due to its importance in structuring their intergroup boundary.

References

BONILLA-SILVA, EDUARDO 2002 'We are all Americans!: The Latin Americanization of racial stratification in the USA', *Race and Society*, vol. 5, pp. 3–16

DUNN, TIMOTHY J., ARAGONÉS, ANA MARÍA, and SHIVERS, GEORGE 2005 'Recent Mexican immigration in the rural Delmarva Peninsula: human rights versus citizenship rights in a local context', in V. Zúñiga and R. Hernández-León (eds), *New Destinations: Mexican Immigration to the United States*, New York: Russell Sage, pp. 155–83

DZIDZIENYO, ANANI and OBOLER, SUZANNE (eds) 2005 *Neither Enemies Nor Friends: Latinos, Blacks, Afro-Latinos*, New York: Palgrave Macmillan

ERWIN, DEBORAH O. 2003 'An ethnographic description of Latino immigration in rural Arkansas: intergroup relations and utilization of healthcare services', *Southern Rural Sociology*, vol. 19, no. 1, pp. 46–72

FENNELLY, KATHERINE 2008 'Prejudice toward immigrants in the Midwest', in D. S. Massey (ed.), *New Faces in New Places: The Changing Geography of American Immigration*, New York: Russell Sage, pp. 151–78

FORMAN, TYRONE, GOAR, CARLA and LEWIS, AMANDA 2002 'Neither black nor white? An empirical test of the Latin Americanization thesis', *Race and Society*, vol. 5, pp. 65–84

GANS, HERBERT 1999 'The possibility of a new racial hierarchy in the twenty-first-century United States', in M. Lamont (ed.), *The Cultural Territories of Race: Black and White Boundaries*, Chicago: University of Chicago Press, pp. 371–89

GRIFFIN, LARRY J. and MCFARLAND, KATHERINE 2007 '"In my heart I'm an American": regional attitudes and American identity', *Southern Cultures*, vol. 13, no. 4, pp. 119–37

GRIFFITH, DAVID 2005 'Rural industry and Mexican immigration and settlement in North Carolina', in V. Zúñiga and R. Hernández-León (eds), *New Destinations: Mexican Immigration to the United States*, New York: Russell Sage, pp. 50–75

HERNÁNDEZ-LEÓN, RUBÉN and ZÚÑIGA, VICTOR 2005 'Appalachia meets Aztlán: Mexican immigration and inter-group relations in Dalton, Georgia', in V. Zúñiga and R. Hernández-León (eds), *New Destinations: Mexican Immigration in the United States*, New York: Russell Sage, pp. 244–73

JIMÉNEZ, TOMÁS R. 2005 'Replenished identity: Mexican Americans, Mexican immigrants, and ethnic identity', PhD dissertation, Department of Sociology, Harvard University, Cambridge, MA

—— 2008 'Mexican-immigrant replenishment and the continuing significance of ethnicity and race', *American Journal of Sociology*, vol. 113, no. 6, pp. 1527–67

JOHNSON-WEBB, KAREN D. 2003 *Recruiting Hispanic Labor: Immigrants in Non-Traditional Areas*, New York: LFB Scholarly Publishing, LLC

KASINITZ, PHILIP, et al. 2008 *Inheriting the City: The Second Generation Comes of Age*, Cambridge, MA: Harvard University Press

KIM, CLAIRE JEAN 1999 'The racial triangulation of Asian Americans', *Politics and Society*, vol. 27, no. 1, pp. 105–38

KIM, NADIA 2004 'A view from below: an analysis of Korean Americans' racial attitudes', *Amerasia Journal*, vol. 30, no. 1, pp. 1–24

KIRSCHENMAN, JOLEEN and NECKERMAN, KATHRYN M. 1991 '"We'd love to hire them but...": the meaning of race for employers', in C. Jencks and P. Peterson (eds), *The Urban Underclass*, Washington, DC: Brookings Institution, pp. 203–34

LEE, JENNIFER and BEAN, FRANK D. 2007 'Reinventing the color line: immigration and America's new racial/ethnic divide', *Social Forces*, vol. 86, no. 2, pp. 1–26

LOEWEN, JAMES W. 1988 *The Mississippi Chinese: Between Black and White*, 2nd edn, Long Grove, IL: Waveland Press

MARROW, HELEN B. 2008 'Hispanic immigration, black population size, and intergroup relations in the rural and small-town south', in D. S. Massey (ed.), *New Faces in New Places: The Changing Geography of American Immigration*, New York: Russell Sage, pp. 211–48

MASSEY, DOUGLAS S. 2007 *Categorically Unequal: The American Stratification System*, New York: Russell Sage

MCCLAIN, PAULA D., *et al.* 2006 'Racial distancing in a southern city: Latino immigrants' views of black Americans', *Journal of Politics*, vol. 68, no. 3, pp. 571–84

—— 2007 'Black Americans and Latino immigrants in a southern city: friendly neighbors or economic competitors?', *Du Bois Review*, vol. 4, no. 1, pp. 97–117

MINDIOLA, TATCHO, NIEMANN, YOLANDA FLORES and RODRíGUEZ, NESTOR 2002 *Black-Brown Relations and Stereotypes*, Austin: University of Texas Press

MONTEJANO, DAVID 1987 *Anglos and Mexicans in the Making of Texas, 1836–1986*, Austin: University of Texas Press

MURGUIA, EDWARD and SAENZ, ROGELIO 2002 'An analysis of the Latin Americanization of race in the United States: a reconnaissance of color stratification among Mexicans', *Race and Society*, vol. 5, pp. 85–101

PERLMANN, JOEL and WALDINGER, ROGER 1997 'Second generation decline? Children of immigrants, past and present – a reconsideration', *International Migration Review*, vol. 31, no. 4, pp. 893–922

QIAN, ZHENCHAO 2002 'Race and social distance: intermarriage with non-Latino whites', *Race and Society*, vol. 5, pp. 33–47

QIAN, ZHENCHAO and LICHTER, DANIEL T. 2007 'Social boundaries and marital assimilation: interpreting trends in racial and ethnic intermarriage', *American Sociological Review*, vol. 72, no. 1, pp. 68–94

QUILLIAN, LINCOLN and CAMPBELL, MARY E. 2003 'Beyond black and white: the present and future of multiracial friendship segregation', *American Sociological Review*, vol. 68, no. 4, pp. 540–66

RICH, BRIAN L. and MIRANDA, MARTA 2005 'The sociopolitical dynamics of Mexican immigration in Lexington, Kentucky, 1977 to 2002: an ambivalent community responds', in V. Zúñiga and R. Hernández-León (eds), *New Destinations: Mexican Immigration to the United States*, New York: Russell Sage, pp. 187–219

ROCKQUEMORE, KERRY ANN 2002 'Negotiating the color line: the gendered process of racial identity construction among black/white biracial women', *Gender and Society*, vol. 16, no. 4, pp. 485–503

ROCKQUEMORE, KERRY ANN and AREND, PATRICIA 2002 'Opting for white: choice, fluidity and racial identity construction in post civil-rights America', *Race and Society*, vol. 5, pp. 49–64

RODRÍGUEZ, CLARA E. 2000 *Changing Race: Latinos, the Census, and the History of Ethnicity in the United States*, New York: New York University Press

ROEDIGER, DAVID R. 2005 *Working Toward Whiteness: How America's Immigrants Became White: The Strange Journey from Ellis Island to the Suburbs*, New York: Basic

SKRENTNY, JOHN D. 2002 *The Minority Rights Revolution*, Cambridge, MA: Harvard University Press

VALLAS, STEVEN P. and ZIMMERMAN, EMILY 2007 'Sources of variation in attitudes toward illegal immigration', Fairfax, VA: Center for Social Science Research, George Mason University

WALDINGER, ROGER and LICHTER, MICHAEL I. 2003 *How the Other Half Works: Immigration and the Social Organization of Labor*, Berkeley: University of California Press

WARREN, JONATHAN W. and TWINE, FRANCE WINDDANCE 1997 'White Americans, the new minority? Non-blacks and the ever-expanding boundaries of whiteness', *Journal of Black Studies*, vol. 28, no. 2, pp. 200–18

WILKES, RIMA and ICELAND, JOHN 2004 'Hypersegregation in the twenty-first century', *Demography*, vol. 41, no. 1, pp. 23–36
YANCEY, GEORGE A. 2003 *Who is White? Latinos, Asians, and the New Black/Nonblack Divide*, Boulder, CO: L. Rienner

An assessment of the Latin Americanization thesis

Christina A. Sue

Abstract

In 2004, Eduardo Bonilla-Silva published an article in which he proposed a provocative thesis – he argued that the US system of race is beginning to resemble that of Latin America. Despite the attention received from the US side, there has been no response from scholars of race in Latin America. This article is a critical reply to Bonilla-Silva's Latin Americanization thesis. In the article, I move the debate forward by introducing a Latin American perspective. I begin by outlining and addressing various claims made by Bonilla-Silva regarding the Latin American system of race. I then discuss how his thesis is put to the empirical test and briefly comment on the model's ability to explain the future of race in the United States. I conclude with a discussion of how the racial terrain is rapidly changing in Latin America and the implications that this has for Bonilla-Silva's theory. Finally, I suggest ways in which the Latin Americanization thesis can be improved.

In 2004, Eduardo Bonilla-Silva published an article in *Ethnic and Racial Studies*, in which he proposed a provocative thesis – he argued that the US racial terrain is reconfiguring to resemble that of Latin America. Specifically, he posits that the US is moving away from a binary black/white model towards a tri-racial model comprised of three tiers: 'whites', 'honorary whites' and a 'collective black' (for details see original article). This publication continued an earlier conversation (Bonilla-Silva 2002a) in which various scholars put Bonilla-Silva's thesis to the test.[1] The Latin Americanization thesis (henceforth LAT) contributes to a growing body of literature aimed at predicting the future of US race relations (Warren and Twine 1997; Gans 1999; Yancey 2003; Lee and Bean 2004). However, the LAT is novel in that scholars have generally predicted the continuance of a bi-polar model, albeit with different racial-group boundaries. Furthermore, scholars have traditionally highlighted the differences, not similarities, between the US and Latin America. Despite the comparative nature of the LAT and the attention received from US scholars, to my knowledge, there has been no response from scholars of race in Latin America. In this article I hope to move the conversation forward by introducing a Latin American perspective. This focus reflects my belief that the starting point of assessing whether or not the US is Latin Americanizing is to clarify what we mean by the Latin American system of race.[2] I will begin by addressing claims made in the LAT and move to a discussion of the methods used to test the thesis empirically.

Claims about Latin America

In his article, Bonilla-Silva characterizes Latin America as a 'tri-racial' system where phenotype is an important determinant of membership in a racial tier. In addition, he describes Latin Americans as strongly identifying with the nation (e.g. 'We are all Mexicans') and holding a colour-blind perspective (i.e. believing racism no longer exists). Finally, he implies that white elites in Latin America, realizing their populations were becoming 'black' and 'Indian', attempted to whiten the population to maintain white dominance. I will address each of these points with the exception of that related to national identities and colour-blindness as I find this aspect of the LAT to be less problematic, especially if we confine our discussion to the twentieth century. I will also address additional concerns I have with the LAT.

Latin America as a 'tri-racial' system

There is still no consensus in the literature regarding how best to characterize the racial system of Latin America; it has been referred to as a colour continuum, a multi-racial system, a tri-racial system (adopted by Bonilla-Silva) and even a bi-racial system. Under the continuum model, skin colour gradations are seen as representing a skin colour hierarchy and there is an absence of discrete racial-group boundaries (Mörner 1967). Evidence to support this description is the high number of popularly used race/colour categories. For example, in Brazil, 135 different responses were given to an open-ended survey question on colour (Telles 2004). More recently, scholars have provided data showing that Brazilians only orient to a small number of these categories. For example, Telles (2004) found that 97 per cent of the non-Asian and non-Indian population in Brazil used just seven colour terms. These findings have led some to refer to Latin America as a multi-racial system (Skidmore 1993).

Others define Latin America as a tri-racial or bi-racial system. Although there is support in the literature for Bonilla-Silva's tri-racial characterization (Duany 1998; Marx 1998 also) scholars have provided evidence that race is sometimes conceptualized in bi-polar terms (Sheriff 2001; Golash-Boza n.d.). Another way in which scholars have asserted a bi-racial characterization is by focusing on the *primary* racial divide. Supporting this emphasis are data which show that mulattos have life chances that are closer to those of blacks than whites (Silva 1985; Lovell 1989; Telles and Lim 1998; Telles 2004; Beck, Mijeski and Stark 2008).

The way race in Latin America is characterized depends on both interpretation and the data being used. For example, in Brazil, the question is not whether mulattoes represent a position between blacks and whites, but whether the gap between mulattoes and blacks is so narrow that it is more appropriate to focus on the white/non-white boundary. Even in the US, which epitomizes a bi-racial system, lighter-skinned blacks do better than their darker-skinned counterparts on a number of measures (Hughes and Hurtel 1990; Keith and Herring 1991). Moreover, in terms of income, light-skinned blacks in the US occupy more of an intermediate position between blacks and whites than they do in Brazil where black and brown incomes are very similar (Telles 2004). Nevertheless, the existence of a skin-colour hierarchy in the US has not been interpreted to mean that a tri-racial system exists as the black/white boundary is seen as marking the *major* racial cleavage in society.

In terms of categorization, the data sources being used largely influence how the Latin American racial system is characterized. For example, the idea of a colour continuum is largely supported by ethnographic, qualitative and open-ended survey data aimed at capturing popular conceptions of race. In contrast, when using official classification systems, intermediate popular categories are oftentimes lumped into a single category for statistical purposes (Duany 1998; Telles 2007). Analysis of official data confines researchers to prescribed categories, which lends itself to depicting a tri-racial or multi-racial system. The popular versus official distinction is less salient in the US, where these categories align more closely, with the exception of the Latino population.

This conversation about how to characterize the Latin American system of race provokes larger conceptual questions relevant to the evaluation of the LAT. For example, what is a tri-racial system and what characteristics does an ideal-type tri-racial system have? In an ideal-type tri-racial system is the strength of the boundary between the first and second tier equal to that between the second and third tier? In the US, although middle groups have existed and continue to exist, the country has not been described as tri-racial, as the focus has been on the primary racial divide. In the LAT, tier one is labelled 'whites' and tier two 'honorary whites' which implies a weaker boundary between tiers one and two compared to that between tiers two and three (the collective black category). A clarification by Bonilla-Silva regarding the relative strength of the boundaries in his model would be useful.

On another point, is a tri-racial system simply a system with three tiers or is it a system where the offspring of two racial categories (representing tiers one and three) are given a social space in tier two? The two options posed in this question highlight the difference between the Latin American model and the future US model as described in the LAT. In Latin America, the idea of three tiers is based on the existence of a separate social category which represents the mixture of two distinct 'races' – either black/white or indigenous/white. In the US, this social space has not existed, as the one-drop rule has usually prevailed, thus the US has been defined as a bi-racial system. However, the future US model, unlike that of Latin America, includes various 'races' and 'ethnicities' in the middle tier (e.g. Asians, Latinos), not just the mixed-race offspring of tiers one and three. Therefore, even if we choose to characterize both systems as having three tiers, the historical development and contemporary construction of these tiers are very different in these two regions.

The importance of skin colour[3]

In terms of skin colour, the LAT correctly captures the importance of colour in Latin America as it relates to dynamics *between two racial poles* such as black/white or Indian/white. The idea of a colour continuum in Latin America has developed based on the treatment of mixed-race individuals who are assumed to be a mixture of the two predominant racial groups in society. In other words, colour is important precisely because *ancestry is assumed to be held constant* as nearly everyone is perceived as representing part of the two poles. For example, it has been found that, in Brazil, 38 per cent of self-identified whites claim some African ancestry and 66 per cent of blacks claim some European ancestry (Telles 2004). Therefore, even at the racial poles, there is a feeling of being part of the black/white mixture. The degree to which an individual represents more of one pole or the other is partially measured by phenotype, a characteristic which affects treatment in society. This dynamic is distinct from how Bonilla-Silva predicts skin colour will function in the US. In his model, there are no clear racial poles as a variety of ethnic and racial groups are represented in the three tiers.

The LAT addresses the importance of skin colour not only *within* a group but also *between* groups. For example, Vietnamese and Laotian individuals (who are generally darker skinned) are in the 'collective black' category whereas Japanese and Chinese individuals are in the 'honorary white' category. Although Bonilla-Silva argues that, at times, factors other than phenotype play a role in group placement and disrupt the pigmentocracy, his model generally demonstrates a colour hierarchy within and between groups. However, in Latin America, outside the continuum of two racial poles, colour is not a strong predictor of classification or treatment (Mörner 1970). For example, lighter-skinned groups such as Asians, Arabs, and Jews have experienced very high rates of discrimination in Latin America (Mörner 1970; Lesser 1999). In addition, colour has not determined which groups have been given preference in the context of immigration. For example, Fitzgerald and Cook-Martin (2008) found that between 1850 and 2000, twenty-one Latin American countries had provisions against Chinese immigration compared to only thirteen having such provisions against African-origin immigration. Therefore, although colour between groups outside the black/white continuum may be important in the US case, this is not so in Latin America. Finally, in a separate publication, Bonilla-Silva, addressing the US case, states that 'all the data points in one direction: that color is a central feature of social stratification' (2002b, p. 110) and uses this conclusion to support his prediction that colour is becoming increasingly important in the US. However, some recent evidence for both Mexican Americans and African Americans suggests that skin colour in the US may actually be *decreasing* in significance (Gullickson 2005; Telles and Ortiz 2008). This contradictory evidence, albeit preliminary, should be addressed.

'White' elites and the darkening of the population

In his thesis, Bonilla-Silva argues that white elites in Latin America realized their countries were darkening and therefore attempted to whiten their populations as a way to maintain white dominance. There are two problems with this narrative. First, Latin American countries were not 'becoming' black and Indian – they had been that way since the beginning. Second, in the early twentieth century when practices of whitening were promoted by importing European immigrants and encouraging race mixture, many elites in countries such as Brazil, Mexico and Peru would not be considered white by North American or European standards[4] (Knight 1990; Davis 1991; Stepan 1991; de la Cadena 2000; Telles 2004). Elites were seen as racially similar to, not distinct from, the general population. The mixed-race elite were *personally* invested in, and thus supported, whitening ideologies. Therefore, the claim that whitening in Latin America was created so that a white elite could maintain white dominance is a misrepresentation, at least for some of the key Latin American countries.[5] If white elites in the US attempt to whiten the population, as Bonilla-Silva predicts, this dynamic would be very distinct from what occurred in Latin America.

Additional concerns

Homogenizing Latin America One of my primary concerns with the LAT is whether or not the racial dynamics in individual Latin American countries are *similar enough* to justify a discussion of a 'Latin American system of race'. Although it is inherent in the nature of theoretical frameworks and ideal-type models to gloss over case specificities, this can be particularly problematic for Latin America which has extreme regional diversity related to race. For example, rates of black-brown/white intermarriage in Brazil are fairly high (Telles 2004), while in Guatemala, Ladino/indigenous intermarriages are exceedingly rare (Ishida 2003). Furthermore, whereas Mexican *mestizos* generally hold a race-blind framework[6] (Sue 2009), the same cannot be said of Afro-Cubans (Sawyer 2006). Finally, although the idea that 'money whitens' has been used in reference to countries such as Ecuador, Brazil and Colombia (Degler 1971; Whitten 1974), the generalizability of this claim is under scrutiny (Telles 2004; Schwartzman 2007; Golash-Boza n.d.). The list of distinctions goes on. A critical barrier to this discussion is the absence of census data on race in much of Latin America, justified by national ideologies which assert racism is not an issue. This has limited scholarly work in a number of Latin American countries.

Within Latin America, there are two distinct types of countries: those with a black/white continuum and/or distinction those with an Indian/*mestizo* distinction. The former, which encompasses parts of the Caribbean and Brazil, has been described as Afro-Latin America and the latter, which includes Mexico, Guatemala and the South American Andes, as *mestizo* America (Harris 1964; Mörner 1967).[7] In Afro-Latin America, phenotype is emphasized and in *mestizo* America cultural markers also play an important role. The phenotype aspect is oftentimes stressed in comparative work on race as Afro-Latin America theoretically overpowers *mestizo* America. Furthermore, census data is more available in Afro-Latin America and it has therefore received more scholarly attention. This emphasis has resulted in a lopsided picture of how race functions in the region. This is especially noteworthy as the majority of countries in Latin America are *not* part of Afro-Latin America.

The regional diversity within Latin America is not recognized in the LAT; instead, almost complete emphasis is placed on Afro-Latin

America, noted in the sole focus on phenotype. My critique invites reflection about what analytical categories are useful when discussing this region. If we are committed to looking at other models to better understand shifts that may be occurring in US society, I propose that we begin by choosing a specific national model, thus avoiding the pitfalls of overgeneralization.[8] In other words, the LAT would avoid a number of conceptual problems if, instead of positing a theory of the 'Latin Americanization' of the US, it predicted the 'Brazilianization' or 'Puerto Ricanization' of the US. In fact, this already appears to be the *de facto* comparison used in the LAT since the general understanding of 'race in Latin America' focuses heavily on data from Brazil and a few Spanish-speaking Caribbean countries. Therefore, a simple change in terminology could solve a number of problems; a more conservative use of terminology would make the LAT more palatable and would sidestep the issue of whether or not Latin America should be treated as an analytically homogenous unit.

Mechanisms versus outcomes In the preceding sections, I have discussed how, in some cases, the US may be moving towards mirroring the Latin American situation in terms of *outcomes* but have stressed that the *underlying mechanisms* that led to these outcomes are quite distinct in these two regions. This discussion brings to the fore a series of questions. For example, should an ideal-type model take mechanisms into account or should the discussion be confined to outcomes (which is the emphasis of the LAT)? Is the US really 'Latin Americanizing' if the end result mirrors some aspects of the racialized social structure in Latin America but the paths to these outcomes are completely different? I would argue that the process is just as important as the outcome and that this is a question all scholars need to address when developing and evaluating theoretical models. In evaluating the LAT, we need to ask ourselves what analytical mileage is gained from the Latin America-US comparison and what is lost in the process.

Operationalizing the theory

Bonilla-Silva puts the LAT to the empirical test by looking at 'objective' (income and education), 'social interaction' (intermarriage and residential segregation) and 'subjective' (racial attitudes and self-classification) measures. Although there are numerous problems that arise regarding the conceptualization and testing of the first two indicators (which he generally acknowledges), due to space constraints, I will focus on the third measure, subjective indicators, and will discuss the crucial relationship between objective and social interaction indicators in Latin America.

In his approach to subjective measures, Bonilla-Silva adopts a group-position perspective on racial attitudes which is widely accepted among US sociologists (Bobo and Hutchings 1996). Blumer (1958), an early contributor to this theory, argued that racial prejudice is rooted in the relationship between racial groups and that racial attitudes are derived from one's sense of racial-group position. Other models adopt a more limited individual or group-interest perspective, arguing that objective material conditions (or one's standing in the socioeconomic hierarchy) determine racial attitudes (see Bobo and Kluegel 1993 for a discussion). In the US context, these perspectives been used to explain differences in racial attitudes have across racial groups (e.g. Bobo and Hutchings 1996; Weitzer and Tuch 2004). Applying these approaches to the LAT, Bonilla-Silva expects levels of racial identification and attitudes to be correlated with membership in a specific tier. He proposes: 'it should not be surprising if objective gaps in income, occupational status, and education between these various groups is contributing to group formation ... If this is happening, [honorary whites] should also be in the process of developing White-like racial attitudes befitting of their new social position' (2004, p. 937). As long as we confine our discussion to the US, and especially to blacks and whites, this group-position or interest-based perspective thesis appears to work. However, when we apply these theories to Latin America, we begin to encounter problems (Bailey 2004; Warren and Sue n.d.).

Research has shown that in Latin America one's place in the racial hierarchy is not a good predictor of racial attitudes (Bailey 2002, 2004; Beck, Mijeski and Stark 2008; Roth 2008). For example, it has been found that people with dark skin are no more likely to perceive racism in society and are no less likely to hold anti-black stereotypes compared to whites (Twine 1998; Sue n.d.). These findings directly contradict the group-position and interest-based perspective. Therefore, not only does research from Latin America force us to re-think the US-based assumption that racial attitudes are derived from membership in a specific tier, it also highlights the problem inherent in the way scholars are testing the LAT. In essence, a US-based understanding of racial attitudes is being used to test a theory about Latin Americanization. If we were to use a Latin-American-based understanding of race, we would not anticipate one's structural standing to be an indicator of one's racial attitudes.

Horizontal versus vertical relations

Bonilla-Silva uses socioeconomic outcomes and social interaction indicators to test the LAT. However, in doing so, he conceptually separates these two dimensions of race relations, overlooking their fundamental connection in much of Latin America. Tying these two dimensions together, Telles (2004) has argued that the paradox of Brazilian race relations is that high levels of sociability coexist with high levels of socioeconomic inequality. In other words, racial inclusion coexists with racial exclusion. However, this paradox is not represented in the way the LAT is being tested. For example, Bonilla-Silva (2004) uses the finding that dark-skinned Latinos exhibit 'blacklike' residential segregation patterns as evidence that this group is becoming part of the 'collective black' category. However, if the US is Latin Americanizing (or maybe just Brazilianizing) we would expect dark-skinned Latinos to be more segregated than light-skinned Latinos although segregation rates would not be 'blacklike'. Instead, segregation rates would be decreasing for all groups, demonstrating more inclusive relations on the horizontal dimension. Therefore, in testing the LAT, we should not be measuring horizontal sociability on the same scale as vertical inequality. If the US is Latin Americanizing, we would expect to see high levels of social interaction coexisting with high levels of inequality. Our focus should not only be on the structure of the hierarchy but also the degree and strength of particular racial boundaries (Bailey 2002).

Conclusion

This article should not be read as an attempt to undermine the entire LAT. We desperately need scholars, such as Bonilla-Silva, to bring forth bold proposals which encourage discussions about the future of race relations. More specifically, the LAT has helped move the discussion of race beyond the painfully outdated black/white model. As Alejandro Portes reminds us: 'All theory worthy of the name requires simplification and abstraction' (1997, p. 803). Nevertheless, we still need to construct our theoretical models with care. In this vein, I have attempted to contribute to the conversation initiated by Bonilla-Silva first and foremost by helping to define the 'Latin American system of race' and then by questioning whether or not this is a productive unit of analysis. Furthermore, this article is intended to prompt reflection on what is needed for systems of race to fall within the same ideal-type model.

There have been different generations of scholarship on race in Latin America. The literature that came out in the first half of the twentieth century continues to dominate general understandings of race in the region, despite recent scholarship which is at odds with previous conclusions. The field is currently undergoing a major transition – a reflection of significant changes occurring in Latin America. For example, in Brazil, racism is increasing recognized both at the popular and government level, a change which manifested in the implementation of affirmative action policies (Bailey 2002, 2004; Telles 2004; Dzidzienyo 2005). Moreover, there is pressure from Brazilian black movement organizations to collapse the brown and black categories on the census, which would move Brazil towards a bi-polar model (Telles 2004; Bailey 2008).

Throughout Latin America, there has been an increase in race-based social movements which has drawn attention to racial inequality in the region. The heightened awareness of racism has led to the creation of public institutions and policies aimed at combating racial discrimination and to constitutional changes aimed at protecting indigenous rights (Stavenhagen 1996; Telles 2004; Oboler and Dzidzienyo 2005; Golash-Boza 2008). Furthermore, countries such as Ecuador, Honduras, Nicaragua, Colombia, Peru, Argentina and Uruguay, which have not traditionally collected data on race, are beginning to do so, demonstrating a weakening of the race-blind ideology (Telles 2007). Finally, there has been a rise of leftist leaders in countries such as Venezuela, Brazil, Bolivia, Chile, Argentina and Nicaragua who are either self-proclaimed members of the indigenous or African-origin populations (e.g. Eva Morales in Bolivia) or who are making race a salient topic in their administrations (e.g. Lula in Brazil). Given these monumental shifts, there is an increasing need to treat Latin America with historical specificity and to recognize that the 'Latin American' model is not a single, ahistorical model that can easily be applied to the US context.

Taking these issues into consideration, one suggestion I would make for revising the LAT would be to choose a specific national model (e.g. Brazil) and to specify a time period (e.g. the first half of the twentieth century) which the model represents. Of course, a theoretical discussion about the 'early twentieth-century Brazilianization' of the US is certainly not as catchy as a discussion about the 'Latin Americanization' of the US, but this specificity would create a much more solid empirical and conceptual foundation, thus avoiding some of the pitfalls outlined in this article. A second suggestion for a revision of the LAT would be to place more weight on the importance of mechanisms and their relationship to outcomes. Doing so would present a more nuanced and less static conception of race relations in both regions and would, in the end, provide a more insightful comparison.

Acknowledgements

I thank Eddie Telles, Stan Bailey, Tanya Golash-Boza, Jason Boardman, Liam Downey and Jonathan Warren for their comments on earlier drafts of this paper.

Notes

1. See *Race and Society*, vol. 5.
2. Bonilla-Silva refers to 'Latin American and Caribbean nations'. When I refer to Latin America, I am including the Spanish-speaking Caribbean in this category.
3. Bonilla-Silva refers to the importance of phenotype and not just skin colour alone. My discussion will focus on colour since this is the aspect of phenotype represented in most data.

4. In a separate publication, Bonilla-Silva and Glover (2004) argue that elites were white by Latin American standards, an important clarification. However, they also claim that Latin Americans perceive most of their politicians as white, an assumption which has not been verified empirically. In my research on Mexico, I found that many Mexicans do not identify former President Vicente Fox (who is fairly phenotypically representative of the Latin American elite) as white.
5. Even in countries where elites were predominantly considered white, many *mestizos*, mulattoes and blacks were represented in politics and in academia (Helg 1990).
6. I argue that a more appropriate term is 'race-blindness' since, in Mexico, there is a clear distinction between 'race' and 'colour', with the national ideology most strongly referencing the former. Furthermore, there is a societal taboo surrounding the term 'race', which does not exist with the term 'colour'.
7. The southern cone has been described as Euro-Latin America (Mörner 1967).
8. This is probably the reason that many race scholars choose specific countries, as opposed to broad regions, when using comparative frameworks.

References

BAILEY, STANLEY 2002 'The race construct and public opinion: understanding Brazilian beliefs about racial inequality and their determinants', *American Journal of Sociology*, vol. 108, no. 2, pp. 406–39
—— 2004 'Group dominance and the myth of racial democracy: antiracism attitudes in Brazil', *American Sociological Review*, vol. 69, pp. 728–47
—— 2008 'Unmixing for race mixing in Brazil', *American Journal of Sociology*, vol. 114, no. 3, pp. 577–614
BECK, SCOTT, MIJESKI, KENNETH and STARK, MEAGAN 2008 'Awareness of racism among self-identified negros and mulatos in Ecuador', paper given at the First Conference on Ethnicity, Race, and Indigenous Peoples in Latin America and the Caribbean. San Diego, CA.
BLUMER, HERBERT 1958 'Race prejudice as a sense of group position', *The Pacific Sociological Review*, vol. 1, no. 1, pp. 3–7
BOBO, LAWRENCE and HUTCHINGS, VINCENT 1996 'Perceptions of racial group competition: extending Blumer's theory of group position to a multiracial social context', *American Sociological Review*, vol. 61, pp. 951–72
BOBO, LAWRENCE and KLUEGEL, JAMES 1993 'Opposition to race-targetting: self-interest, stratification ideology, or racial attitudes?', *American Sociological Review*, vol. 58, no. 4, pp. 443–464
BONILLA-SILVA, EDUARDO 2002a 'We are all Americans! The Latin Americanization of racial stratification in the USA', *Race & Society*, vol. 5, pp. 3–16
—— 2002b '*Where is the love?* A rejoinder by Bonilla-Silva on the Latin Americanization thesis', *Race & Society*, vol. 5, pp. 104–14
—— 2004 'From bi-racial to tri-racial: towards a new system of racial stratification in the USA', *Ethnic and Racial Studies*, vol. 27, no. 6, pp. 931–50
BONILLA-SILVA, EDUARDO and GLOVER, KAREN 2004 '"We are all Americans": The Latin Americanization of race relations in the United States', in Maria Krysan and Lewis Amanda (eds), *The Changing Terrain of Race and Ethnicity*, New York: Russell Sage Foundation, pp. 149–83
DAVIS, JAMES 1991 *Who is Black? One Nation's Definition*, University Park, PA: Pennsylvania State University Press
DEGLER, CARL 1971 *Neither Black nor White: Slavery and Race Relations in Brazil and the United States*, New York: Macmillan
DE LA CADENA, MARISOL 2000 *Indigenous Mestizos: The Politics of Race and Culture in Cuzco, Peru, 1919–1991*, Durham, NC: Duke University Press

DUANY, JORGE 1998 'Reconstructing racial identity: ethnicity, color, and class among Dominicans in the United States and Puerto Rico', *Latin American Perspectives*, vol. 25, no. 3, pp. 1–14

DZIDZIENYO, ARIEL 2005 'A region in denial: racial discrimination and racism in Latin America', in Ariel Dzidzienyo and Suzanne Oboler (eds), *Neither Enemies nor Friends: Latinos, Blacks, Afro-Latinos*, New York: Palgrave Macmillan, pp. 39–60

FITZGERALD, DAVID and COOK-MARTÍN, David 2008 'Race, immigration, and citizenship in the Americas', paper given at the Americas Plural: Regional and Comparative Perspectives conference, University of London, Institute for the Study of the Americas, 19–20 June 2008

GANS, HERBERT 1999 'The possibility of a new racial hierarchy in the twenty-first-century United States', in Michele Lamont (ed.), *The Cultural Territories of Race: Black and White Boundaries*, Chicago, IL: University of Chicago Press, pp. 371–90

GOLASH-BOZA, TANYAA 2008 '"My grandmother is black, so I am not a racist": racial discourses in a multicultural era in Lima, Peru', paper given at the First Conference on Ethnicity, Race, and Indigenous Peoples in Latin America and the Caribbean, San Diego, CA.

—— n.d. 'Negro, Moreno, Zambo: the use of racial labels in Peru', unpublished manuscript

GULLICKSON, AARON 2005 'The significance of skin color declines: a re-analysis of skin tone differentials in post civil rights America', *Social Forces*, vol. 84, no. 1, pp. 157–80

HARRIS, MARVIN 1964 *Patterns of Race in the Americas*, New York: Walker

HELG, ALINE 1990 Race in Argentina and Cuba, 1880–1930: theory, policies, and popular reaction, in Richard Graham (ed.), *The Idea of Race in Latin America, 1870–1940*, Austin, TX: University of Texas Press, pp. 37–69

HUGHES, MICHAEL and HERTEL, BRADLEY 1990 'The significance of color remains: a study of life chances, mate selection, and ethnic consciousness among black Americans', *Social Forces*, vol. 68, no. 4, pp. 1105–20

ISHIDA, KANAKO 2003 'Racial intermarriage between Indígenas and Ladinos in Guatemala', Master's thesis, Department of Sociology, UCLA, Los Angeles, CA

KEITH, VERNA and HERRING, CEDRIC 1991 'Skin tone and stratification in the black community', *American Journal of Sociology*, vol. 97, no. 3, pp. 760–78

KNIGHT, ALAN 1990 'Racism, revolution, and indigenismo: Mexico, 1910–1940, in Richard Graham (ed.), *The Idea of Race in Latin America 1840–1940'*, Austin, TX: University of Texas Press, pp. 71–113

LEE, JENNIFER and BEAN, FRANK 2004 'America's changing color lines: immigration, race/ethnicity, and multiracial identification', *Annual Review of Sociology*, vol. 30, pp. 221–42

LESSER, JEFFREY 1999 *Negotiating National Identity: Immigrants, Minorities, and the Struggle for Ethnicity in Brazil*, Durham, NC: Duke University Press

LOVELL, PEGGY 1989 *'Income and racial inequality in Brazil'*, PhD dissertation, Department of Sociology, University of Florida, Gainesville, FL

MARX, ANTHONY 1998 *Making Race and Nation: A Comparison of the United States, South Africa, and Brazil*, Cambridge: Cambridge University Press

MÖRNER, MAGNUS 1967 *Race Mixture in the History of Latin America*, Boston, MA: Little, Brown

—— 1970 *Race and Class in Latin America*, New York: Columbia University Press

OBOLER, SUZANNE and DZIDZIENYO, ARIEL 2005 'Flows and counterflows: Latinas/os, blackness and racialization in hemispheric perspective', in Ariel Dzidzienyo and Suzanne Oboler (eds), *Neither Enemies nor Friends: Latinos, Blacks and Afro-Latinos*, New York: Palgrave Macmillan, pp. 3–35

PORTES, ALEJANDRO 1997 'Immigration theory for a new century: some problems and opportunities', *International Migration Review*, vol. 31, no. 4, pp. 799–825

ROTH, WENDY 2008 *'"There is no racism here": Dominicans' and Puerto Ricans' perceptions of racial discrimination'*, paper given at the First Conference on Ethnicity, Race, and indigenous Peoples in Latin America and the Caribbean, San Diego, CA

SAWYER, MARK 2006 *Racial Politics in Post-Revolutionary Cuba*, Cambridge: Cambridge University Press
SCHWARTZMAN, LUISA 2007 'Does money whiten? Intergenerational changes in racial classifications in Brazil', *American Sociological Review*, vol. 72, no. 6, pp. 940–63
SHERIFF, ROBIN 2001 *Dreaming Equality: Color, Race and Racism in Urban Brazil*, New Brunswick, NJ: Rutgers University Press
SILVA, NELSON DO VALLE 1985 'Updating the cost of not being white in Brazil', in Pierre-Michel Fontaine (ed.), *Race, Class, and Power in Brazil*, Los Angeles, CA: UCLA Center for Afro-American Studies, pp. 42–55
SKIDMORE, THOMAS 1993 'Bi-racial U.S.A. vs. multi-racial Brazil: is the contrast still valid?', *Journal of Latin American Studies*, vol. 25, no. 2, pp. 373–86
STAVENHAGEN, RODOLFO 1996 'Indigenous rights: some conceptual problems', in Elizabeth Jelin and Eric Hershberg (eds), *Constructing Democracy: Human Rights, Citizenship and, Society in Latin America*, Boulder, CO: Westview Press, pp. 141–59
STEPAN, NANCY 1991 *The Hour of Eugenics: Race, Gender and Nation in Latin America*, Ithaca, NY: Cornell University Press
SUE, CHRISTINA 2009 'The dynamics of color: *mestizaje*, racism, and blackness in Veracruz, Mexico', in Evelyn Nakano-Glenn (ed.), *Shades of Difference: Transnational Perspectives on How and Why Skin Color Matters*, Palo Alto, CA: Stanford University Press, pp. 114–28
—— n.d. 'Racial common sense: the social reproduction of national ideology in Mexico', unpublished manuscript
TELLES, EDWARD 2004 *Race in Another America: The Significance of Skin Color in Brazil*, Princeton, NJ: Princeton University Press
—— 2007 'Race and ethnicity and Latin America's United Nations millennium development goals',*Latin American and Caribbean Ethnic Studies*, vol. 2, no. 2, pp. 185–200
TELLES, EDWARD and LIM, NELSON 1998 'Does it matter who answers the race question? Racial classification and income inequality in Brazil', *Demography*, vol. 35, no. 4, pp. 465–74
TELLES, EDWARD and ORTIZ, VILMA 2008 *Generations of Exclusion: Mexican Americans, Assimilation, and Race*, New York: Russell Sage Foundation
TWINE, FRANCE 1998 *Racism in a Racial Democracy: The Maintenance of White Supremacy in Brazil*, New Brunswick, NJ: Rutgers University Press
WARREN, JONATHAN and SUE, CHRISTINA n.d. 'What the south can teach the north about antiracism', unpublished manuscript
WARREN, JONATHAN and TWINE, FRANCE 1997 'White Americans, the new minority? Non-blacks and the ever-expanding boundaries of whiteness', *Journal of Black Studies*, vol. 28, no. 2, pp. 200–18
WEITZER, RONALD and TUCH, STEVEN 2004 'Race and perceptions of police misconduct', *Social Problems*, vol. 51, no. 3, pp. 305–25
WHITTEN JR., NORMAN 1974 *Black Frontiersmen: A South American Case*, New York: Wiley
YANCEY, GEORGE 2003 *Who Is White? Latinos, Asians, and the New Black/Nonblack Divide*, Boulder, CO: Lynne Rienner

Are the Americas 'sick with racism' or is it a problem at the poles? A reply to Christina A. Sue

Eduardo Bonilla-Silva

Abstract

Christina A. Sue commented on my 2004 article in *Ethnic and Racial Studies* on the Latin Americanization of racial stratification in the USA. Almost all her observations hinge on the assumption that racial stratification in Latin American countries is fundamentally structured around 'two racial poles'. I disagree with her and in my reply do three things. First, I address three major claims or issues in her comment. Second, I point out some methodological limitations of American-centred race analysis in Latin America. Third, I conclude by discussing briefly the Obama phenomenon and suggest this event fits in many ways my Latin Americanization thesis.

> The Americas are sick with racism, blind in both eyes from North to South.
>
> (Eduardo Galeano 2000, p. 56)

Since I unveiled my Latin Americanization thesis in 2001,[1] I have received plenty of critical feedback – some negative, but mostly positive. Accordingly, I welcome Christina Sue's comment. Although we see race matters in *both* Americas quite differently – I believe the Americas are 'sick with racism' and Sue seems to believe racism is a problem at the 'racial poles'[2] – our exchange may stimulate further debate about the racial question in Latin America and the USA.

In this rejoinder I do three things. First, I address some of Sue's criticisms. Second, I advance several methodological observations orthogonally related to Sue's comments. Third, I briefly tackle the big elephant in the contemporary American racial room (the election of a black man as president) and suggest it fits my Latin Americanization thesis.

Different perspectives on race in the Americas

Sue raises numerous points – some interesting, several unfounded. I respond to three here, mention others in endnotes (endnotes in this article are *very* important) and the methodology section, and leave the rest for another time and venue.

An ideal type of racial stratification in the Americas?

Sue contends that I classify all Latin American countries as having a 'tri-racial' order. Although in the *Ethnic and Racial Studies* article I described tri-racialism as one central racial stratification feature in the Americas, I also (a) included references to societies with more than three racial and ethnic groups, (b) stated in *all* long versions of this work that I was providing a *sketch* of racial formation in the Americas, (c) added the notion of 'plural' racial orders in many recent versions of this work (Bonilla-Silva 2006, p. 182) following – but not biblically – Smith (1965) and Kuper (1975), (d) referred to 'intermediate groups' (in plural) as inhabiting the middle racial strata[3] in these societies and (e) mentioned in *all* my public presentations and writings that racial stratification in the Americas (indeed, in the world) is complex and, thus, that I was not advancing an 'ideal type'.

This charge is also puzzling because, if true, I would be violating my own theorization about racial stratification. I proposed a structural interpretation that requires analysts to uncover the specific practices that reproduce white supremacy in racial orders (Bonilla-Silva 1997).[4] I urged scholars to engage in comparative work, examine the particularities of 'racial structures', and stated that my own theorization should *not* be seen as a 'universal theory explaining racial phenomena in societies' (Bonilla-Silva 2001, p. 47).

Whitening in the Americas

Sue self-identifies as a 'Latin Americanist' but her comments on 'whitening' prove the sociological adage that 'all self-reports are full of measurement error'. For instance, despite Sue's commentary, few analysts dispute that most nations in Latin America attempted whitening projects in the nineteenth century (Scarano 1989; Stepan

1991; Andrews 2004), particularly after the 'unthinkable event', as Trouillot (1996) has called the Haitian revolution, raised the spectrum of race rebellions against white and *criollo* (creole) rule (Greggus 2003). Few also dispute that, for various reasons,[5] not many countries (Argentina, Chile, Uruguay and perhaps Costa Rica) succeeded in this effort leaving the racial demographic 'problem' in place. This is why I argued that the 'solution' to the problem of maintaining white rule in majority non-white polities was establishing multiracial orders where phenotypical and non-phenotypical elements (see below) were given social weight to foster racial distinctions among the masses.[6]

But whitening was not just a population policy. Whitening was also an ideological practice (Pêcheux 1994) that touched almost every aspect of these societies (Skidmore 1990; Twine 1997; Torres 1998). Spanish elites, and later *criollos*, maintained their race-class power through complex hierarchical racial orders bonded by the *logic* of white supremacy (Knight 1990; Gould 1998; Grandin 2000). For a theoretical discussion, see Mills 1997). Race-mixing with Africans and Indians transpired[7] yet white power remained; nation-states emerged in the nineteenth century (Castellanos-Guerrero 2005), but ideologies of *mestizaje* arose which subordinated everything deemed black or Indian (Stutzman 1981; Almeida-Vinueza 1999). And whitening still (partially) organizes social relations and interactions and affects Latin Americans quite intimately – many abuse their hair, skin and body to look or feel like *Blancanieves* (Snow White) (Godreau 2002).

Colourism, phenotype, and the construction of race

Sue postulates that I do not appreciate the salience of 'phenotype', suggests I have a colour-based view of racial stratification and claims I miss the significance of the 'two poles' she believes drive the racial question in the Americas (on this pole business, please see endnote 3 and the second and third points in the next section). However, I wrote: '"color" (in quotation marks because in addition to skin tone, phenotype, hair texture, eye color, culture and education, and class matter in the racial classification of individuals in Latin America)' (Bonilla-Silva 2006, p. 182). Furthermore, I classified Asian Indians and other relatively dark-skinned groups as 'honorary whites' which suggests I do not have a colour-deterministic stand. Lastly, to make my point abundantly clear, 'colourism'[8] is about the construction of racial categories based on notions of whiteness. Phenotypical elements are not the sole building blocks in 'racialization' processes (Omi and Winant 1994) as non-physical attributes such as education, culture, citizenship and language can enter the equation.[9]

Sue also displays a rather simplistic understanding of how 'race' works. For example, in discussing whitening, Sue writes 'when practices of whitening were promoted by importing European immigrants and encouraging race mixture, many elites in countries such as Brazil, Mexico, and Peru would not be considered white by North American or European standards' (2009), to which I say, *so what*? Since races are socially constructed, what matters is how they are constructed in different localities. Hence, a 'white' from Mexico not being regarded as such by USA standards does not deny the 'whiteness' of that person or how her 'race' affects her life chances in that locality.[10]

Lastly, Sue states that, since Jews, Arabs, Indians and Chinese experienced discrimination and even exclusion in the region, therefore, 'outside the continuum of the two racial poles, colour is not a strong predictor of classification and treatment' (2009). This is rubbish. Although these groups experienced (and some still do) discrimination, this is not the end of the story. All of them, as *groups*, were able to attain race-class mobility and (1) receive today higher levels of socioeconomic benefits and social estimation than blacks and native peoples and (2) are racially either in the middle 'racial space' (see footnote 4) or gained admission to the white or white-like elites (Bryan 1996; Hanoonmansingh 1996; Tsuda 2003).[11] The mobility these groups experienced was due to their particular 'racialization' in the Americas, a process that included 'colour', culture, phenotype, class and even strength of country of origin considerations.

Methodological and interpretative matters

Sue contends that one reason why analysts find 'tri-racial' orders is because of the way census data are gathered in the Americas. Sue is partially right. Many analysts have examined the role of the Census in 'race-making' and documented how it can produce artificial categories or miss others altogether (Nobles 2000; Kertzner and Arel 2001; Rodríguez 2009). Curiously, after making this point, Sue cites without any hesitation findings from Brazilian Census data (Telles 2004)[12] and from surveys on racial attitudes (Bailey 2002) to criticize me. To counter her arguments, I make a few *lanzamientos* (pitches) on methodology and race analysis in the Americas:

1. Collapsing categories (e.g. the 'pardo' and 'preto' categories in Brazil) because the socioeconomic gaps between groups are seemingly small is an ill-conceived sociological practice. Social life is not a statistical matter and, as social psychologists have amply demonstrated (Ridgeway *et al.* 1998), small differences can create significant social distance[13] between actors and lead to group formation. More significantly, census data may not reveal the true extent of inequality between these groups because many

'pretos' self-classify as 'pardos' (see Winant 1992; Harris *et al.* 1993; Wade 1997).
2. One must work analytically *and* politically not from 'what if' but from 'what is'. We must cease assuming people are 'black' or 'Indian' based on our experiential or statistical prejudices.[14] Hence, recognizing the extreme importance of the middle racial space is but the first step to develop an analytical strategy that appreciates how individuals navigate their lives and how others interact with them in Latin America (Hoetink 1967; Lancaster 2003). This appreciation may be the foundation for a fitting political strategy that will ultimately produce the desired unity among people of colour in the Americas.
3. Telles has suggested that racial stratification in Brazil works strongly vertically (e.g. income, education, etc.), but not equally horizontally (e.g. marriage, residential, etc.). I believe this interpretation is somewhat descriptive of Brazil and many Latin American countries, however, ultimately, (a) it is still the product of American-centred lenses, (b) lacks qualitative sensibility and (c) does not help explain *how* Brazil's – or other Latin American countries' – 'comparative mild' racial relations are deeply structured by racial hierarchy (Telles 2004, p. 223).[15] Residential segregation in Latin America has *always* been lower than in the USA due to the *different* racial rules and 'racial etiquette' of those orders. Thus, for example, in nineteenth-century Puerto Rico, *even during slavery*, free people of colour lived close to whites in San Juan (Kinsbrunner 1996) and Ponce (Quintero-Rivera 2003) – a fact that did not signify social equality or mild race relations, but a different way of structuring racial interactions (for a recent discussion on Brazil, see Lowy 2003). Similarly, the higher rate of 'interracial marriage' (again, calculated from census data which produces some serious distortions) in these countries must be tempered by the fact that many unions are still affected by the premise, stated or not, of *'mejorar la raza'* (improve the race) (Caulfield 2003; Quiñones-Rivera 2006).

I have much more to say, but will leave the rest for another occasion.[16]

Latin Americanization and Obamerica[17]

The American public has interpreted Barack Obama's election as president as all but the fulfilment of Martin Luther King's dream. In contrast, I have argued that his election is perhaps the last stage in the forty-year transition from Jim Crow to the 'new racism' (Bonilla-Silva 2001; for a full elaboration of my thesis, see Bonilla-Silva and Ray 2009). More significantly for this exchange, *Obamerica* may bring the nation closer to my Latin Americanization predictions. Let me explain.

First, Obama, like most politicians in the Americas, worked hard during the campaign at making a nationalist, post-racial appeal. Second, like some racially mixed leaders in the Americas, Obama was keen to signify the peculiar character of his 'blackness' (his half-white, half-black background) and the provenance of his blackness (his father hailed from Kenya and in the USA African blackness is perceived as less threatening). Obama has cultivated an outlook where his 'blackness' is more about style than political substance; Obama is the 'cool', exceptional black man not likely to rock the American racial boat. Third, Obama has exhibited an accommodationist stand on race (Street 2009). In a speech in Selma, Alabama, he stated the USA was '90% on the road to racial equality' (Obama 2007) and continued this path in his so-called 'race speech' (Obama 2008). Fourth, whites see Obama as a 'safe black' who, unlike traditional black politicians, will not advocate race-based social policy. Fifth, Obama will formulate 'universal' (class-based) policies that are unlikely to remedy racial inequality (Obama 2004). Sixth, his election, in conjunction with other developments in the last decades, evinces the ascendance to political power (with a small 'p') of 'neo-mulattos' (Horton and Sykes 2004), will exacerbate the existing colour-class divide within the black community, and reinforce 'multiculturalist white supremacy' (Rodríguez 2008).

Obama's blackness is becoming whites' new weapon of choice for singing their colour-blind lullaby. As I write these last lines, the space for talking about race in the USA is shrinking by the minute and making the USA feel much like a Latin American country. Therefore, I can still paraphrase George Orwell and conclude, with a minor amendment, that in *Obamerica* 'some will still be more equal than others' (Bonilla-Silva and Glover 2004, p. 172).

Acknowledgements

I want to thank Elizabeth Hordge Freeman and Victor S. Ray, two outstanding graduate students in sociology at Duke with expertise on racial matters in Brazil and the USA respectively, for their able assistance on this article. I also want to thank Professors Tyrone A. Forman and Amanda E. Lewis, from Emory, and Professor David G. Embrick, from Loyola University in Chicago, for helpful editorial comments. Needless to say, I am responsible for the entire content of this article.

Notes

1. The *ERS* article (Bonilla-Silva 2004) emanated out of a presentation I gave at a national conference on race at the University of Illinois-Chicago in 2001 (Bonilla-Silva and Glover 2004). Since then, versions of the work have appeared in multiple outlets. This is an important detail to point out as the *ERS* article was an abridged version of the original paper with data from the 1990 Census (more recent versions include 2000 Census data) and did not include the full sketch of racial stratification features of Latin American and Caribbean societies (but see Bonilla-Silva and Glover 2004; Bonilla-Silva 2006).
2. Sue's observations suggest she holds a binary view of race matters in Latin America and, perhaps, even in the USA. She ponders the significance of 'primary' and 'secondary' racial contradictions and the distance between the boundaries of racial groups. Her questions and observations indicate she believes that racial orders (1) have two primary races, (2) one main racial contradiction and (3) those I claim are in the middle strata have at best a derivative standing. Her view is akin to the vulgar Marxist view that simplifies the class structure of modern capitalist societies and regards it as comprised of two main classes. But the history of racial (and class) formations shows that most evolved from their earlier simple forms into complex orders, an evolution that increased their sociopolitical resiliency.
3. In the original piece I used the term 'strata' to refer to the emerging groups in the USA as well as to the 'races' in Latin American societies. That choice, I assumed, would denote the 'in itself', rather than 'for itself', state of racial groups in these societies. But in recent presentations on this work and in work in progress I have replaced this term altogether with the notion of 'racial space' and included a more explicit discussion of how racial groups in contemporary Latin American and Caribbean societies seldom cohere as *groups* and of how the space they share has cracks that allow for upward as well as downward individual mobility. On the malleability of 'races' in the Americas that I am trying to describe with the notion of 'racial space', see Mintz (1984, pp. 318–24).
4. I make a point here for those interested in the history of ideas in sociology. Sue accuses me of having a Brazilian-inspired race analysis. She is wrong. Anyone who knows me and my work knows that *all* of it, from my first publication in *ASR* to my most recent work on racial grammar (Bonilla-Silva 2008), is *fundamentally* connected to my experiences in my native Puerto Rico. In the final version of her piece, Sue added that my analysis could be labeled the '"the Brazilianization or Puerto Ricanization" of the USA' (2009). I may plead guilty to *this* charge so long as Sue and my other American critics admit they are limited by their social, racial and scholarly training in the 'belly of the beast,' too.
5. In many Caribbean nations, the whites that came in this period brought slaves and thus whitening failed. But overall, the strategy failed in the region because most 'countries lacked the conditions to attract European laborers and their families' (Andrews 2004, p. 153).
6. This forced a racial 'challenge' to the European and American eugenic view as white supremacists in the Americas had to reverse the traditional arguments and claimed that 'constructive miscegenation' (racial mixing) would ultimately eliminate the 'lower races' in a few generations. That is, instead of claiming more whites were needed to replace non-whites, Latin American leaders claimed that *mestizaje* would ultimately produce the desired whitening of the population. See Stepan (1991).
7. I want to be careful here as 'Indians within Latin America can be located within a continuum from isolated, uncontacted Indian populations to full-fledged ethnic groups, on a par with other recognized ethnic groups within the nation-state' (Urban and Sherzer 1991, p. 5).
8. It is unfortunate that the centrality of the logic of white supremacy in organizing racial evaluations in the Americas was coded conceptually as 'colourism' or 'pigmentocracy'. Either term is based on skin tone rather than on the extensive elements involved in the racial construction at play in Latin America and, for that matter, in the world. And both terms have led far too many analysts, including Sue, to believe that so-called colour-based distinctions are not as deep as the main one between the poles in societies.

9. This explains why, for instance, presumably racially homogeneous countries such as Japan (Weiner 1997) or Haiti (Trouillot 1995) have racially based divisions. It also explains why people who were phenotypically 'white' were regarded as non-white or 'not-yet-white' in the early part of the twentieth century in the USA (Roediger 1991).

10. Some Latin Americans who are classed as 'white' in their countries of origin are 'shocked' when they come to the USA and are not regarded as such. But I would be remiss if I did not point out that some white Latin Americans were able to have their whiteness ticket validated in the USA parking lot in the nineteenth century (Montejano 1987; Almaguer 1994) and that a larger number achieved a status that Laura Gómez characterizes as 'contingent whiteness' (2009).

11. Too many authors (including the ones I cite), after demonstrating the advantageous socioeconomic and racial standing of these groups, explain their success as the product of their 'ethnicity' or 'culture'. For a critique of this type of explanation, see Steinberg (1989).

12. For the record, I disclose that Professor Telles is my friend and, in many ways, one of my role models. And, despite some of my disagreements with his take on race matters in Latin America (and I have pointed some out to him in conversations and exchanges), his work on race matters in Brazil and the USA is invaluable. Thus, I hope readers appreciate that my engagement emanates from the beauty and genuineness of Nietzsche's dictum: 'Digressions, objections, delight in mockery, carefree mistrust are signs of health; everything unconditional belongs in pathology' (1966, p. 90).

13. Harry Hoetink alluded to this problem in his magnum opus *Caribbean Race Relations: A Study of Two Variants* (1967, esp. pp. 34–5).

14. I learned this lesson in Saint Lucia in the 1990s. I spoke there with a 'black' woman about the importance of Pan-African unity. She looked at me in disbelief and told me, 'I am not black and neither are you', and proceeded to denigrate 'Africans' in her country. 'So, what are you?' I asked her, and she told me, 'I am a "Dougla" (mixture of Indians and Africans).' I gave her some business about how confused she was. *But I was wrong.* I should have inquired about Douglas to assess whether her claim was an identity one or had any social validity as a status marker of a 'real' racial group. For a discussion on the Douglas, see Reddock (2001).

15. Let me explain this by analogy. The index of residential similarity in the southern part of the USA is about ten points lower than in the North. Does this suggest that horizontal racial relations are better in the South than in the North? No, this is indicative of a regional racial order that historically has been more rigid and, therefore, has not necessitated the same level of residential exclusion as the North (Massey and Denton 1993).

16. I feel compelled to make one more point. Researchers must be extremely cautious when using indices derived from the USA experience for assessing race matters in Latin America. An example of why these tools cannot be applied in straightforward fashion is the work of Bailey (2002). His finding that white Brazilians appreciate the significance of discrimination more than blacks is nonsensical. Why would those at the top of *any* social structure be more cognizant of their advantages and of the way in which they are produced and maintained than those at the bottom? And how does he square his finding with white Brazilians' current (and growing) opposition to affirmative action (Htun 2004; Santos 2006)? When a finding does not fit, you must acquit, that is, the analyst must dig deeper to make sense of things. Interestingly, and apparently without being aware of it, Bailey (2008) may have solved the 'puzzle' in this most recent work. Now he specifies that white Brazilians agree to affirmative action *only* for very dark-skinned blacks who are about 6 per cent of the population. Hence their 'support' for affirmative action – and, by extension, their appreciation for the significance of discrimination in Brazil – is quite limited as it excludes *most* of the Afro-Brazilian population. Worse yet, since dark-skinned blacks tend to be extremely poor and undereducated, they are less likely to be in a position to take advantage of affirmative action. (For the limitations of using surveys on racial attitudes in the Americas, see Wade (1997) and Mitchell (2003). For a critique of the survey strategy for understanding whites' racial views in post-civil rights USA, see Bonilla-Silva (2006)).

17. I have used this term in my writings on the Obama phenomenon to capture the fact that Obama was elected president without the backing of a social movement, a fact that limits the possibilities for meaningful change during his presidency.

References

ALMAGUER, TOMAS 1994 *Racial Fault Lines: The Historical Origins of White Supremacy in California*, Berkeley, CA: University of California Press

ALMEIDA-VINUEZA, JOSE 1999 'Racismo, construción nacional y mestizaje', in Jose Almedia-Vinueza (ed.), *El Racismo en Las Américas e el Caribe*, Quito: Ediciones Abya-Yala, pp. 189–217

ANDREWS, GEORGE. R. 2004 *Afro-Latin America, 1800–2000*, New York: Oxford University Press

BAILEY, STANLEY 2002 'The race construct and public opinion: understanding Brazilian beliefs about racial inequality and their determinants', *American Journal of Sociology*, vol. 108, no. 2, pp. 406–39

—— 2008 'Unmixing for race making in Brazil', *American Journal of Sociology*, vol. 114, no. 3, pp. 577–614

BONILLA-SILVA, EDUARDO 1997 'Rethinking racism: toward a structural interpretation', *American Sociological Review*, vol. 62, no. 3, pp. 465–80

—— 2001 *White Supremacy and Racism in the Post-Civil Rights Era*, Boulder, CO: Lynne Rienner Publishers.

—— 2004 'From bi-racial to tri-racial: towards a new system of racial stratification in the USA', *Ethnic and Racial Studies*, vol. 27, no. 6, pp. 931–50

—— 2006 *Racism without Racists: Color-Blind Racism and the Persistence of Racial Inequality in the USA*, 2nd edn, Lanham, MD: Rowman & Littlefield

—— 2008 'The invisible weight of whiteness: the racial grammar of everyday life in contemporary America', Lewis A. Coser talk, American Sociological Association Meeting, Boston, MA, August

BONILLA-SILVA, EDUARDO and GLOVER, KAREN 2004 'We are all Americans! The Latin Americanization of race relations in the USA', in Amanda E. Lewis and Maria Krysan (eds), *The Changing Terrain of Race and Ethnicity: Theory, Methods, and Public Policy*, New York: Russell Sage Foundation, pp. 149–83

BONILLA-SILVA, E. and RAY, V. 2009 'When whites love a black leader: race matters in Obamerica', *Journal of African American Studies Online*, vol. 1, no. 1, www.springerlink.com/content.112866/?Content+Status=Accepted

BRYAN, PATRICK 1996 'The creolization of the Chinese community in Jamaica', in Rhoda E. Reddock (ed.), *Ethnic Minorities in Caribbean Society*, St. Augustine, Trinidad and Tobago: Institute of Social and Economic Research, pp. 173–272

CASTELLANOS-GUERRERO, ALICIA 2005 'Para hacer nación: discursos racistas en el México decimonónico', in Jose Izquierdo and Guy Rozat Dupeyron (eds), *Los Caminos del Racismo en México*, México, D.F. [Puebla]: Plaza y Valdés; Benemérita Universidad Autónoma de Puebla, Instituto de Ciencias Sociales y Humanidades, pp. 117–45

CAULFIELD, SUSAN 2003 'Interracial courtship in the Rio de Janeiro courts, 1918–1940', in Nancy Appelbaum, Anne Macpherson and Karin A. Rosemblatt (eds), *Race and Nation in Modern Latin America*, Chapel Hill, NC: University of North Carolina Press, pp. 163–86

GALEANO, EDUARDO 2000 *Upside down: A Primer for the Looking-Glass World*, New York: Picador

GODREAU, ISAR P. 2002 'Peinando diferencias, bregas de diferencia: el alisado y el llamado "pelo malo"', *Caribbean Studies*, vol. 30, no. 1, pp. 82–132

GÓMEZ, LAURA E. 2009 'Opposite one-drop rules: Mexican-Americans, African-Americans, and the need to reconceive turn-of-the-century race relations', in José Cobas,

Jorge Duany and Joe R. Feagin (eds), *How the United States Racializes Latinos*, Boulder, CO: Paradigm, pp. 87–100

GOULD, JEFFREY, L 1998 *To Die This Way: Nicaraguan Indians and the Myth of Mesti Zaje, 1880–1965*, Durham and London: Duke University Press.

GRANDIN, GREG 2000 *The Blood of Guatemala: A History of Race and Nation*, Durham, NC: Duke University Press

GREGGUS, DAVID 2003 'The influence of the Haitian revolution on blacks in America and the Caribbean', in Nancy Priscilla Naro (ed.), *Blacks, Coloureds and National Identity in Nineteenth-Century Latin America*, London: Institute of Latin American Studies, University of London, pp. 38–59

HANOOMANSINGH, PETER 1996 'Beyond profit and capital: a study of the Sindhis and Gujaratis of Barbados', in Rhoda E. Reddock (ed.), *Ethnic Minorities in Caribbean Society*, St. Augustine, Trinidad and Tobago: Institute of Social and Economic Research, pp. 173–272

HARRIS, MARVIN, CONSORTE, JOSILDEM G., LANG, JOSEPH and BRYNE, BRYAN 1993 'Who are the whites? Imposed census categories and the racial demography of Brazil', *Social Forces*, vol. 72, pp. 451–62

HOETINK, HARRY 1967 *Caribbean Race Relations: A Study of Two Variants*, London: Oxford University Press for the Institute of Race Relations

HORTON, HAYWARD DERRICK and SYKES, LORI 2004 'Toward a critical demography of Neo-mulattos: structural change and diversity within the black population', in Cedric Herring, Verna Keith and Hayward Derrick Horton (eds.), *Skin Deep: How Race and Complexion Matter in the "Colour-Blind" Era*, Chicago: University of Illinois Press, pp. 159–173

HTUN, MALA 2004 'From "racial democracy" to affirmative action: changing state policy on race in Brazil', *Latin American Research Review*, vol. 39, no. 1, pp. 60–89

KERTZNER, DAVID and AREL, DOMINIQUE 2001 'Censuses, identity formation, and the struggle for political power', in David Kertzner and Dominique Arel (eds), *Census and Identity: The Politics of Race, Ethnicity, and Language in National Censuses*, Cambridge: Cambridge University Press, pp. 1–42

KINSBRUNNER, JAY 1996 *Not of Pure Blood: The Free People of Color and Racial Prejudice in Nineteenth-Century Puerto Rico*, Durham, NC: Duke University Press

KNIGHT, FRANKLIN W. 1990 *The Caribbean, the Genesis of a Fragmented Nationalism*, 2nd edn, New York: Oxford University Press

KUPER, LEO 1975 *Race, Class, and Power: Ideology and Revolutionary Change in Plural Societies*, Chicago: Aldine

LANCASTER, ROGER N. 2003 'Skin color, race, and racism in Nicaragua', in John Stone and Rutledge Dennis (eds), *Race and Ethnicity: Comparative and Theoretical Perspectives*, Malden, MA: Blackwell, pp. 99–113

LOWY, MICHAEL 2003 'Brazil: a country marked by social apartheid', *Logos: A Journal of Modern Society and Culture*, vol. 2, no. 2

MASSEY, DOUGLAS and DENTON, NANCY 1993 *American Apartheid: Segregation and the Making of the Underclass*, Cambridge, MA: Harvard University Press

MILLS, CHARLES W. 1997 *The Racial Contract*, Ithaca, NY: Cornell University Press

MINTZ, SYDNEY W. 1984 *Caribbean Transformations*, Baltimore, MD: Johns Hopkins University Press

MITCHELL, MICHAEL 2003 'Changing racial attitudes in Brazil: retrospective and prospective views', in Georgia A. Persons (ed.), *Race and Democracy in the Americas*, New York: Transaction Publishers, pp. 35–52

MONTEJANO, DAVID 1997 *Anglos and Mexicans in the Making of Texas, 1836–1986*, Austin, TX: University of Texas Press

NIETZSCHE, FRIEDRICH 1966 *Beyond Good and Evil: Prelude to a Philosophy of the Future*, New York: Vintage

NOBLES, MELISSA 2000 *Shades of Citizenship: Race and the Census in Modern Politics*, Stanford, CA: Stanford University Press

OBAMA, BARACK 2004 *The Audacity of Hope: Thoughts on Reclaiming the American Dream*, New York: Crown Publishers
—— 2007 'Selma voting rights commemoration', speech at Brown University Chapel, Selma, AL, 4 March.
—— 2008 'A more perfect union', speech in Philadelphia, 18 March.
OMI, MICHAEL. and WINANT, HOWARD 1994 *Racial Formation in the United States: From the 1960s to the 1990s*, New York: Routledge
PÊCHEUX, MICHEL 1994 'The mechanism of ideological (mis)recognition', in Slavoj Zizek (ed.), *Mapping Ideology*, London: Verso, pp. 141–51
QUIÑONES-RIVERA, MARITZA 2006 'From Trigueñita to Afro-Puerto Rican: intersections of the racialized, gendered, and sexualized body in Puerto Rico and the U.S. Mainland', *Meridians*, vol. 7, no. 1, pp. 162–82
QUINTERO-RIVERA, ANGEL G. 2003 *Ponce: La Capital Alterna*, Ponce, Puerto Rico: Centro de Investigaciones Sociales
REDDOCK, RHODA 2001 'Douglarisation and the politics of gender relations in Trinidad and Tobago', in Christina Barrow and Rhoda Reddeck (eds), *Caribbean Sociology: Introductory Reading*, Princeton, NJ: Markus Weiner, pp. 320–33
RIDGEWAY, CECILIA L., BOYLE, ELIZABETH H., KUIPERS, KATHY J. and ROBINSON, DAWN T. 1998 'How do status beliefs develop? The role of resources and interactional experience', *American Sociological Review*, vol. 63, no. 3, pp. 331–50
RODRÍGUEZ, CLARA E. 2009 'Counting Latinos in the U.S. Census', in José Cabas, Jorge Dunay and Joe R. Feagin (eds), *How the United States Racializes Latinos*, Boulder, CO: Paradigm, pp. 37–53
RODRÍGUEZ, DYLAN 2008 'Inaugurating multiculturalist white supremacy', *ILLVOX: Blog of Anarchist People of Color*, 14 November
ROEDIGER, DAVID R. 1991 *The Wages of Whiteness: Race and the Making of the American Working Class*, London: Verso
SANTOS, SALES AUGUSTO DOS 2006 'Who is black in Brazil? A timely or a false question in Brazilian race relations in the era of affirmative action', *Latin American Perspectives*, vol. 33, no. 4, pp. 30–8
SCARANO, FRANCISCO 1989 *Inmigración y Clases Sociales en el Puerto Rico del Siglo XIX*, Río Piedras: Editorial Huracán
SKIDMORE, THOMAS 1990 Racial ideas and social policy in Brazil, 1870–1940, in Richard Graham (ed.), *The Idea of Race in Latin America*, Austin, TX: University of Texas Press, pp. 7–36
SMITH, MICHAEL G. 1965 *Stratification in Grenada*, Berkeley, CA: University of California Press
STEINBERG, STEPHEN 2001 *The Ethnic Myth*, 3rd edn, Boston, MA: Beacon Press
STEPAN, NANCY L. 1991 *The Hour of Eugenics: Race, Gender, and Nation in Latin America*, Ithaca, NY: Cornell University Press
STREET, PAUL L. 2009 *Barack Obama and the Future of American Politics*, Boulder, CO: Paradigm
STUTZMAN, RONALD 1981 'El mestizaje: an all-inclusive ideology of exclusion', in Norma E. Whitten (ed.), *Cultural Transformations and Ethnicity in Modern Ecuador*, Urbana, IL: University of Illinois Press, pp. 45–94
SUE, CHRISTINA 2009 'An assessment of the Latin Americanization thesis', *Ethnic and Racial Studies*, DOI: 10.1080/01419870902802262
TELLES, EDWARD 2004 *Race in Another America: The Significance of Skin Color in Brazil*, Princeton, NJ: Princeton University Press
TORRES, ARLENE 1998 'La gran familia Puertorriqueña "El Prieta de Beldá"', in Arlene Torres and Norma E. Whitten (eds), *Blackness in Latin America and the Caribbean*, Bloomington, IN: Indiana University Press, pp. 285–336
TROUILLOT, MICHEL-ROLPH 1995 *Silencing the Past: Power and the Production of History*, Boston, MA: Beacon Press

TSUDA, TAKEYUKI 2003 *Strangers in the Ethnic Homeland: Japanese Brazilian Return Migration in Transnational Perspective*, New York: Columbia University Press

TWINE, FRANCE WINDDANCE 1998 *Racism in a Racial Democracy: The Maintenance of White Supremacy in Brazil*, New Brunswick, NJ: Rutgers University Press

URBAN, GREG and JOEL, SHERZER 1991 'Introduction: Indians, nation-states, and cultures', in Greg Urban and Joel Sherzer (eds), *Nation-States and Indians in Latin America*, Austin, TX: University of Texas Press, pp. 1–18

WADE, PETER 1997 *Race and Ethnicity in Latin America*, Sterling, VA: Pluto

WEINER, MICHAEL 1997 *Japan's Minorities: The Illusion of Homogeneity*, London and New York: Routledge

WINANT, HOWARD 1992 Rethinking race in Brazil', *Journal of Latin American Studies*, vol. 24, no. 1, pp. 173–92

Index

Page numbers in *Italics* represent tables.

accommodation 7
acculturation 46–7, 73; life course 77; reconceptualization 79
action hero 38
adolescent friendships: across races 115
affirmative action: Brazil 142; regulations 7
African Americans 113; Hispanic relationship 124
African ancestry 137
African-origin: political leaders 143
Afro-Latin America 139
agricultural industry: racialization of employees 93–110
Agron, Salvador 28
Alba, Richard 45
Albuquerque 50
American colour line: models of 114–16
American labor force: Latino/a 93–4; race 94
American Me (film) 33–4
American racial hierarchy 113
American-Latino gang masculinity 80
Americanization 44, 105
Americas: different perspectives on race 148–50
ancestry 137
anti-racist social movements 40
apartheid: global 109
Argentina 143
Arguinzoni, Sonny 75
ascription 7
Asians: panethnicity 5; social mobility 114; worker experience 96
assimilation 39, 46, 47, 74; barriers to 74; classical 74; life course 77
Atlanta 50

Bankston, C.L. 75, 89

barrio gang members 82
barrio symbols 79–80
Barth, F. 9
Basch, Linda 8
Bean, Frank 114
Bedford County 116, 117
Beltrán, Mary 38
bi-racial identity 116
bi-racial system 40, 136
biases: film makers 25
bilingualism 2, 59; advantages of 60; biculturalism 47; economic benefit 50; forces against 62; global economy 60; Hispanic residential clustering 52; pay premium 49, 52, 60, 61; transnational ties 61
bilingualism among US-born Latinos: analysis and findings 52–6; best models of bilingualism *70*; coefficients for regression (MSAs/PMSAs) *53*; contexts 43–4; data, variables and measures 48–52; discussion and conclusion 61–2; endpoint of linguistic assimilation 45–6; ground floor contexts 56–60; lagged models coefficients for regression (MSAs/PMSAs) *54*; modelling contexts 48; pay premium regressions *71*; Pearson correlations *66–9*; theorizing language choice 46–8
biliterate 59
binary colour line 114
biologization of culture 103
bisexuality 36
black: stereotypes 121
black-Hispanic tension 125
black/nonblack divide 116
black/nonblack model 115
black/white segregation 118

INDEX

blackness 114, 115; devalued 121; Obama 152
blacks: social interaction with whites 120–8; socioeconomic disadvantage 118
Blanc-Szanton, Cristina 8
Blancanieves 149
Blood In, Blood Out (film) 31–4
Bolivia 143
Bonilla-Silva, Eduardo 100, 103, 134–42; *Ethnic and Racial Studies* 3, 134
borderlands 75
Born in East L.A. (Marin) 27, 33
Boston 8
boundary marker 43
Bracero Program 96
Brazil 135, 138, 139, 143; affirmative action 142; race relations paradox 141–2
Brazilianization 140, 153
Brigante, Carlito 28, 33, 39
Bronx 35
Brooklyn 37
Brusco, Elizabeth 76, 77, 79, 85, 87, 88

California 51, 52, 55, 59
call-and-response 82
Cao, N. 75
capitalism 34
Caribbean: migration from 9
Carlito's Way (film): Latino masculinity 28–31
carros públicos 19
Carter, P. 75
Catholicism 30
census 2; classifications 5; race making 150
Central American Free Trade Agreement 21
Central Americans 115
change 82, 83, 88
Charlotte 50
Chicago 5, 7, 50
Chicano 30; male culture 34; male violence 27
Chicano ex-gang members 2; Christian asceticism in Victory Outreach 84–5; conclusion 88–90; data and methods 78–9; household relationships 85–6; introduction 72–3; literature review 73–7; muscular Christianity 87–8; reformed barrio masculine acculturation 84–5; religious optimism 82–4; upward mobility 84–5; values, style and masculinity 79–81; work 86–7
child-bearing: early 77
Children of Immigrants Longitudinal Survey (CILS) 74, 77
Chile 143
Chinese category 138
Christian conversion 75
church: ethnic 74; participatory black Protestant 82, 83; Spanish mass 58
citizenship 108; marginal 33
civil rights 114; linguistic rights 51
class 116
class demarcation 35
classification system: United States 7
collective blacks 115, 120, 134, 142
Collins, Patricia Hill 82
Colombia 76, 88, 139, 143
colonial subjects 115
colonialism 114
color: people of 38
color demarcation 35
color line: triracial 115
color-blind 108, 135
colorism 149–50
community: language 50
consonant acculturation 74
consumption 77
Cook-Martin, David 138
Courtney Smith, Robert 76
criminality 28, 33
criollos 149
Crow, Jim 151
crystal methamphetamine 85
Cuban Americans 51
Cubans 13, 51
cultural commonalities 15
cultural difference 108
cultural events 14
cultural identity 29
cultural products 6
cultural representations 25
cultural xenophobia: racial hatred 123
culturally white 116
culture: as explanation for subordination 102–3, 108

darkening of the population: white elites 138–9
De Genova, Nicholas 95, 96
demand: supply 100
democracy 33
demographics 101
DePalma, Brian 28, 31

INDEX

dependability 104
Despierta America 17
deviant barrio masculinity 80, 83
deviant masculinity 31
discipline 31
discrimination 19–20, 33, 123–4; skin colour 138
dissonant acculturation 46, 74
distancing 115, 125, 128; anti-black 116; social 120
diversity 59
division of labour: racial 109
Dominican Republic 2, 115; colonial history of 9–10; compared with Puerto Rico 9–11; history 10; panethnic label use *12*; panethnicity and US contact *18*; relationship with US 10; research interview data 11–12; returning migrants 9; Santo Domingo 6; telecommunications industry 15
downward assimilation 74
downward mobility: sheltering from 87
drug addicts 82; Christian conversion 75
drug taking 80
drugs 28, 32; dealing 35; selling 85
dual frame of reference 108
dual-language: education 60, 61; movement 57; programmes 59
DuBois, W.E.B. 103

economic benefit: bilingualism 50
economic competition 125, 128
economic utility: language 44
economic vulnerability 106
economy 84
Ecuador 139, 143
education: under-performance 76
El Salvador 81
electoral politics 5
emotional segregation 26
Empire (film) 34, 35, 36, 40
employers: race practices 94; recruitment practices 94; white 100
English language 32; US government 43
English monolingualism 44
Espiritu, Yen Le 5, 7
ethnic boundaries: shifting 6; transnationalism 8–9
ethnic church 74
ethnic difference 26
Ethnic and Racial Studies (Bonilla-Silva) 3
ethnicity: race 100; reactive 90
ethno-racial composition: jobs 99

European Americans 26
European ancestry 137
exclusion 33
exclusionary politics 108
exploitation 106, 114; racialization 110
extra-marital affairs 85

families: broken 31
family breakdown 28
female empowerment 39
femininity 39
feminism 87
feminization: fear of 88
Filipino agricultural workers 96
filmmakers: biases 25
Finney County 56
Fitzgerald, David 138
Flores, Edward 2
Florida 51, 52, 55
food 13, 14
Food Stamps 107
Fordham, S. 73
Fort Lauderdale 50
freedom 33
functionalist theory 47

Galeano, Eduardo 147
gangs 32; transnational 81
Gans, Herbert 77, 79
Garden City 56, 57
gender 88, 98; hierarchies 102; identities 8; second-generation immigrant mobility 76
Gibson, Margaret 74
Girlfight (film) 25, 27, 34, 37–40
Glick Schiller, Nina 8
global apartheid 109
global economy: bilingualism 60
globalization 44
good old Americanness 29
Gordon, M. 46
growth: Latino/a communities 1
Guatemala 139
guest worker 94

Haiti 10
Haitian revolution 149
Harlem 30–1
Hawaii 96
health and wealth gospel 83
hero: new Latina 38
heroes 36
Hispanic: label 7; term 12
Hispanic culture 102

INDEX

Hispanic identity 4
Hispanic isolation 50
Hispanic jobs 103
Hispanic newcomers: racial/ethnic identifications 119–20; responses to perceived discrimination by blacks 123–8; social interactions with whites and blacks 120–8
Hispanic politicians 55
Hispanic population: North Carolina 117
Hispanic relationship: African Americans 124
Hispanic residential clustering: bilingualism 52
Hispanics 98; distinct group 120
Hollywood 39–40; Latino identity 25–6; Latino masculinity 28–31; methodological approach 27–8; whiteness in scripts 26–7
homogenizing Latin America 139–40
Honduras 143
honorary whites 115, 122, 134, 138, 141
honour 76
horizontal citizenship axis 125
horizontal versus vertical relations 141–2
hot-blooded temperament 31
household 88
household consumption 77
human capital theory 47

identification 7
illegal economy 84
illegal immigrants 33
illegal migrant workers 115
illegals 105–6
immigrant acculturation: language shift 46; remaking the mainstream 59
immigrant optimism 84
immigrant replenishment 47
immigration: anti 62; religion 74–5
immigration controls: labour shortages 106
Immigration and Naturalization Services (INS) 33
immigration policies: racial views 127–8
incarceration 77
independent films 34–9
inequality 27
inferiority 26, 96
institutionalization: Asian panethnicity 5
intergenerational language shift 45

invisible groups 95
isolation index 55
Italian gangster 30

Jackson, Reverend Jesse 83
Jamaica Plain 8
Japanese agricultural workers 96
Japanese category 138
Jiménez, Tomás R. 2, 46, 47, 126
jobs: ethno-racial composition 99; segmentation 108
Jung, Moon-Kei 96

Kao, G. 84
Kasinitz, P. 81
Kim, C.J. 96, 125
King, Martin Luther 151

label: Hispanic 7
labour: coalitional politics 110; sexual division 88
labour force: cheaper 107
labour market participation 86
labour shortages: immigration controls 106
language: community 50; generational change 46; national identity 43
language minority 55
language shift: immigrant acculturation 46
Latin America: system of race 136; tri-racial system 135–7; US 16
Latin Americanization 140, 151–2; claims 135–40; conclusion 142–3; introduction 134–5; operationalizing the theory 140–2
Latina bodies 38
Latina Community: New York 17
Latinidad 15, 26, 31, 34, 39
Latinidad: and masculinity 31–3
Latino 1.5 generation 43–4, 48–57, 61–2, 66–8, 70–1, 127
Latino: term 12
Latino Billboard Awards 17
Latino identity: introduction 1–3; outline of chapters 1–3; Puerto Ricans 4; sending societies 12–15
Latino masculinity 26; Hollywood 28–31
Latino media: globalization of 15–17
Latino metros 50
Latino music 17
Latino panethnic identity 20–2
Latino political mobilization 14

INDEX

Latino/a employers 100
Latinos: third-plus generation 78
Lee, Jennifer 75, 114
legal status 105, 108
Levitt, Peggy 8
Liberato, Ana S.Q. 2
Lichter, Michael 94, 106–7, 108
life course 77
linguistic dissimilation 62
linguistic rights: civil rights 51
Linton, April 2, 46
Lopez, Jennifer 39
los americanos 9
Los Angeles 50
low-wage jobs 94
loyalty: US 96

machismo 76
macho 76
macho behaviour 29
Maldonado, Marta Maria 2
management 102
management positions 108
marginality 31–3
marginalization 89; structural relations of 27
Marin, C.: *Born in East L.A.* 27, 33
market dynamics 101; racial content 108
markets: broadening 15
marriage 40; inter-racial 115, 116, 139, 140, 151
masculinities: competing 76
masculinity 31; and Latindad 31–4
mass culture: politicizing 25
Massey, Douglas 9
materialism 34
meatpacking 97
Medicaid 107
mestizaje 149
mestizos 139
Mexican Americans 5, 7, 33, 45, 56; informal Spanish lessons 57; New York 76; subculture 73
Mexicans 13, 115; Puerto Ricans 96
Mexico 16, 51, 138; size of immigrant population 45
Miami 30–1, 45, 50
Miami-Dade County 55
Milwaukee 50
Minaflores 8
minorities 40
minority cultures 75
minority groups: tensions between 125
Mirandé, Alfredo 76, 77

mixed-race individuals 137
mobility 79, 84; race-class 150; religious participation 77; upward 74, 77, 81, 84–5
money whitens 139
Montana, Tony 28–30, 33, 39
moral depravity 38
mulattoes 136
multicultural awareness 60
multiculturalism 39, 40, 44; high value 46
multiculturalist white supremacy 152
multinational programming 17

nativism 126
natural tendencies 103
naturalization of racism 100
Neckerman, K. 75
neo-mulattos 152
neoclassical economic theory 47
networks: migrants 19
new destinations 113
New Haven 50
new identity politics 40
new racism 151
New York 35, 50; Mexican-American 76; Puerto Rican 36–7
Nicaragua 143
No Child Left Behind 57
non-black identification: factors behind 120
non-whites 114
North Carolina: Hispanic population 117
Nuyorican poetry movement 36

Obama, President Barack: blackness 152; election 3, 151
Obamerica 151–2
Ogbu, J. 73
Okamoto, D. 5
Olmos, Edward James 34, 39
oppositional culture 73, 75, 81
oppositional groups 74
oppression 114
Orwell, George 152
Othering 26, 27, 29
outsiders 107, 125

Pacino, Al 28
Padilla, F. 5, 7
Panamanians 13
panethnic entrepreneurs 15

INDEX

panethnic label use: Dominicans and Puerto Ricans *12*
panethnicity: boundary formation 5; origins of 6–8; sentiments 4; shaping of 2; spreading 7
parenting 85
patriarchy 76
pay premium: bilingualism 49, 52
Pearson correlations: bilingualism among US-born Latinos *66–9*
Pentecostalism 75, 76, 79, 83, 85
Peru 138, 143
phenotype 149–50
physical labour 104
Piñero (film) 34, 36–7, 40
political leaders: African-origin 143
Portes, A. 45, 74, 75, 142
press 15
prison 84, 87; avoiding 80–1
privilege: whiteness 121
profit 103
Promise Keepers 87
propensities 103
Proposition 187: California 14
Protestantism 30
public sector labour market 52
Public Use Microdata Sample (PUMS) 48
Puerto Ricanization 140, 153
Puerto Ricans 115; Latino identity 4; Mexicans 96; New York 36–7; panethnic label use *12*; panethnicity and US contact *18*; research interview data 11–12; US citizenship 10
Puerto Rico 2; colonial history of 9–10; Commonwealth 9; compared with Dominican Republic 9–11; nineteenth century 151; status and national identity 10; unique case 21; US protectorate 10
Puerto Rico Community Survey 5
Punjab: Sikhs 74

race 40; construction of 149–50; employers practices 94; ethnicity 100; mixing 149; perception of 19; segregation in workplace 98; talking about 98–9, 101, 152
race making: Census 150
racial content: market dynamics 108
racial divide: primary 136
racial etiquette 151
racial hatred: cultural xenophobia 123
racial hierarchy 113; workplace 108

racial ideology 40
racial inferiority 96
racial meanings 94
racial minorities 114
racial oppression: resisting 83
racial space 150
racial structures 148
racial triangulation 96
racial violence 5
racialization 39, 114; exploitation 110; how it occurs 95
racialization of Latino/as: agricultural work 97–8; case study 96–7; colour as explanation 102–3; colour-blindness in agriculture 98–101; discussion and implications 108–10; relative valorization of workers 103–7; sample description *97*; theoretical considerations 95–6
racializations: different 95–6
racialized differences 96
racism 28, 34; multiple 95–6
radio 15
Ramos-Zayas, Ana 95, 96
ranchero masculinity 76
rapper masculinity 76
reactive ethnicity 90
reformed barrio masculinity 80, 83
refugees 115
religion: immigration 74–5
religious optimism 84, 89
religious participation: socio-economic mobility 77
replenishment hypothesis 55
resentment 128
residential segregation 115, 142
responsibility 86
return migration 9
rhetorical incoherence 100
rights 14
Robles, Rudy 33
Rodriguez, Michelle 37
Roth, Wendy D. 1–2
Rumbaut, R.G. 45, 74, 75, 77

San Diego 45
San Juan 13; Puerto Rico 6
Sanchez-Walsh, Arlene 88
Santa Barbara 56
Santa Maria 56, 57
Santo Domingo 19; Dominican Republic 6
Sayer, Andrew 103

INDEX

Scarface (film): Latino masculinity 28–31
schools: dual-language 46, 56, 60, 61
second generation: decline 77; immigrant mobility by gender 76; males 76
segmentation: jobs 108
segmented assimilation theory 73–4, 77, 79, 81, 87, 89
segregation: emotional 26; racial 151; residential 115, 142; workplace 98
selective acculturation 47, 74
self-identification 137
sending societies 6; Latino identities 12–15
sexism 28, 29
sexual division: labour 88
sexuality 36
Sikhs: Punjab 74
Silva, Bonilla 40
Singer, Audrey 50
skin color 116; discrimination 138; hierarchy 135; importance of 137–8; range 117
slavery 151
social class 124
social remittances 8
social service funding 5
social stratification 138
socio-economic mobility 73; religious participation 77
Spain 14
Spanish church: masses 58
Spanish Harlem 30–1
Spanish language 7; at home 50; longevity 44; media 2, 46, 51, 58
Spanish-American War 10
Spanish-language television 15, *see also* television
stereotypes 26, 40; anti-black 120; black 121; upward mobility 81
stereotyping 27, 125, 128
Stevens, Gillian 45, 50
stratification 40
structural racism 96
style 75
subordination 108; culture as explanation 102–3
success 31
Sue, Christina A. 3, 147–50
supervisory positions 102
Suro, Roberto 50

Telemundo 15, 16

television 15, 16, *see also* Spanish-language television
Television and Cable Factbook 49
Telles, Edward 135, 141, 151
Texas 51, 55
Thai workers 109
Thailand 107
third-plus generation Latinos 78
Tienda, M. 84
Tinker Salas, M. 8
transnational contact 2, 9, 17–20
transnational social fields 5, 6, 21, 22
transnational ties: bilingualism 61
transnationalism: ethnic boundaries 8–9
tri-racial color line 115
tri-racial model 116, 119, 120
tri-racial system 40, 135; Latin America 135–7
Trouillot, M.-R. 149
Trujillo, Rafael 10, 15

unemployment 107
United States of America (USA): classification system 7; descriptive statistics for metro areas *49*; immigrant receiving society 5; Latino identity phenomenon 8; loyalty 96; population 40, *see also* American ...
Univisión 15, 16, 17
upward assimilation 47
upward mobility 74, 77, 89; Chicano ex-gang members 84–5; stereotypes 81
Uruguay 143
US Census (2000) 11
US Census data 44

valorization 96
Venezuela 14, 143
Versailles residents 89
vertical skin color axis 125
Victory Outreach 73, 75, 78, 82, 89
Vietnamese 89, 138
Vietnamese Catholic Church 75
villains 36
violence 28, 32, 38; Chicano men 27

Waldinger, Roger 94, 106–7, 108
Walker, Richard 103
Washington: agriculture 96
Washington State University's Cooperative Extension 97
WASPism 26
Waters, Mary 65

white elites: darkening of the population 138–9
white employers 100
white privilege 108
white racial identification 119
white rule: maintaining 149
white superiority 120
white supremacy 108, 149, 153
white/black divide 115
whiteness: benefits of 40, 103; privilege 121
whitening 138, 148–9, 149–50
whites 114, 134; preferences for Hispanics over African Americans 121–3; social interaction with blacks 120–8

Wilcox County 116–17
Winant, Howard 108
women: changing roles 8; in charge 102
work ethic 87, 104
workers: desirability 108; racialized assessment 108
working conditions 106
workplaces 97, 98; racial hierarchies 108
worth: sense of 26

Yancey, George 40

Zhou, M. 75, 89

 Routledge
Taylor & Francis Group

African and Black Diaspora: An International Journal

Publication of the DePaul Center for Black Diaspora

EDITORS:
Fassil Demissie, *DePaul University, USA*
Sandra Jackson, *DePaul University, USA*
Abebe Zegeye, *University of South Africa, South Africa*

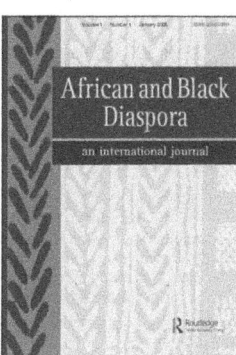

This is the first academic journal that directly addresses the needs of scholars working in the important field of African Diaspora studies. It advances the analytical and interrogative discourses that constitute this distinctive interdisciplinary study of the deterritorialised and transnational nature of the African and Black Diaspora.

Beyond essentialist modes of theorizing, the journal will locate the movement of African descended populations (geographical, cultural, social, political and psychological) in the context of globalized and transnational spaces by emphasizing the centrality of African and Black Diaspora.

For details on how to submit a paper to *African and Black Diaspora* please visit www.tandf.co.uk/journals/rabd and click on the 'Instructions for Authors' link.

Recent Articles

Sam Selvon's The Lonely Londoners and the structure of Black metropolitan life **Mpalive-Hangson Msiska**

Paradoxes of diaspora, global identity and human rights: the deportation of Nigerians in Ireland **Elisa Joy White**

Rethinking diasporicity: embodiment, emotion, and the displaced origin **Bibi Bakare-Yusuf**

To sign up for tables of contents, new publications and citation alerting services visit **www.informaworld.com/alerting**

 **updates**
Taylor & Francis Group

Register your email address at www.tandf.co.uk/journals/eupdates.asp to receive information on books, journals and other news within your areas of interest.

 Powered by **informa**world

For further information, please contact Customer Services at either of the following:
T&F Informa UK Ltd, Sheepen Place, Colchester, Essex, CO3 3LP, UK
Tel: +44 (0) 20 7017 5544 Fax: 44 (0) 20 7017 5198
Email: subscriptions@tandf.co.uk
Taylor & Francis Inc, 325 Chestnut Street, Philadelphia, PA 19106, USA
Tel: +1 800 354 1420 (toll-free calls from within the US)
or +1 215 625 8900 (calls from overseas) Fax: +1 215 625 2940
Email: customerservice@taylorandfrancis.com

View an online sample issue at:
www.tandf.co.uk/journals/rabd

Social Identities
Journal for the Study of Race, Nation and Culture

New look for 2009

EDITORS:
Pal Ahluwalia, *University of California, San Diego, USA, and University of South Australia*
Toby Miller, *University of California, Riverside, USA*

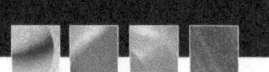

Recent years have witnessed considerable worldwide changes concerning social identities such as race, nation and ethnicity, as well as the emergence of new forms of racism and nationalism as discriminatory exclusions. **Social Identities** aims to furnish an interdisciplinary and international focal point for theorizing issues at the interface of social identities.

The journal is especially concerned to address these issues in the context of the transforming political economies and cultures of postmodern and postcolonial conditions. **Social Identities** is intended as a forum for contesting ideas and debates concerning the formations of, and transformations in, socially significant identities, their attendant forms of material exclusion and power, as well as the political and cultural possibilities opened up by these identifications.

Besides the regular range of articles, **Social Identities** also features Specificities and Debate sections, an occasional book review section, and special issues on topics of note.

All research articles published in this journal have undergone rigorous peer review, based on initial editor screening and anonymized refereeing by at least two anonymous referees.

To sign up for tables of contents, new publications and citation alerting services visit www.informaworld.com/alerting

 Register your email address at www.tandf.co.uk/journals/eupdates.asp to receive information on books, journals and other news within your areas of interest.

For further information, please contact Customer Services at either of the following:
T&F Informa UK Ltd, Sheepen Place, Colchester, Essex, CO3 3LP, UK
Tel: +44 (0) 20 7017 5544 Fax: 44 (0) 20 7017 5198
Email: subscriptions@tandf.co.uk
Taylor & Francis Inc, 325 Chestnut Street, Philadelphia, PA 19106, USA
Tel: +1 800 354 1420 (toll-free calls from within the US)
or +1 215 625 8900 (calls from overseas) Fax: +1 215 625 2940
Email: customerservice@taylorandfrancis.com

View an online sample issue at:
www.tandf.co.uk/journals/csid